Praise for Wes Wheeler and *The Turnaround Leader*

Wes is an accomplished leader whose career has been defined by driving results through action. His story, as told in this book, reflects his journey to become the 'turnaround' leader whose 'can do' attitude has led to world class performance throughout his career. Overcoming insurmountable obstacles on a daily basis to find 'the art of the possible' is routine for Wes. This is a great book for anyone who wants evidence that one person can make a difference.

–**Timothy C. Tyson**, Chairman and CEO, TriRx Pharmaceutical Services, LLC

Wes Wheeler was the right leader at the right time! He clearly understood the importance of being a great teammate, team builder and challenger of status quo. At the end of the day his leadership was instrumental in our overall success!

–**General Gus Perna**, US Army (r); Chief Operating Officer, Operation Warp Speed

I had the privilege of working with Wes Wheeler during my time as UPS's Chief Operating Officer, where his expertise and stellar leadership were paramount. Under Wes's guidance, UPS Healthcare grew remarkably fast. Though I had retired when COVID-19 hit, I watched from afar as Wes spearheaded UPS's pivotal role delivering billions of vaccines globally, saving countless lives through his perseverance and integrity. I wholeheartedly recommend this inspirational book for the universal leadership lessons it imparts.

–**Jim Barber**, Former COO, UPS

THE TURNAROUND LEADER

WES WHEELER

THE TURNAROUND LEADER

REBUILDING GREAT ORGANIZATIONS

IN THE FACE OF ADVERSITY

Advantage | Books

Published by Advantage Books, Charleston, South Carolina.
An imprint of Advantage Media.

Printed in the United States of America.

10 9 8 7 6 5 4 3 2 1

ISBN: 979-8-89188-034-4 (Hardcover)
ISBN: 979-8-89188-035-1 (eBook)

Library of Congress Control Number: 2024905315

Book design by Megan Elger.

To my wife, Marianne,
who has stood by me for these past forty-two years.

Nothing I have accomplished, including all the events and stories told in this book, would have been possible without her unconditional love and support.

CONTENTS

ACKNOWLEDGMENTS xiii

PREFACE xvii

CHAPTER 1. 1
Beginnings (1978–1989)

CHAPTER 2 13
Exxon (1978–1989)

CHAPTER 3 39
Glaxo (1989–2002)

CHAPTER 4 85
DSM Pharmaceuticals, Inc. (2002–2003)

CHAPTER 5 123
Valeant Pharmaceuticals International, Inc. (2003–2007)

CHAPTER 6 171
Patheon, Inc. (2007–2010)

CHAPTER 7 203
Marken (2011-2019)

CHAPTER 8 247
Bushu Pharmaceuticals Ltd. (2017-2021)

CHAPTER 9 261
UPS Healthcare (2019-2020)

CHAPTER 10 275
UPS Healthcare (2020-2023)

CHAPTER 11 315
What's Next (2023 and After ...)

APPENDIX 329

LEGAL DISCLAIMER

The views and opinions expressed in this book are solely those of the author, Wes Wheeler, and do not necessarily reflect the views, opinions, or official stance of any company or organization mentioned or any of its affiliated entities. The book represents the personal experiences, thoughts, and beliefs of Wes Wheeler and should be understood as such.

While Wes Wheeler held various positions within the companies mentioned in this book, it is important to note that the content presented in this book is not endorsed, supported, or sanctioned by any of those companies. The book is a product of the author's independent expression and does not purport to represent the companies' values, policies, or strategies.

The information, anecdotes, and ideas presented in this book are intended for informational and entertainment purposes only. They should not be considered as professional advice, business recommendations, or official statements from Wes Wheeler. Readers are encouraged to exercise critical thinking, form their own opinions, and consult relevant experts or sources for specific guidance or advice pertaining to any aspect discussed in the book.

This book contains information based on historical events and personal experiences. This information is not meant to be used as a source of financial or professional advice.

The author and publisher do not recommend making any investment or professional decision based on the content of this work without prior consultation with a financial or professional advisor. The author and publisher disclaim liability if the information and opinions in this book are interpreted to be legal advice, professional advice, or investment advice and actions based on this book's content end with poor results. Readers assume the risk for their decisions when relying on this book's content.

The author and publisher have made every effort to assure that the events and data contained in this work are accurate and presented under fair use principles. We have sourced and quoted material from individuals and media respected for their integrity and their commitment to accuracy. Any inaccuracies are regrettable, but the author and publisher disclaim liability to the full extent of the law.

Financial information presented for companies represented in this book was internally sourced, and it is presented from statements, reports, and other documents available to the author during his service at those companies.

Wes Wheeler assumes no responsibility or liability for any errors, omissions, or inaccuracies in the content of this book. Readers are advised to independently verify any information presented herein and bear full responsibility for their own interpretations and actions.

By reading this book, you acknowledge and agree that the views expressed are solely those of the author and not representative of the companies or any of their affiliates. You understand that the author's opinions are subject to change and that he has no obligation to update or correct any information contained in this book.

In conclusion, this disclaimer emphasizes that the views expressed in this book are the personal opinions of the author, Wes Wheeler, and do not reflect the views, opinions, or official positions of any mentioned companies or their affiliated entities. Readers are encouraged to consider the book from an individual's perspective and exercise their own judgment and discretion when interpreting its content.

ACKNOWLEDGMENTS

Thirty-five people were interviewed for this book, several of them multiple times. I am profoundly thankful for their contributions. I chose each of them carefully for each chapter to ensure accuracy and balance. They gave their time and candid portrayals of the stories from their own viewpoints. The list of contributors is listed below, and I offer each individual my sincere gratitude:

- Ariette van Strien
- Bary Bailey
- Chuck Bramlage
- Dan Gagnon
- Doaa Fathallah
- Ed Casanova
- Erica Wheeler
- General Christopher Sharpsten
- General Gustave Perna
- Greg Wheeler
- Hans Engels
- Jim Barber

- Jim Coughlan
- Jim Scandura
- John Pattullo
- Kate Gutmann
- Ken Somers
- Laura Lane
- Marcela Quinonez
- Marianne Spinner Wheeler
- Mark Blough
- Mark Hembarsky
- Paul Vassallo
- Ramsey Frank
- Robert Blaha
- Scott Evangelista
- Tadashi Maruoka
- Takanobu Hara
- Tanya Alcorn
- Terry Novak
- Terry Tipple
- Tim Tyson
- Todd Snyder
- Tom Page
- William Van

I have to acknowledge some of the leaders who have mentored me over the years and who believed in me, even when the going got tough.

I have worked for Tim Tyson for seventeen of my forty-three years, first at Glaxo (now GlaxoSmithKline) and then at Valeant Pharmaceuticals (now Bausch Health). Tim has been my mentor and the leader I have most aspired to be. He is a military man who graduated from the United States Military Academy at West Point. More importantly, during my early years at Glaxo, he pushed me to do my very best as a project manager and then allowed me to lead people for the very first time as a director.

He took a chance on me with an important career change after earning my MBA at night. He offered me a chance to move from engineering to marketing, a very unconventional career path in our industry. It was that move that allowed me to grow, first as a division president and ultimately a CEO of three companies.

I want to acknowledge John Pattullo, who became chair at Marken at a particularly sensitive time in my career. John believed in me and supported me while navigating out of the darkest period in Marken's history. He is my gold standard for how effective a board chair can be.

I also want to acknowledge Jim Barber, now retired and formerly the chief operating officer at UPS. Jim was the executive responsible for the acquisition of Marken, which put healthcare in the spotlight at UPS. The success of the Marken acquisition led to the company's decision to design and build the first-ever business vertical at UPS, which we branded UPS Healthcare. It was this transformational move, made at a critical time in history, that enabled my team to take a leading role during the pandemic as part of Operation Warp Speed.

I want to particularly thank Charles McNair, who was instrumental in writing this book. Charles was the inspiration for transforming what was meant to be a series of business case studies into a book that encapsulates the entirety of my forty-three-year career. He personally interviewed more than thirty people—sometimes multiple times—compiled hundreds of pages of notes, and endured multiple drafts of each chapter. Charles is an accomplished business writer and novelist in his own right. His writing and communication consulting career spans forty years, and he has written speeches and thought leadership works for executives at many top companies. I am forever thankful for Charles's countless hours of thoughtful work and devotion to this project.

My mother, Beverly Wheeler, has been an inspiration to me throughout my entire life. After my parents' divorce, when I was twelve, she became a single working Mom. She earned a Master's Degree while working two jobs, commuting to graduate school at night, and teaching high school full-time. She powered through these difficult years and still managed to maintain a happy, nurturing home for the three of us. For as long as I can remember, she had a poem hung on her kitchen wall entitled *Children Learn what they Live*, by Dorothy Law Nolte. I never forgot that poem and realize now how important those words are while children are growing up, developing their character and moral compass. I have done my best to become the man she wanted me to be.

And finally, I want to thank my wife, Marianne, and my two children, Greg and Erica. Marianne and I have moved fifteen times in our forty-two years together. We moved Greg and Erica many times during their formative years, including two years in the United Kingdom, after growing up in Chapel Hill and then went on to California. My family has supported me through all these moves and all my posts, during the best and worst of times, and for this I am forever grateful.

PREFACE

I wrote *The Turnaround Leader* for two reasons.

First, as a lifelong reader of histories and biographies, I have always found immense value in seeing past events documented and described so that others can remember them and understand how they led to where we are today. My personal story spans six decades of history and happenings so far. I hope the depictions of my career and life memories during these years can bring value to readers of *The Turnaround Leader*.

Second, I hope to present current and future business leaders with case studies they might find useful in their decision-making. The challenges I faced in my business career have been unique, but the solutions I implemented as a leader are universal—they're the same ones all leaders must create, in their own ways, if they are to succeed.

For more than forty years, I devoted much of my life to seven important business roles throughout my career, beginning with Exxon, my project management "bootcamp," concluding with UPS Healthcare and the important work we did to grow a new $10 billion business unit while managing the movement of nearly two billion doses of the COVID-19 vaccines to more than one hundred countries.

These seven important roles in my career, including three as CEO, have given me a unique perspective on how to fix and grow companies. These roles have also taught me lessons in leadership that I gladly pass on to others throughout these pages.

I have made mistakes, and I have experienced successes. Fortunately, the upsides have exceeded the downsides. I became a better executive as a result of all my experiences.

It also must be said that none of these experiences would have been possible without the support of my family, especially Marianne, my wife of forty-two years. We have moved fifteen times during our marriage, from New Jersey to Japan and back, then to California and North Carolina. We next moved to England, came back to California, and then finally settled in North Carolina.

Our family members have become citizens of the world. My two children, Greg and Erica, have received gifts of experience, humility, understanding, and diversity through these travels.

I am grateful to have been given such opportunities in my life, and I'm equally grateful now for the chance to pass them on.

Again, as a chronicle of work and life through the decades and as a users' guide for leaders, I hope you find *The Turnaround Leader* of value.

—WES WHEELER

CHAPTER 1

BEGINNINGS (1978–1989)

Turning Around Family Failures ... and Finding a Path to My Purpose

My childhood years were defined by two major failures: one in business and, shortly after, one in a marriage.

The business failure came when I was seven.

My family and I had lived in Spain for two years, returning to Clason Point, New York, in the spring of 1963 to witness the tail end of a disaster—the still-smoking embers of the Wheeler Yacht Company. The shipyard had burned to the ground. We were told a grass fire had swept through the Bronx and into the yard.

It was the third shipyard the Wheeler family had lost.

The family business crafted mostly pleasure boats from 1910 until 1965, but the Wheelers also built more than four hundred ships to support the Allied war effort in World War II (Appendix C1.1). After one last eighty-three-foot Coast Guard cutter came off the line just after the war, the Wheeler Shipbuilding Corporation handed back the Whitestone shipyard, leased to us by the City of New York. Our

The Wheeler Shipyard in Whitestone, Queens, in 1942

Howard E. Wheeler (center) surrounded by the Wheeler Family. Wesley L. Wheeler, my grandfather, is on the far right

company was rewarded for its war effort, receiving a highly coveted Navy-E Award in 1942 for outstanding performance in war production. Four stars were later placed on the E pennant to recognize four additional extraordinary performance events.

After the war, the US government made tax disclosure claims against Wheeler Shipbuilding and, more specifically, the Wheeler brothers who ran it.

The corporation filed for bankruptcy in 1946, seeking financial protection. Two years later, the Wheelers purchased a company called Dawn Boat Works in Clason Point in the Bronx and, for the next fifteen years, built some of the finest pleasure yachts of the day. Rebranded, Wheeler Yacht Company vessels starred at every New York boat show for a decade. The Wheeler logo on the bow meant something.

In total, we built nearly four thousand boats, including vessels used long before the Second World War, in Brooklyn, where my great-grandfather, Howard E. Wheeler, founded the company. His yard crafted *Pilar*, Ernest Hemingway's famous boat, in 1934 (AC1.2). The writer claimed to have written *The Old Man and the Sea* standing upright at the helm of the thirty-eight-foot fishing boat, a posture that helped ease the pain of a chronically bad back. Hemingway paid Wheeler Shipbuilding $7,455 for *Pilar* the year it launched.

Then, three shipyards later, Wheeler Yacht Company burned to the ground in 1963.

I still remember as a seven-year-old rummaging through ashes with Dad, salvaging anything we could. Some old boatbuilding plans had been protected in metal files. My four-year-old brother, Jonathan, and my mom were also with us. We found lots of photographs and awards. I still have those in storage, covered with char marks. Years later, my brother took those photos and tried his best to restore them

Hemingway's Pilar *in Havana*

for posterity. Sadly, the original 1930s-era design drawings, including those of *Pilar*, were lost.

The fire devastated my dad. He had gone to the University of Michigan to study naval architecture with the sole intention of one day taking over the family business.

That never happened. The financially challenged Wheelers handed the business over to new owners. Dad instead went to work for various ship builders and ultimately created his own consulting business. His lifelong dream, though, had turned to ashes.

Dad jumped from job to job. He was not home during most of my school years, preferring to travel overseas, far from our family.

When I was twelve, he divorced my mother and went on to remarry twice. Dad never fulfilled his dream of being a wealthy boat-

One of many photos recovered from the fire

building baron like his forebears and, in fact, died with little more than a house full of memories.

It was a shame. Dad had a brilliant mind. He had traveled the world. He was easy to talk to. His gifts to me were his ability to thrive overseas, his knowledge of the world's many cultures, and his love of history. But his divorce from my mother turned nasty, and the ensuing years were difficult for all of us. My father had failed our family.

I helped Mom at home, especially with baby Debbie, my sister, who is nine years younger than me. Mom needed to go back to college to earn her master's degree, which would get her a higher teacher's salary. Wanting to be responsible, I started working at age ten, washing cars, shoveling snow, and mowing lawns.

At twelve, I got lucky. I nabbed a paper route.

My mom drove me down to the offices of the *Port Chester Daily Item* on Main Street in Port Chester, New York, the town where we then lived. I had to prove I was twelve years old. (I think that was the age requirement at the time.) And I needed a permit to throw papers, so I quickly acquired that, excited about a new way to make money.

My mom and dad had just divorced, and Dad hadn't been around for a very long time. He was with me during my early days of Boy Scouting, but then he disappeared for long stretches, living in Malta and enjoying Europe without us.

I had a wonderful grandfather, Howard Vinton Potter. We called him Pop. He was the patriarch of the family, smart, lovable, and very helpful to us after the divorce. My Aunt Lee and Uncle Ron were also there for us.

So, as the man of the house at age twelve, I went to work delivering newspapers—what I considered a real job, one to take more seriously than mowing lawns and shoveling snow.

My route ran for a mile or so, and I carried afternoon papers to fifty houses. Every day, a *Daily Item* vehicle dropped a bundle of newspapers at the corner of Upland Drive and Fairview Avenue, just opposite King Street School, where I attended grade school.

Each day after classes, I opened the bundle, folded the papers a certain way, stuffed them in a big canvas bag that I carried over one shoulder, and trudged up the long hill, making my deliveries. The special way I folded the papers made it easy to throw them from a sidewalk onto front porches. This came in especially handy when it snowed, because the plows made huge piles in front of driveways and sidewalks.

If it rained, the bundle dropped at the street corner arrived wrapped in plastic. I would take time to slip my fifty newspapers, folded just so, into plastic sleeves to keep them dry before making my deliveries. I took my job very seriously.

On Saturday, I delivered a little earlier in the day and then made my collections. That was the worst part of the job. Some people wouldn't pay. Some couldn't pay. Some just forgot they had to pay. I would have to loop back to the unpaid houses to collect, but if the customer still didn't pay, I had to make up the difference out of my own pocket. (I did get tips sometimes, which helped.)

Sundays presented a different challenge. Because the Sunday paper held all the ads and coupons, plus the cartoons and classifieds, customers really looked forward to it, but the Sunday edition had so many pages that it was impossible to fold and throw. Sunday papers were heavy, and I broke a sweat delivering them, even on the coldest winter days.

After a year on my original route, I took a different one farther from my house. I used my bicycle for this new route, as it was longer, two or three miles in all, with lots more houses. I got paid better, and I developed a much better aim as I calculated, house by house, the best approach and throw from my loaded-down bike.

I got to know people. I got to know their pets. I learned how important it was for me to be reliable and deliver on time.

No internet existed back then, and only a few television channels kept people informed. My neighbors—my community—relied on the newspaper for news, weather, and social events. I saw how the daily paper gave them a lifeline to people and activities around them. I could never skip a day, or even be a few minutes late, because I felt a responsibility to them and to Port Chester, and I took it seriously. I consider my paper route my first real job.

All my life, I have felt that my early job as a paperboy gave me valuable lessons that have helped me succeed in all my jobs since.

Next, I caddied at Apawamis Golf Club, carrying two golf bags over eighteen holes for $10, plus lunch and tips. After a few years, I got a job at Rye Ridge Hardware store, where I worked after school and in the summers through junior high school and high school, and even a couple of summers home from college.

While I worked on my engineering degree at Worcester Polytechnic Institute (WPI) in Worcester, Massachusetts, I delivered refrigerators and big appliances for a local store. I broke my ankle one day carrying a washing machine up a steep staircase.

I worked in the university machine shop, turning a lathe. Then, with a few engineering classes under my belt, I held a summer job in downtown Manhattan as a piping draftsman for a small company called Rosenblatt & Sons. My job was drawing piping components for the Trident-class submarines being built in Groton, Connecticut (AC1.3). (Boatbuilding, obviously, is a recurring theme for us Wheelers.)

I even spent one summer aboard a Liberian cargo ship. I carried a US Merchant Marine credential card, certifying me as an engine wiper. The ship, *Roman Bernard*, cruised from Charleston, South Carolina, to Caracas, Venezuela, and then to Georgetown, Guyana. That was hot, hard, difficult work spent with a mostly Spanish-speaking crew in miserable conditions. Still, it gave me an experience in life I'll never forget.

The point of all this?

My first job as a paperboy led to a lifetime of work and discipline. It stood as the first of those part-time jobs I held along the way that allowed me to pay for all my living expenses and some of my tuition at college. Far more important, though, was how my paper route established habits for a life of hard work that I continue to keep to this very day. It's where my work ethic was born.

From all these experiences, and many to come later, I learned firsthand that people can achieve great things from failure—of a business, a marriage, whatever—if they are willing to work hard enough.

In the past, I've told people that I may not be the smartest person in the room, but there is nobody in the room who can outwork me.

I believed that then. I believe that now.

Marianne Spinner, the love of my life, is part of my beginnings. She's been Marianne Wheeler for forty-two years now and counting.

We met each other in junior high school in Port Chester. I was a grade ahead and six months older. Marianne came from this big, lively Italian family. Her Marine dad was a second-generation Italian, and her mom had been born in Italy. Marianne loved to dance. She has gifts of balance and style, and she has an artistic bent that I never had. She was good enough during her youth to study to be a prima ballerina.

Marianne in high school

In high school, we found things in common. We both played in the marching band—me in the trumpet section, Marianne with the flutes. Our band was modeled after the British Royal Marines, with navy blue uniforms and pith helmets. In formation, everybody in the band looked like men—even Marianne. We traveled on weekends for competitions. One year, the band marched in the Macy's Thanksgiving Day Parade in New York City. Before my time, the band marched in the Tournament of Roses Parade in Pasadena.

Marianne and I both liked math, and it came easy for her. She considered a career as an engineer, talking seriously about that with her dad, a construction superintendent who later studied and got his engineering degree at the same time Marianne graduated from college.

Marianne decided, though, that her true calling lay in teaching. She had known this in her heart since second grade, when she discovered she could explain things to classmates that the teacher had a hard time getting across.

We had one official date in high school. We went to the Franco Zeffirelli movie version of *Romeo and Juliet*. The two teenage actors in the main roles had a nude scene on-screen. It was awkward.

After we graduated from high school—we both finished in the top 10 percent of our class of four hundred or so—Marianne went on to Pace University in New York City to major in education. She took loads of math, too, and it really helped when the time came for her to look for teaching jobs. A job at Bloomingdale's also helped Marianne look great for interviews and student teaching. She earned her education degree in just three years and then started work on her master's.

I attended Worcester Polytechnic Institute, a private university in Worcester, Massachusetts. It was, at the time, one of the most respected engineering schools in the country. I had planned on going to the University of Michigan, but WPI came through with a very important scholarship that, combined with a National Student Direct Loan from the US government, allowed me to afford college. Today, WPI is still among the top engineering schools in the country and, according to one source, it's the seventh most expensive college in the United States.

Marianne and I lost touch with each other through college. I had a steady girlfriend for a while. Meanwhile, Marianne was teaching in Greenwich. I stayed busy studying, and I filled my summers at the hardware store, and as a draftsman working at my dad's firm and on boat projects. It would be six years from the time I last saw Marianne in Port Chester to the time we later reconnected.

I earned my mechanical engineering degree from WPI in 1978. It had been a four-year grind, some of the hardest days and nights of my life, especially the competency exam, the engineering equivalent to the bar exam. We all had to pass it to graduate. I graduated with distinction, the WPI equivalent of cum laude, and then I got several solid job offers.

I said yes to one of the world's largest oil companies, Exxon.

That began a long, rewarding, and adventurous career in business.

LESSONS LEARNED

Failures can lead to opportunities. Struggling through early failures–even those not of one's own doing–often instills a natural instinct and a burning drive to make the future better. Working hard at a real job from an early age will establish a healthy, lifelong work ethic.

N

CHAPTER 2

EXXON (1978-1989)

A Whole New World

I like to refer to my time at Exxon as "career bootcamp," where I learned professional discipline. It is a very structured and well-run engineering company, and I learned that it's true that hard work and going the extra mile pay off.

From 1978 to 1989, I absorbed management lessons—and life lessons—at Exxon Research & Engineering Company (ER&E). In five of those twelve years, I worked overseas on assignments in the United Kingdom, Japan, South Korea, and Italy. Stateside, I held posts in New Jersey and California.

In July 1978, I launched my professional career, entering Exxon offices in Florham Park, New Jersey. I was twenty-one, and I didn't know a soul in the Garden State.

I had not planned on living in New Jersey, but Exxon offered me $300 more per year than my other offers. My salary was a modest $18,300 with good benefits but no bonuses.

In the late seventies, Exxon was hiring fresh talent in droves, skimming cream-of-the-crop graduates from strong university engineering programs. The company offered new hires, almost all single and male in those times, the promise of good careers, plus setup money to ease their transitions into professional life and to help them stay focused on work instead of financial worries. As you can imagine, an Exxon job was coveted.

I rolled into Exxon with that wave of new engineers. The company loaned me $1,000 to get my life started.

I took a cheap apartment in Budd Lake, nearly thirty miles from the Exxon offices. My furniture was mostly stuff I took from my mom's home: a lobster trap for a cocktail table, cinder blocks, and plywood for shelving.

I found myself alone in a tiny town in a state where I'd never lived, my closest friends and family members two hundred miles away.

What saved me was the team that surrounded me.

I think of my first year at Exxon as an extension of college but with a boss. Exxon had hired twenty-five new college graduates into my unit that year, a fraternity of engineering colleagues that worked hard, played hard, and made enduring friendships, some lasting entire careers and even beyond.

We were all in the same boat. Nobody knew anybody else, and we all depended on one another.

Mark Blough, another new hire, arrived at Exxon in June 1978, a month before me. Mark and I had grown up in New York State and were kindred spirits. We had our training together and worked on the same projects. Forging what became a lifelong friendship, Marianne and I would one day even ask Mark to be the godfather of our first child.

In the office, Mark and I did serious work. We also enjoyed hitting a local bar a couple of times a week, talking over what we were learning.

"Our class of new hires went through something like a mass indoctrination program," Mark recalled. "Our training ranged from safety requirements to corporate structure to functions of the parts of Exxon to the basics of the petroleum industry. It was very broad based, and it lasted months."

Mark and I served in the Project Management Division of ER&E. Our training focused on how to create cost estimates and working schedules for massive refinery projects. We spent much of our time punching cards with data. Those cards were then fed into a mainframe computer across the campus. If you got those cards perfectly right, and in the correct order, the program would run and spit out hundreds of pages of cost estimates.

We both wanted to shine.

"Wes was a type A personality. Very focused," Mark responded when asked to weigh in on my work ethic. "He always wanted to do what was right for the company. He was far less concerned with impressing a supervisor.

My first employee ID

"Wes also always had a very high level of humility. In his dealings at work or when out in public, he never acted like he was superior or knew more than other people on a subject—even when he did."

Nine months after my first paycheck, Exxon rewarded me with my first real assignment: London Calling.

My reaction?

What? I'm having way too much fun to move, and I love where I work now!

Like other Exxon engineers, I quickly learned that overseas assignments were part of the deal. Many of the 1978 hires, in fact, ended up living all over the globe in their careers. Exxon knows how to manage very complex projects, and it is masterful at moving talent around the world to carry out that work.

I got one of the first calls among all the new hires, a plum assignment to the European headquarters of Exxon Research, known inside simply as "Triple-E L," for its continental name, Esso Engineering (Europe) Limited.

I packed practically nothing because I owned practically nothing. I gave my brother a car inherited from my grandfather. I took some clothes. Nothing with a plug would work in the UK, so I couldn't even take my stereo.

In July 1979, one year after starting with Exxon, I landed in London.

The England Years

I knew nobody—not one person—in all of England. It dawned on me that not only did I not know anybody, but I also did not have a clue how to function there.

England made a bewildering first impression. That was especially true in 1979. We all know about driving on the left, but what was not apparent to the casual visitor was how difficult it was to shop or get anything done while living in a flat. There were no supermarkets. No Uber Eats. Everything had to be paid in cash. I would physically go to five or six different stores to shop for the basics. Of course, that has all changed today.

In August 1979, not long after I arrived, Lord Mountbatten, the great-grandson of Queen Victoria, was assassinated by the Irish Republican Army, starting the Troubles, years of bloody unrest between England and the Irish. I remember that assassination like it was yesterday.

This was the world I entered with my new assignment.

Mostly, though, politics and news events were all background noise. I was a single young man focused on a job at hand, handling first-time projects like revamping refinery units in Rotterdam and expanding a refinery in Trecate, Italy.

Esso took good care of me. It provided a flat in Chelsea, a bank account, healthcare coverage, and a steady paycheck. For the first time in my life, I had money. Esso paid for everything but the beer.

London was home, but my work took me all over Europe, mostly Italy, the Netherlands, and Germany.

Languages, of course, posed a challenge. So did managing various currencies in pre–European Union and pre-euro nations. In airports and rail stations, I shuffled British pounds, Dutch guilders, German marks, and Italian lira.

I also couldn't always figure out how to get around or make calls from a pay phone in these countries, many years before cell phones. Sometimes that was a serious problem—I would occasionally forget the address of my hotel. But I learned fast, and this was the beginning of my lifelong journey into our huge, strange, wonderful world.

I fell in love with London and England. They were wonderful then, and they're wonderful now, decades later, when I visit my daughter, Erica, who lives and works in London.

At the office, I was learning the ABCs of project management from the best in the industry. The skill set used in project management has been the foundation of everything I've done for the rest of my career.

Kindred Spirits and New Friends for Life

Those defining years had just one problem.

I led a lonely life.

Most of the Exxon guys who moved to London had families, and many lived out of town. I was in the middle of the city, in Chelsea, pretty much by myself.

Again, cell phones didn't exist in 1979. Calling the United States when I got homesick always tested my patience.

I would reserve time on Sunday nights on the WATS line to use the undersea cable connecting the United States and the UK to talk to Mom. I called once a week, without fail.

To pass free time, I took up banjo, inspired by the comedian Steve Martin. I went on pub crawls, a ritual for many well-paid young single men in an exciting foreign capital. I took a photography class, and for a while, I tooled around in an MG BGT convertible, a classic British sports car, until it got broadsided.

Then, I found a new hobby, one that became a lifelong passion: I took to the waves.

One of the married guys, Rich McGreal, asked if I wanted to crew a 470 Olympic-class sailboat for him. I agreed. We bought one, and soon we were racing on Queen Mary Reservoir, just a few miles from Heathrow Airport. Rich and I have been close friends ever since.

About a year into my London post, another Exxon friend for life, Ed Casanova, appeared, newly transferred from the United States.

Ed was like a gift from heaven. At last—another single guy in London!

My boss asked me to welcome Ed to London. We didn't know each other well when we walked into a restaurant for dinner, but four bottles of wine and many stories later, we did. We became inseparable, working late, then staying out even later.

Ed Casanova and I in 1980

"My boss told me that Wes and I had found a third end of the candle to burn," Ed confessed.

Ed and I went on double dates, drove all over Europe together, took many trips into the heart of England, and drank in pubs, listening to old locals talk about World War II.

As two young bachelors, we put on top hats and tails to view horse races at the Royal Ascot. We dressed down, too, buying tickets to watch Chelsea soccer matches, standing right behind the goalposts in a stadium a short walk from my apartment. Chelsea tickets today are like gold—if you can even get them.

I fell in love with soccer, and I would coach my kids' teams later on.

All good things come to an end, of course. Ed took an assignment in Colombia. I would go back to the United States and then on to a new assignment.

In those London years, Ed had a unique, close-at-hand view into my work ethic and my professionalism.

"I think Wes's secret sauce—the secret of his career success—came to him in those early years at Exxon," Ed said.

"That was when he learned project management. It works in so many walks of life. You have certain logical steps. You define a need. You figure out: *Is that going to be profitable or not?* Then you achieve that need by capital investment or changing the organization or developing a new product. It was so clear to Wes: Design it. Procure what you need. And go build it.

"Managing a project is simply a microcosm of managing a business," Ed said. "Exxon planted that seed, and Wes nurtured it."

Placing My Bet

After countless travels in England and on the Continent, I added one more trip at Christmas in 1979—my first return home to New York State in more than a year.

It would turn out to be the most important journey I ever took.

When Marianne Spinner, my friend from high school, heard from a mutual friend that I was back in town, she gave me a call. It came completely out of the blue. Nearly six years had passed since we'd seen each other.

We went out to dinner. We caught up on our lives. We talked over old times.

And something felt new.

"We went to a little Italian restaurant," Marianne remembered, "and all during dinner, renewing our friendship, I thought, *Wes has grown up, we've got so much in common, he's gotten taller, and his eyes are so blue.*"

Marianne was dating a West Pointer at the time. I gave her a kiss on the cheek the night we parted. That was it.

After the holidays, I returned to England, my intense work, my bachelor life, and my adventures with Ed.

Two months later, Marianne learned that her soldier boy had been cheating. They broke up in early February.

On Valentine's Day, she came home from school to a surprise.

"Lo and behold, there was a bunch of roses from Wes," Marianne said. "It was so sweet. He was placing his bet."

A year and a lot of correspondence later, Marianne came to visit me in England. She and a girlfriend flew over in February on a school break. They did touristy things and just hung out.

Marianne asked to see the English countryside. I booked a cute bed-and-breakfast spot in Hazlemere, south of London.

Now it was my turn for something out of the blue.

I asked Marianne to marry me.

She couldn't believe it. The next day, she pressed me. "Wes, are you serious? Really?"

Really.

Marianne had realized something important about me.

"He's the kind of guy," she said, "who goes right after something once he's pretty sure about it."

The Japan Years

We lived apart for the next year, tying up loose ends as we readied to tie the knot.

Then Exxon brought me back to the states. Once again, I took up residence with colleagues in New Jersey. I would live out my remaining bachelor days with them. We went back to working hard and playing hard. But I was different now, with new things to think about.

Marianne and I walked down the aisle in June 1982, a month after she'd earned her master's degree in education. We found an apartment in Summit, New Jersey, and set about making it a home.

We almost got the paint dry.

Six months after Marianne had moved out of her parents' home and into married life, Exxon asked me to take a new assignment—halfway around the world.

We packed up and moved to Japan.

It would be an amazing time for us—two of the best years of our married lives together. I was barely twenty-six years old, and we were living in Japan with more money than I ever dreamed of having. Sometimes I wonder if that assignment that moved us together away from our families, with just us two and nobody else, was what has kept our marriage strong now for more than four decades.

I joined a select team designing and building a massive new refinery in Sakai, an industrial suburb of Osaka. Exxon's design team was based at a contractor's office in Kamiooka, near Yokohama. Marianne and I first lived in Yokohama, then later moved to Kobe, a suburb of Osaka.

As the project took shape, our Exxon design team moved on-site. I took up residence in a field office. I wore a uniform each day, packed a bento box for lunch, and even led the daily workforce exercises, known in Japan as Radio Taiso.

The project was a beehive, with four thousand workers on-site at the peak of construction. Despite its complexity, I and other Exxon project managers planned project coordination and implementation so well that not a single lost-time accident occurred in more than twelve million man-hours of work.

That project taught me to appreciate the specialness of Japanese culture.

Japanese employees are tremendously loyal to their companies and all their policies. Honor has a special meaning, and part of that is following through on one's commitments. It's extremely important in Japan.

The largest lift at Sakai was a 200-ton reactor

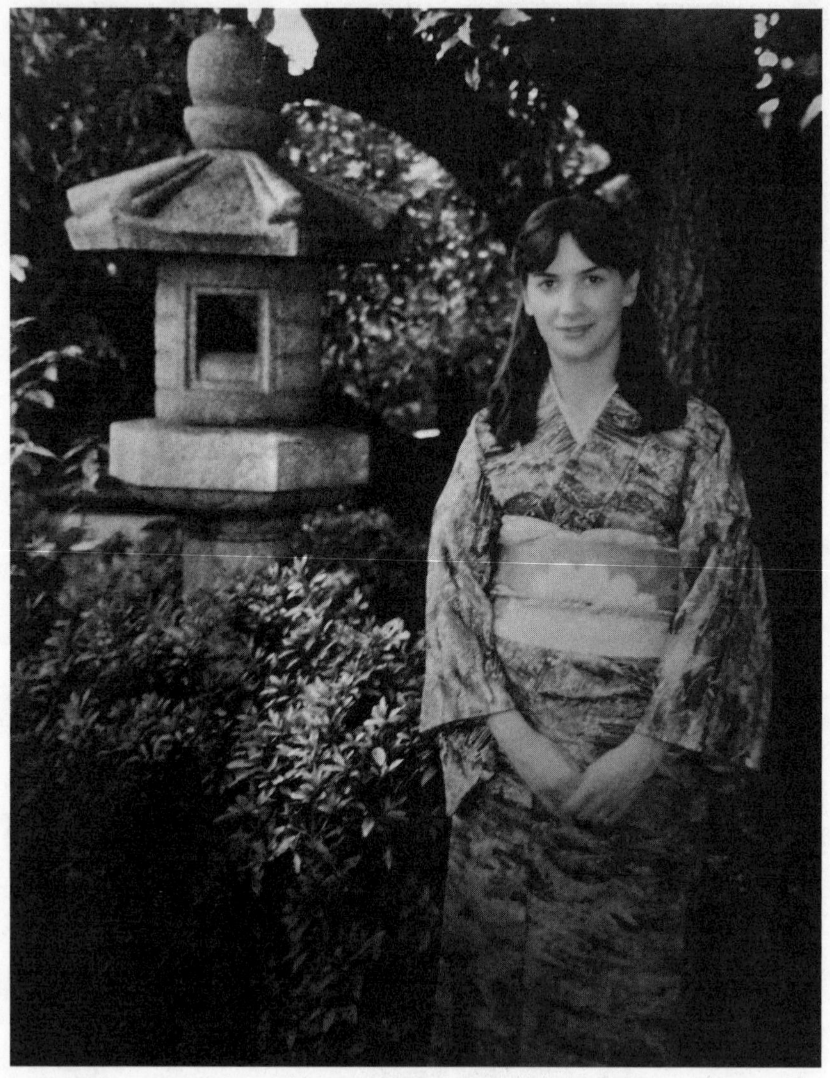

Marianne in her kimono

That powerful strength of the culture in Japan is why the project succeeded. We were pushing our contractors hard, typical of our American style of work. But in the end, we succeeded because of personal commitments made late at night in hostess bars, man to man. (There were no women in the key jobs then.) That's how business is done in Japan. Understanding that made all the difference.

Sakai conversion needed very large vessels

My controls team in Sakai

The deal-making was deeply Japanese—personal bonding forged with my Japanese counterparts and their bosses over multiple glasses of *mizu wari*, whiskey and water, often amid raucous sessions of karaoke.

I got my job done by making myself Japanese, as much as a gaijin—the Japanese term for a foreigner—is able.

Also, I enthusiastically absorbed the Eastern world around me. It would prove of great value later in my career.

I learned how deeply to bow in various circumstances. I learned what to say and how to say it. I learned how to take *o furo* (a bath) without embarrassing myself. I learned how to read the two phonetic alphabets, katakana and hiragana, and I even memorized about one hundred kanji symbols—kanji are Chinese logographic characters used in Japanese writing. Our team went to sumo matches, and we adopted our favorite local baseball team, the Yokohama Whales. We met loads of people, and we felt like a family at work.

The Sakai project was a ringing success. Completed right on time, its design and execution would become a model for Exxon projects elsewhere.

As the schedule control engineer, I wrote up a summary of how the company managed the massive project from design to completion in twenty-five months, on deadline, without one lost-time accident. The project's consummate execution and results kept me top of mind when Exxon leadership conducted annual rankings.

Here's what that meant.

Each year, Exxon's leaders evaluated the twenty-five of us who were in the same grade and same department—mostly the guys I started with in 1978. A manager for our work group ranked direct reports, then met with other managers who had done the same thing, and they determined top performers based on performance input from superiors, peers, and subordinates. Senior managers chaired the meetings, kept things on track, and broke ties when employees had similar rankings.

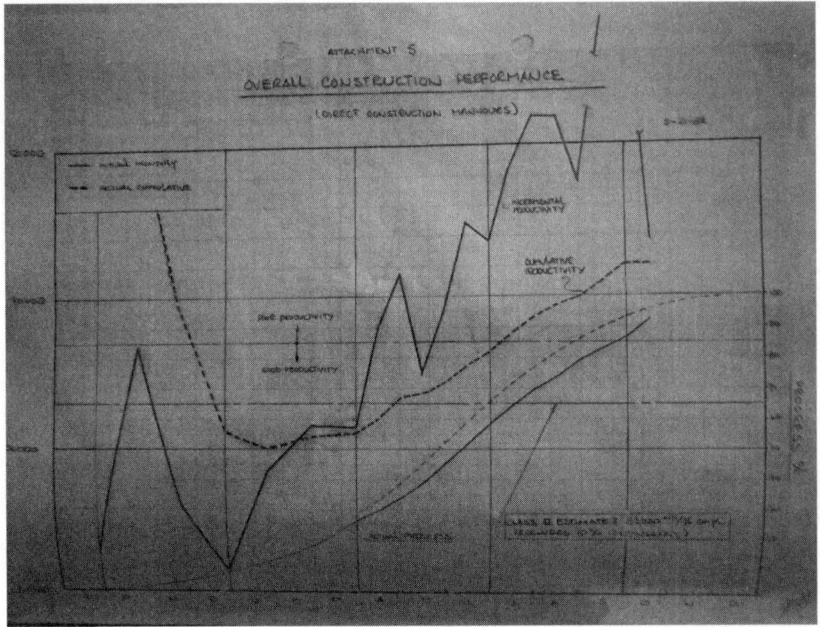

Managing the project by hand

For all twelve years I worked at Exxon, I was in the top 10 percent of my grade. For a few of those years, I was either number one or number two.

I fit the mold at Exxon. An article from 1978 in *Texas Monthly* magazine (Appendix C2.1) neatly captured the essence of the successful Exxon manager. (Keep in mind that this profile appeared more than a half century ago. Times have changed.)

From the article:

It's generally agreed, among those who love the company and those who don't, that the successful Exxon executive is a person (almost always a man) of a particular type. Above all, he is extremely able; the system is good at weeding out incompetents. Like many men who have risen in our large corporations, he comes from a stable, middle-class background, usually not a big city and usually not the East or West Coast.

He's a family man, happily married to an attractive woman and the father of several children. He and his wife take care to be active in respectable community affairs. He's not an eccentric, a maverick, or an entrepreneurial type. He's not a flashy or sloppy dresser. He's bright, aggressive, good with numbers, less good with people. Very likely he is a veteran of the military.

He's willing to relocate frequently (though this is becoming less the case) and to work hard on any assignment he's given. "The people who did best there," says one former employee, "were those who kept plugging, who never questioned authority, who said, 'If this is what the company wants, I'll do it.'

"Anyone who said, 'Why the hell am I staying up all night Sunday to finish this when nobody needs it till Thursday?' didn't have the right spirit."

HAPPINESS ON THE HOME FRONT

Marianne and I were very happy on our Japanese home front.

As newlyweds, we toured Japan and Asia, only coming home for Christmas one time. Free of children, free of pets, we dove into the culture and saw all we could.

I served as best man at two weddings in classic Japanese settings. Marianne and I skied in Sapporo, sailed on Tokyo Bay, and visited Hiroshima and Nagasaki. We experienced earthquakes for the first time. We toured Hong Kong, Singapore, Thailand, and Bali. We lodged in *ryokan* and the more rustic *minshuku*, traditional Japanese inns with tatami mats and communal baths. We relaxed in hot springs and tried our hands, literally, at an ancient form of pottery making in Japan's mountains.

Marianne tutored, did some work for Encyclopaedia Britannica, and taught aerobics. In a surreal twist, she landed on Japanese television as part of a team-led morning aerobics show popular with Japanese housewives.

Marianne on Japanese TV every morning

"I was a doo-wop girl on the back row," Marianne said. "I had the same height and the same haircut as the other girls. You could only tell I was the one gaijin when the camera panned us, and there were my round eyes."

Japan was amazing from every perspective. Marianne and I did all we could find to do there.

The Santa Ynez Project in California

The Sakai Conversion Project reached a successful end. Then I got another call.

This time, Exxon wanted me in Norway, a four-year project working out of Oslo.

At this point, I was a company man. I said yes and, with Marianne, started packing two years of possessions and Japanese memories. We boxed it all, and Marianne flew ahead to the United States to handle storage and visit her parents. She would meet me in Oslo once I settled there.

But days before my flight to Scandinavia, news came. No Oslo project. Canceled at the last minute. Instead, I would report back to New Jersey and wait for my next assignment.

It worked out fine. Marianne and I bought our first house and adopted our first dog, a golden retriever named Monty, after Monty Python, the British satirical comedy troupe.

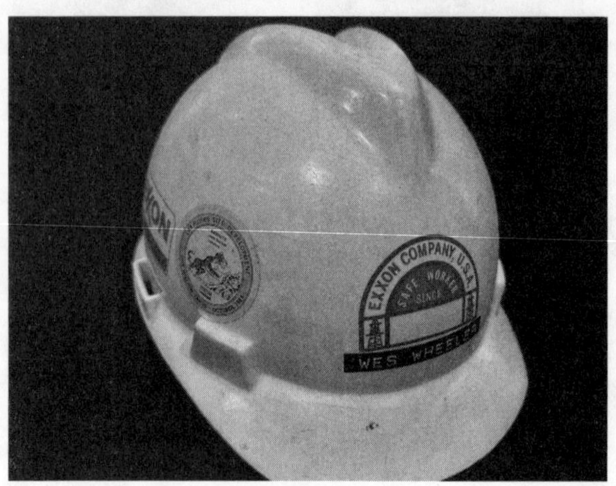

My Exxon hard hat

Then the six-month bug bit again.

Within a few months, I was asked to move to California for an eighteen-month assignment. So Marianne and I sold our first house and moved to the Exxon Western Division Headquarters in Thousand Oaks, California, just up the coast from Los Angeles.

The Santa Ynez Unit Project, as it was called, was the highlight of my time at Exxon.

The project involved design and construction of two offshore drilling platforms, each one the size of the World Trade Center and each one built with thirty-five thousand tons of steel. Construction and assembly of the structure took place in Dong Ulsan, South Korea. The 850-foot-long launch barge was built in the Netherlands, the platform topsides in Texas. The rigs would ultimately tap a big oil deposit off the California coast near Santa Barbara.

Before even starting the assignment, Exxon had to finalize the project financials and ensure viability. Geologists had to determine the exact placement of the offshore platforms, the routing of the undersea pipelines, and how the pipelines would travel onto land at Las Flores Canyon, the project site.

Execution planning was always a strength at Exxon, and for this work, contracting made up a whole department within the project team. The project schedule would be long, four to five years. Negotiations and mutual agreements with state and county governments and with environmental groups were all major milestones.

I reconnected with Mark Blough on the project control side. We got busy developing a unique way of controlling the project.

"We had a cost control system to set up," Mark explained. "It broke the project into different areas, different groupings, with different budgets, and people had to report against the different budgets.

"Some of the old-timers wanted just to wing it, saying, 'Don't worry, we'll give you the cost when it's done.' But our system at ER&E was disciplined and more demanding than the 'upstream' division at Exxon, which manages drilling and pipelines. We brought structure and accountability and cost controls that the project needed."

Exxon's upstream prided themselves on their self-reliance and independence—a cowboy mentality.

"Some people who weren't familiar with our system," said Mark, "didn't totally buy into it. Some thought it was stupid, a waste of time. Sometimes there was friction."

Mark recalls working with me during some of the tense meetings with the upstream team in Houston.

"We'd be in meetings where people raised their voices and called each other names," Mark said. "Wes would never do that. He had found a diplomatic way of dealing with work and with people. I found that to be an excellent example of good leadership."

Two massive steel structures built in Dong-Ulsan, South Korea

Step by step, I set up the project management system for construction of the offshore drilling platform in South Korea. Each platform would be built in one piece at Hyundai Shipyard in Dong Ulsan, then towed across the Pacific Ocean and launched off the coast of Santa Barbara during a tight, six week weather window.

The project required me to be on-site in South Korea for six weeks of 1986. Dong Ulsan was a gritty, blue-collar town. It teemed with tough, working-class Koreans. It was a place on the water but was nothing like the California coast, where Marianne and I had sailed, played golf, and sat on the beach with Monty and our new friends.

That was a rough time. Marianne was home with her teaching, and I was on the other side of the world. By now, we wanted to start a family, but it couldn't quite happen yet.

Finally, my work in Korea ended. I came home to a joyful reunion—and news. My job would move now to Goleta, a town at the base of the same mountain as Ronald Reagan's ranch just north of beautiful Santa Barbara and not far from the Las Flores Canyon jobsite.

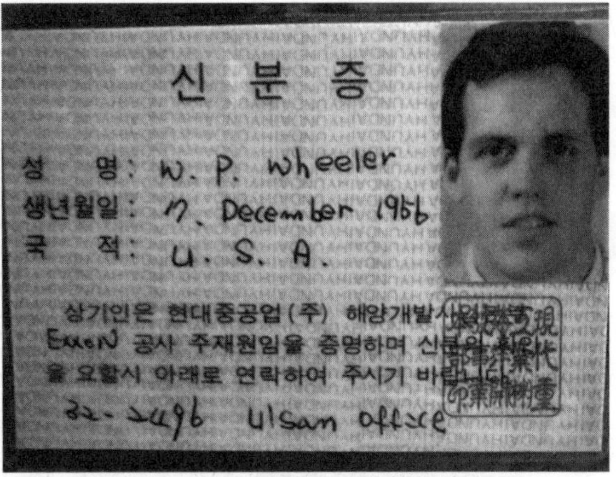

My Hyundai Shipyard ID

So we moved again. And we settled in—again.

I happily spent the next two years at a worksite where I put on my Red Wing boots (steel toed, of course) and a hard hat every day. From a small trailer office, I helped manage the development of the onshore oil processing site, where petroleum from the offshore rigs would be piped in, sulfur scrubbed out, and the crude oil stabilized and stored prior to shipment by cross-country pipelines to refineries in Texas.

The Santa Ynez Project site

When I got out of the trailer in my off-hours, open water called.

I raced sailboats out of Santa Barbara Harbor. Marianne and I spent our nights on State Street in Santa Barbara, at Joe's, the iconic bar near the beach. We biked to Isla Vista, where the University of

Santa Barbara overlooks the channel from a cliff. We discovered great wineries nearby.

Marianne and I had each other. We had Monty. We had friends.

Marianne, Monty, and I

Then we had Greg.

Our first child was born in Ventura County Medical Center. I held my little boy in my arms and made some grown-up decisions.

I got rid of the motorcycle. I got rid of the sports car. We were a family—Greg, Monty, Marianne, and me.

It was perfect.

Leaving the Mother Ship

My role in the Santa Ynez Project came to an end in November 1989.

I brought my two-year portion of a multi-year project in exactly on time and on budget. I did so despite two major landslides on our site, a few unfortunate and deadly accidents, and protests by Chumash native peoples over their ancient homelands. I did it at the same time I managed through routine interventions by local Air Pollution Control District and fire department officials, community protesters, and environmental activists.

My team and I had stayed the course and met the rigid timelines set for the Santa Ynez planning phase. The work required more than fifty thousand horsepower of earthmovers and bulldozers day after day during the project. My team moved five million cubic yards of earth. We carved out eight platform sites for oil facilities to be used in the project's next phase. We put in place all the infrastructure, including the firewater systems, the electrical systems, and the roads that would be required for future operations.

It was grinding work, but the place was spectacular, and our team loved it. I loved it most of all.

A moment of accomplishment came with the arrival of the first of two oil platforms. They had been completed on time and floated across the Pacific during a calm weather window.

Marianne and I, along with many proud Exxon team members, watched the first barge arrive with its completed twelve-hundred-foot-long drilling structure. The barge was flooded in a way that allowed the thirty-five-thousand-ton structure to slide off into the water and onto its side. The structure consisted of hundreds of steel tubes that were airtight, allowing it to float. Then a single man climbed aboard, entered a control room, and carefully flooded the tubes in a sequence that allowed the platform to right itself.

A massive earthmoving project

It was a spectacular feat of engineering. No one who saw the launch will ever forget the vision of the gargantuan, man-made structure crashing into the blue Pacific, then slowly rising right-side up. Cheers rose from shore and from every boat in the operation.

I felt a profound sense of achievement.

I also felt, deep down, I needed more.

I wanted a promotion. I told Marianne I'd be willing to stay longer with Exxon if one came my way. I had already started working on my MBA at night to strengthen my credentials.

I waited expectantly for the reward I knew would come from my company after a dozen years of outstanding work.

What didn't happen next changed my life.

Exxon told me that I would stay on the project—but only at my current level and with my current responsibility. I would remain a cost-and-schedule engineer on the project's next phase.

I appealed, but the promotion I felt I'd earned for more than a decade of outstanding service would not come, I was told, for at least a few more years.

That frustrated me. I lost my patience. After twelve years of being in the top 10 percent of my peer group, I wasn't promoted. I couldn't help but feel that if I stayed at Exxon, everything would just stay the same for my career, and I would remain stagnant.

But things *weren't* the same for me anymore.

I was a father now. I had more than one future to plan. I felt grateful to Exxon for many things, but I knew in my heart I had earned a chance to play a bigger role.

A phone call changed my life.

It came out of the blue. A North Carolina area code. A man named Tim Tyson. A West Pointer, born to lead. A chieftain in the pharmaceutical industry, of all places.

Tim asked me if I might consider a career change.

Yes. Yes, I would.

Boot camp was over.

Even so, a dozen years at Exxon had meant the world to me.

When Marianne came to pick me up at the jobsite on my last day, I cried like a baby.

LESSONS LEARNED

I believe it's valuable to start a career with a large, established company. Why? It teaches you how to work with leaders and colleagues of all types–brilliant, demanding, lazy, or loser. It creates structure in a work life. You learn how to navigate the labyrinth of rules, policies, mood swings, deadlines, and dramas the business world presents. Use this period in your career to figure out how to distinguish between the brilliant and the losers, and how you can differentiate yourself from others.

I learned during my construction days to wake up early. I had to, or I was already behind. This is just as important in an office job, where people rarely show up early. If you have the discipline to get to the office before all the others, you are already ahead of the game.

CHAPTER 3

GLAXO (1989-2002)

Acquisitions, Mergers, Launches, and Carving Out a Global Operation

I had never heard of Tim Tyson before his call. I had never heard of his company.

After our talk, I turned to Marianne with a puzzled look. "Glaxo?" I asked. "What's a Glaxo?"

I learned that Glaxo was a century-old player in the pharmaceutical industry. Tim Tyson was a leader there. He needed help with a big project, and he heard I might be the man for the job.

In 1978, Glaxo had staked out a presence in the United States by purchasing Meyer Laboratories. Five years later, in 1983, the company set up the North Carolina-based US headquarters, Glaxo Inc., in Research Triangle Park, with ambitious plans to conduct R&D and manufacturing.

Tim Tyson, my surprise caller, had grown up in the fields and woods of rural New York State. In high school, he played three sports and was the lead guitarist in a rock band. Tim graduated into the United States Military Academy at West Point, where he earned a mechanical engineering degree. He put in his time with Uncle Sam, then entered civilian work, first at Procter & Gamble, then Bristol-Myers Corporation, then Glaxo.

Tim would become one of the great influences in my life, a mentor for fifteen years, and a lifelong friend.

I sensed none of this immediately after the call. I only knew that the more I thought about Tim Tyson and Glaxo, the more mystified I became.

I had spent twelve years studying oil refineries and building big things in Europe, Asia, and California. Now I'd gotten a call about a possible job in rural North Carolina for a company that made tiny pills.

At that moment, it did not compute.

I learned more. It started to compute.

Glaxo's showcase drug was called ranitidine. The company marketed this stomach-acid reducing product as Zantac, and it was making a fortune.

The launch of Zantac had transformed Glaxo into the fastest-growing pharma company in the world.

Glaxo wanted to keep its profits in the United States. To do so, it was investing in a massive new greenfield R&D campus in the RTP in North Carolina, a science and pharma research hot spot anchored by fine universities at Raleigh, Durham, and Chapel Hill.

The $350 million project (more than $700 million in today's dollars) was just coming out of the ground. By completion, the immense development would employ every major contractor in the Tarheel State.

On his call, Tim had been plainspoken. He told me he needed a great project manager.

Tim's timing was nearly perfect.

I had just returned, disappointed, to Goleta after that trip to Exxon headquarters in New Jersey. I had appealed the company's decision to extend my current role for the next phase of work at Santa Ynez without a promotion.

It left me unsettled and raw.

I had truly loved the work at Santa Ynez.

I wore my Red Wings and took my lunch to the jobsite every day. I drove a well-loved company Jeep Cherokee—it went through some pretty brutal conditions on the five-hundred-acre mountainside property. The work had felt almost too good to be true.

Like a soldier's stripes, my hard hat displayed stickers telling the Santa Ynez story.

One decal commemorated the completion of one million cubic yards of moved earth. (That would go on to exceed five million cubic yards.) Another marked a key safety record. Others celebrated second and third earthmoving milestones. Even with all that, my hard hat still had room for an American flag decal and one of Exxon's famous "Tony the Tiger" logos.

I wore my Exxon hard hat with pride.

Until I didn't.

Meeting My Mentor

I flew to Raleigh, North Carolina, with Marianne and Greg. The next morning, I visited the Glaxo jobsite.

I immediately ran into an old friend—Bob Diefenderfer, a former Exxon executive and one of my early mentors. "Deef," as Exxon folks knew him, had come out of retirement to consult with Tim Tyson and Glaxo.

Deef was dressed in full construction gear, holding court at the center of a beehive swarm of men, vehicles, and moving equipment.

Seeing an old friend in his element, busy and happy at important work, gave me the right first impression. The sight of Deef also helped me connect a few dots. I realized that he was the one who had told Tim Tyson about me. Deef was the reason Glaxo called.

I later learned what else he told Tim Tyson:

Wes Wheeler is the best there is, but he will never leave Exxon.

Deef proved better at engineering than prophecy.

I shook hands with Tim Tyson for the first time that day. The moment changed both our lives.

I was incredibly impressed. I told Marianne that night, "I'd really like to work with this guy."

And what was Tim Tyson looking for?

"The first thing at Glaxo I looked at when my boss, Mike Herriott, the vice president of engineering, hired me, was the structural setup," Tim said. "Honestly, that's usually a major deficiency in the pharma world, but it's a key to success.

"You need a controls group on construction projects. It's essential. Three things matter if you talk with an engineer—scope, cost, and schedule. Those all need controls oversight. If a job candidate doesn't talk about that, he doesn't know what he's doing."

Tim continued. "So I'm looking for a controls engineer with capability. But the last place I would look is pharma, because when it comes to engineering and construction, pharma projects are often miserably out of control. Pharma is not going to be the place to look for a project manager. But Exxon is a *great* place to look for engineers.

"Wes and I hit it off," Tim said. "We both grew up in New York. Wes's positive, can-do attitude impressed me. He had a discipline for execution. He was a family man with a good moral background. We had much in common."

Tim also said, "I always interview eight to ten people. No one else compared to Wes. I was looking for a superstar with the ability to step in right away. I saw no problem with Wes's youth or his ability to go top to bottom and bottom to top on a project. I was very impressed."

I felt the same about Tim, so I took the job.

So here I came, to a new company, a new industry, a new part of the world. I took a strictly lateral move. I got less pay. I received no bonus.

My incentive?

It gave me a major challenge where I could use my experience—and gain experience—in a whole new industry.

That decision would prove to be one of the most consequential of my life.

The Glaxo R&D Project

The mammoth Glaxo project would develop ten buildings and more than 1.5 million square feet of new space for the firm's growing R&D activities.

The project had a sense of urgency. The United States was becoming Glaxo's main driver of company profits. Zantac, its blockbuster product, plus the asthma/COPD inhaler drug Ventolin and more promising drugs in the pipeline, were giving Glaxo a golden opportunity to carve out a bigger share in the world's most lucrative pharma marketplace.

Seizing the moment, Glaxo had gone all-in at the North Carolina site. It hired notable Philadelphia architects, The Kling-Lindquist

Partnership, Inc., and Rhode Island-based Gilbane Building Company was hired to manage the construction.

The design included an enormous signature central administration building and auditorium. It would have two large laboratory buildings, two animal facilities for preclinical research, a pilot plant where small quantities of test drugs could be manufactured, a sales training building, and a central plant that produced all the utilities for Glaxo facilities. Just down the road, other buildings would fill out the vast campus.

When I arrived in November 1989, only a few foundations showed above the scraped ground.

As at Exxon, I worked from a trailer, one of several in a project oversight complex. I took an office next to Tim's. I went to work, as I had for the past dozen years, setting up cost-and-schedule controls for various parts of the project. I had no direct reports. I showed up before 6:00 a.m. every morning, the first person on the job, just as at Exxon in California.

I was thirty-three years old and still doing just about the same thing I'd done all my career.

As I waited for bigger opportunities at Glaxo, I took night courses at North Carolina State University in nearby Raleigh to finish my MBA.

My family arrived in Chapel Hill, and our second child, Erica, arrived around the same time. She was born on March 1, 1991, a healthy, 6-pound-15.5-ounce baby girl—and another compelling reason for me to make good on a gamble to relaunch my career at a pharmaceutical company in the American South.

The Life of a Project Manager

Tim had assembled an able team, but despite its best efforts, the Glaxo project fell behind. Gilbane was not able to catch up. The construction project's deadline loomed large, barely more than two years ahead.

Tim saw firsthand how I pulled my weight.

"The nemesis of the controls engineer is the customer," Tim said. "Changes cost money. The controls engineer is always trying to minimize change to the design. It's tough when the customer is involved—in this case, a customer named Glaxo."

An example?

If a Glaxo executive wanted to move a light switch, on paper, that would look like a small thing. But it could cost $5,000 by the time materials were bought, the HVAC overhead adjusted, the conduit run, the structural column located, and the painting completed. A change to one light switch might also affect four other light switches; then the job could cost $25,000.

"Small can get complicated in a hurry," Tim said, "and small changes can create major issues with major costs.

"In pharma, the R&D people are gods. Telling them no? It's just not happening. But here's Wes Wheeler. He's probably thirty years old, but he looks a lot younger. And he's from a different industry. And to scientists he's just a dumb engineer—*any* engineer is a redheaded stepchild in the pharma industry.

"But Wes had a unique ability to say no in a professional way, so people heard him and respected him. 'Look,' he'd say, 'if we do this, then this happens, and it means this.' He was so competent and able to articulate issues and say no without saying no."

For hardheaded customers, of course, I escalated issues to Tim.

"Wes and I spent a huge amount of time together," Tim said. "We had 128 subcontractors, and the work of everyone had implications for our cost, scope, and time. We'd spend half a working day together designing things necessary to keep our controls in place.

"*Everything* is critical to a controls engineer. Project management requires a lot of babysitting. If pipe was supposed to be laid, Wes would be out checking it. If electrical contractors were scheduled today and they planned on having ten people on hand, but only eight showed up, Wes was right there asking, 'Where are the other two?' If people aren't there, work doesn't get done."

Tim stressed, "Wes kept that kind of vigilance every day. He constantly measured, codified, and put cost data into the system. In our work, details were critical.

"Wes was a master of detail."

A Consequential Stranger Onsite

One evening, alone at the trailer site, I found a stranger wandering through. By now, I knew everyone on the team, and I had never laid eyes on this particular guy.

"Who the hell are you?" I demanded. (Yes, years of Exxon project work had refined my construction site manners.)

The stranger answered with equal refinement.

"Who the hell are *you*? I'm here taking a look around; that's all you need to know."

At that point, I was ready to escort him off the jobsite.

The stranger glared, then added, "It doesn't matter who I am. But you can get anything you want from me as long as you have a checkbook."

It turned out that Bill Van, the stranger, was on-site courtesy of the boss. Tim had previously hired Bill for assignments at Bristol-Myers. A career electrician, Bill was a highly skilled, union-trained (via the International Brotherhood of Electrical Workers), rough-and-tumble professional. He was a genius when it came to practical problem-solving.

Bill laughs these days, remembering our first encounter.

"I didn't know how to spell the word *pharmaceutical*," Bill said, "but the last thing I needed was a snot-nosed college grad to tell me anything. I could see Wes was younger than me, and probably not as experienced."

From that unpromising start, a lifelong friendship would grow.

Bill became one of the most important people in my career and in my life. He would end up working alongside me for the entire Glaxo project. And beyond.

"OK, fine," I told Bill. "We will probably need something. And we have a checkbook."

Glaxo did, in fact, need help like Bill's.

Bill could be raw. Bill could be rude. But Bill was always right. He became my wingman in the field and an important part of the reason we finally pulled off the project on time.

The work took me into the field often

Another great resource appeared. Jim Scandura arrived as a contractor from Johnson Controls. Our styles matched.

"When I met with Tim's project team," Jim said, "Wes was the one who consistently said things of substance. And he was the only one who acted like it was OK that I was there to help finish the construction project."

Jim wasn't your typical team member.

"I was the guy that came in to make things happen without caring about collateral damage." Jim described his work personality. "I knew we just needed to get the job done. I could be the nice guy. Or I could be the 'You're-going-to-do-it-this-way' guy. Whatever it took.

"I was a lot like Wes that way. That's why we got along. He would get extremely frustrated when people weren't doing what they were supposed to do. It drove him nuts. He had no tolerance for slowness, sloppiness, or stupidity."

Glaxo R&D Campus

With Bill and Jim at my side, we took over completion of the most complicated facility in the project. Leadership at the Pharmaceutical Development Pilot Plant had been lacking, especially for the complex equipment and systems required to make the drugs. Things had to change.

That was true for the whole project.

Tim had grown gravely worried. We were now midway through 1990; the completion deadline of year-end 1991 looked as imposing as Mount Everest.

Always a man of action, Tim stepped up.

He brought the entire project team to an off-site hotel. There must have been one hundred people there. And Tim gave one of the most compelling speeches I heard in my entire career. With emotion and determination, he set a deadline of October 18, 1991, as our completion date. We were not going to fail.

Suddenly, the project caught fire. A tremendous amount of work remained, but our team now attacked the challenge instead of allowing ourselves to be daunted by it.

We started managing the project from the back end, rather than the front end. In other words, we started measuring, in great detail, all the activities it would take to complete the work rather than reporting on how much work had already been done. We perfected this novel concept in those final months of the project.

The grind went on for weeks, right up to the night before the site's formal opening event. It was a big deal—Sir Paul Girolami, the company's Italian chair and CEO, would attend. So would North Carolina governor James Martin.

I remember Bill Van wandering around construction areas hours prior to the opening ceremony with fists full of $20 bills, offering them to workers who would stay later and work longer. I had turned off the lights in the trailer many nights, the last member of management on the job. But that night, I remained on the job until 3:00 a.m., leaving for home only to change out of my paint-spattered suit.

I returned to the jobsite at 8:00 a.m.

We were still painting, fixing, correcting mistakes, and cleaning in the lobby when Sir Paul Girolami came through the front door.

Against all odds, the build-out of the Glaxo R&D project met the deadline.

The project was a success. It came in on time and *under* budget. It was approved for $350 million and completed for $339 million. This was an achievement virtually unheard of in the pharmaceutical industry.

At Last: An Opportunity to Lead

The successful completion of the huge flagship project brought my long-sought promotion. I took a new title as director of engineering for all Glaxo's RTP facilities.

I now had a team reporting to me. Some of them had been my peers for the length of the R&D project.

After changing companies in a quest for more challenges and a higher profile, I now had gotten all I had bargained for.

I led development of a Glaxo system to monitor the big projects and dozens of smaller ones approved each year. I sharpened my leadership skills by delegating and monitoring assignments to project managers. For one assignment, Glaxo annexed the Durham Southern High School to build a small adjacent campus. We expanded the laboratories and the central plant. We were managing more than one hundred projects at a time.

I especially relished "fun projects," as we called them. On one, we guided construction of a house for a Glaxo division president. We created an office in Washington, DC, for lobbyists, and even built a company skybox at the Durham Bulls's minor league baseball stadium.

To help with our leadership development, Tim called in Terry Tipple, PhD, a young consultant who specialized in organizational development.

Terry needed to solve an immediate workplace problem.

Two of Tim's engineering directors couldn't get along. Their clashing styles and attitudes were affecting work and those around them.

One director was me.

Terry Tipple met first with the other director.

"He did the usual thing you would expect," Terry said. "He started going on for an hour about how difficult Wes was, how it was just impossible to work with him, how evil Wes was, how he wasn't interested in working together, how he wasn't interested in creative solutions, how he was driving people crazy, etcetera."

Terry then sat down with me.

"I expected to hear the exact same thing," Terry said. "But Wes blew me away.

"He just said, 'Tell me what to do differently, and I'll do it. What do I need to do?'

"Wes shelved his ego. He did not accuse the other director of any wrongs. He focused on solving the problem, not the man behind the problem.

"At that moment," Terry said, "I knew I was dealing with a pretty significant individual. How many young directors are that self-aware?"

Tim Tyson added, "Hearing about that meeting always stayed with me. Wes was not a touchy-feely guy. He wasn't into backslapping, but he wasn't defensive about learning to lead. He had an openness to criticism and feedback. He was willing to self-analyze. It was a distinguishing characteristic from day one."

My Move from Engineering to Marketing

In July 1993, Glaxo had rewarded Tim for his vast campus construction oversight with a long-sought promotion of his own. He was now vice president and general manager of Glaxo Dermatology, one of the company's fast-growing units.

In short order, Tim then received a *second* promotion, to vice president of sales and marketing, an even bigger position.

He immediately saw that several of his marketing functions deserved better leadership. After a close look, Tim decided to hire someone to run marketing research, physician-related events, the art studio in charge of graphics and divisional creative, the forecasting area, financial reporting, and data management.

He wanted me.

Tim asked me to take the title of group director of marketing services. To get our CEO's approval, Tim leveraged the fact that I had just completed my MBA.

It was a pivotal moment in my career.

I had built labs and research facilities for Glaxo, and now I moved to marketing, where I learned how businesses were run. This was the single most important move of my career. My MBA had opened a door into the commercial side of the company. I jumped from being a staffer to being a leader in business.

Just a blink after I had become a director, now I was group director, suddenly leading a team of 140 people, with several directors of my own. I had my own creative playground—an art studio—and eighty market researchers, event planners, and a handful of analysts.

I went to work mastering this new trade. I read, talked to marketing experts, and experimented. I learned everything there was to learn about marketing and drugs and how the development-to-launch cycle worked.

I had to learn. And fast.

My team supported the entire Glaxo portfolio and the launches of Imitrex, Flonase, Flovent, Zofran, and other commercially important products. On my watch, the company would launch thirty-two new drugs, a dozen of which would far exceed $1 billion in global revenue.

I brought a project engineer's mindset from the construction and engineering world to the white-collar, free-play world of the commercial space. I demanded commitment and performance at a high level. I knew my no-nonsense style could rub people the wrong way, but I also knew how to make things happen—the right way.

I brought back Dr. Terry Tipple to help develop my new organization—an eclectic group of creative and analytical professionals who had seldom worked together. Terry would become my personal coach—and my friend—for decades.

Terry attended the marketing team's first off-site meeting under my leadership, in Pinehurst, North Carolina. Directors from groups that worked both for and with me met for the first time.

Terry found a private opportunity to ask people about me, to "crack the formality," as he put it.

Their blunt comments of my directors surprised him.

"Wes? The guy's a machine," Terry heard. "He's working ninety hours a week. He's taking all the art out of marketing. He's trying to engineer the whole marketing function. We're wondering if he's really human ..."

"After dinner," Terry remembered, "we found ourselves all together in the bar. Wes was there too. And, lo and behold, the bar had a foosball machine."

Terry remembers that a smile spread over my face. Glaxo's badass, inhuman marketing services chief stepped up to the foosball machine and began to spin handles and slam home points.

I picked up right where I'd left off in my college life at Worcester Polytechnic, where members of my fraternity played twenty-four seven on a foosball machine in our house.

"The hard-driving man whose team considered him a super technocrat all of a sudden did this thing called foosball," Terry said. "It had nothing to do with work.

"And just like that, everyone suddenly saw that Wes Wheeler was just a guy. He had a family. He had a wife. He had a mortgage. And he knew how to play foosball.

"I watched the team's perception of Wes Wheeler change that night."

My Marketing Boot Camp

Through foosball, adaptation, and burning a lot of midnight oil to learn about life on the commercial side, I soon found my comfort zone in marketing services, supporting the company's commercial business.

I worked hard. I wanted to show Tim that his faith in me was well founded. Sometimes the work meant coloring outside the lines.

I came up with a unique forecasting methodology and produced a series of reports that would become required reading all the way up to the C suite. These reports were summarized in a monthly document that became known as "the Green Book," which Tim described as "the Glaxo commercial one source of truth."

Before the Green Book became mainstream, nearly every executive relied on the daily sales report. It told only what we sold yesterday, a snapshot in time. Waiting for the daily sales report was like a Pavlovian response each morning. But it really didn't tell you much. One day would be great, another terrible.

This Green Book went to every corner of the company and out into daily operations. The reports could create controversy, but I defended them the way a good engineer would—by pointing out facts, algorithms, and trends. As I said, it became required reading.

It was a wild time at Glaxo. The average employee age on the entire campus was twenty-seven years old. We had the best sales team in the industry. We were growing fast.

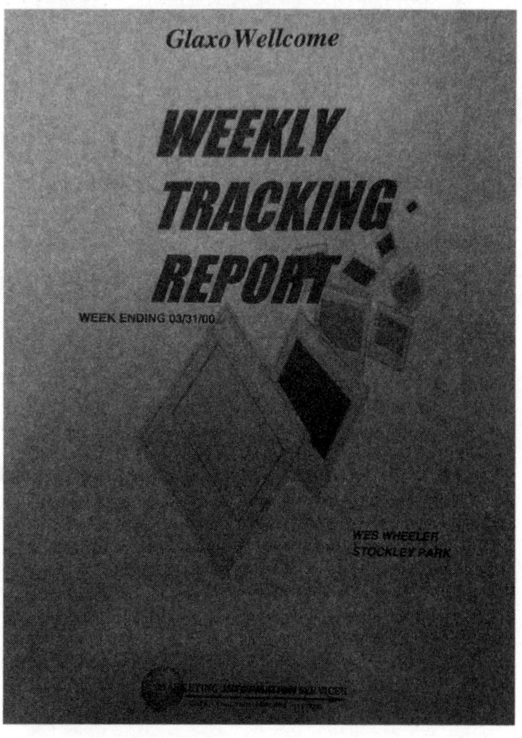

The Green Book became essential reading for all of our commercial executives

What did I learn?

About marketing? Everything.

Glaxo was my marketing boot camp. The company is masterful when it comes to marketing.

It became clear to me that the path to success in the pharmaceutical industry boiled down to just seven words: *find a way to differentiate your product.*

You need to find something special, or invent something new, in your product versus the current gold standard and then exploit the hell out of it with your sales force.

In 1995, Glaxo took a step to expand its portfolio and scientific expertise by acquiring Burroughs Wellcome Company (BW).

A pair of visionary giants in pharma, Dr. Gertrude Elion and George Hitchings, had affiliations with BW. They developed the world's first leukemia drug, and for that and other achievements received a Nobel Prize for Physiology or Medicine in 1988.

At the time of the Glaxo merger, Dr. Elion still had an association with BW. She had most recently in her illustrious career played a crucial role in developing that company's breakthrough antiviral drug Retrovir, or AZT, one of the first effective treatments against HIV and AIDS.

The BW buyout brought us new and promising products to market: Zovirax for genital herpes, and a new form of Zovirax in development, to be marketed as Valtrex and used to treat herpes infections like shingles, cold sores, and chicken pox. Older products included a minor cancer drug.

Glaxo hired Boston Consulting Group (BCG) to manage integration of the two companies. Separate teams formed, managing all aspects of the transition. I joined Ward Swift, a Glaxo legacy marketing director, to lead the integration of the two marketing units.

The intention to make a seamless transition hit potholes.

The BCG people tried to run things, but their inexperience in pharma showed, and we were not having any of it. About halfway through the integration, we pushed the consultants aside and took over.

After that, the integration of the two marketing units went exceedingly well.

Now I felt a deepening sense of purpose.

We were building a whole new company, with new therapies, new people, new ways of thinking, and new leaders. Every day in our integration team room, we could feel a new Glaxo being born.

Our integration room even had its own mascot—a Mr. Potato Head, the familiar Hasbro toy. As we realized we were creating something new—mergers in the pharma world were still pretty rare then—we looked at combining the best practices of both companies to make 1 + 1 = 3. So each day, Mr. Potato Head stood at the center of our table, and our team would change the way he looked. It perfectly symbolized our work designing a whole new company.

When we finished the integration, we held a celebration dinner. Everyone got a Mr. Potato Head on a trophy base with this inscription: "Creating the Industry's Best Marketing Organization."

Building a Corporate Brand before It Was Popular

About this time, Glaxo's chief change agents, Tim Tyson and I, found ourselves at the center of a controversy.

It happened when we came forward with a bold, outside-the-box idea: We proposed that GlaxoWellcome, as a new company, leverage the brand-name popularity of its products to bolster its own corporate brand.

The reason seemed pretty simple. Patients and doctors know the names of drugs, but they rarely know who makes them. Our idea was to build on the reputation of our drugs to benefit the company brand.

It shouldn't have been controversial.

The new pharma power had a commanding and visible portfolio: Flovent, Flonase, and Ventolin to combat respiratory ailments. Retrovir to fight HIV/AIDS. Imitrex to halt migraines. Zantac to treat ulcers.

Even with all this potential brand power, our efforts to leverage reputable brands on behalf of GlaxoWellcome didn't fly internally. Branding this way never made it out of the boardroom.

Tim and I had pioneered a concept, though.

Soon, using product brands to publicize corporate brands would be standard operating procedure in pharma. Who doesn't know today that the COVID-19 vaccine came from Pfizer?

That's today, but back then, few people knew who made their drugs. Tim had envisioned it way back then, though, in the late eighties. We gave it our best shot.

Our biggest win in corporate branding came when Tim negotiated with *TIME* magazine to run two special editions: "The Heroes of Medicine" and a follow-up, "The Frontiers of Medicine." We worked directly with *TIME* publisher Jack Haire and editor Walter Isaacson.

The *TIME* editions were a great success, introducing the GlaxoWellcome brand to millions of readers and staking out a powerful thought leadership position.

The work also rewarded us with special invitations to a magical evening on March 3, 1998, when *TIME* held its seventy-fifth birthday event at Radio City Music Hall. The publication transformed Radio City from an art deco performance space to an enormous and lavish dining hall with expensive … everything.

Everybody still alive who had ever been on the cover of *TIME* magazine showed up—except Saddam Hussein, Osama bin Laden, and the pope. I sat with the Olympic skater Peggy Fleming. I ran into former Russian premier Mikhail Gorbachev in the men's room. What an incredible night.

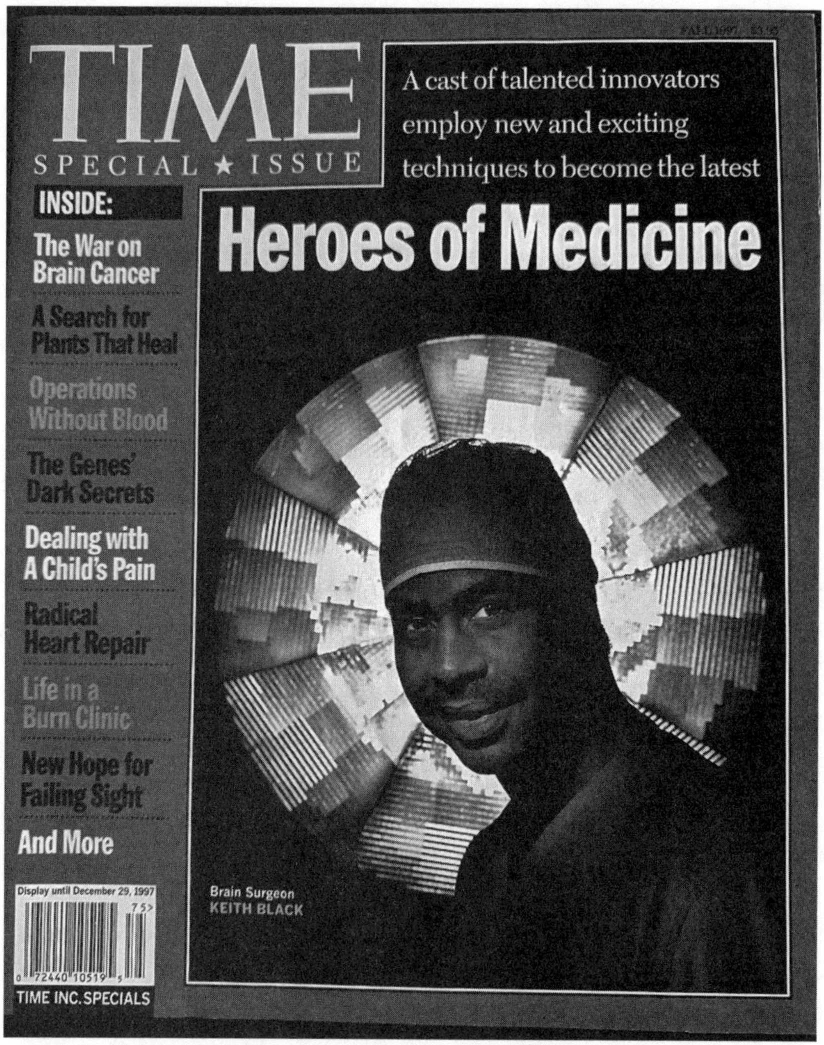

The Heroes of Medicine (AC3.1)

TIME put exactly two representatives from GSK up at the Waldorf Astoria for the event—my great friend Chuck Bramlage and I earned that honor. We spent starstruck hours gawking at the crowd as *TIME* editor Walter Isaacson presided and as President Bill Clinton spoke. We recognized indelible famous faces by the hundreds—Hank

Aaron, Steve Jobs, Sean Connery, Raquel Welch, Toni Morrison, Steven Spielberg, Barbara Walters, and many more.

"Wes and I wore our tuxes, of course, and walked the red carpet," Chuck said. "I cased the event and decided I wanted to meet three people there, and I did. One was John Glenn, an Ohioan like me—such a quality man. I spent fifteen minutes with him. I met Bill Gates, the world's greatest capitalist of that day. And I shook hands with Bill Clinton after waiting for him to stop chatting with Tom Cruise, who is very short. The president had very large hands and the biggest physical head I've ever seen on a human."

Chuck and I, back at the Waldorf Astoria, stayed awake most of the night chattering like schoolboys after a first double date.

"We both talked about how no one would ever believe the things we would tell them," Chuck said. "It was like nothing either of us had ever imagined would happen in our lives."

Convincing the FDA to Think Outside the Box

Successes like the *TIME* editions and my high-visibility forecasting work brought me a 1998 promotion to vice president of marketing.

At that same time, a new change agent appeared on the scene. This executive would one day be knighted by Queen Elizabeth II.

Andrew Witty parachuted in from South Africa and took over marketing. He would continue to climb, brilliantly differentiating himself at every level of the company. Eventually, Witty became CEO of Glaxo's future iteration, GlaxoSmithKline. His knighthood came in 2012, denoting the importance of the pharma company, the largest in the UK.

And what happened to Tim?

He moved on to run the GlaxoWellcome sales team, more than two thousand young men and women in the field, calling on doctors' offices as many as eight times a day. He stayed busy.

I now reported to Witty, who held responsibility for marketing drugs for treating gastrointestinal, metabolic, and antibiotic diseases. My portfolio was carved out to include Zantac (today off-patent); Zovirax; Valtrex (then in development); Ceftin; Fortaz; a new quinolone antibiotic to be called Raxar (ultimately discontinued); and Relenza for flu.

Each drug faced unique marketing issues, common for pharma products.

I developed a commercial strategy for Relenza then rolled it out in a massive launch.

Raxar, in phase 3 clinical trials, showed tremendous potential as an antibiotic in the emerging quinolone class. Hearts broke, though, when the newly launched drug caused intolerable cardiac side effects. That drug, along with Trovan and a number of others in the class, all failed.

Ceftin, then one of the leading antibiotics in the world and widely used for ear infections, sinusitis, pneumonia, and other bacterial infections, worked but had a problem—it tasted terrible. My team went to work to mask the taste and expand the label, adding Lyme disease to its many indications. Some trial-and-error work yielded a suspension formula that kids wouldn't actually spit out.

A newly launched product, Tritec, a unique combination of ranitidine and bismuth citrate and effective against *H. pylori* infections, also fell into my portfolio. It was a poor product but survived the portfolio review because our CEO at the time insisted it be launched. I worked with the team to discontinue Tritec soon after taking charge of it—not a difficult decision.

One of our company's most serious financial challenges came to a head on my shift.

Zantac, at that time the biggest product in GlaxoWellcome's portfolio, was set to go off-patent in 1997. My marketing unit worked with legal to help delay that expiration of exclusive marketing rights by six valuable months, and company CEO Bob Ingram went to Washington and convinced regulators to defer generic entry the extra half year. The interval let GlaxoWellcome salvage millions in revenue.

Meanwhile, our team worked with the managed care team to develop a business-to-consumer Zantac sales arrangement through Medco Health Solutions. Even so, GlaxoWellcome eventually lost most of the Zantac market to generics. In April 2020, the FDA requested manufacturers of Zantac and all generic versions withdrawn from the market due to an impurity.

Of all my time in the new marketing post, though, I spent the bulk of my energy launching Valtrex, used to treat genital herpes zoster. It would succeed Zovirax, the existing gold standard, which was coming off-patent.

We had a consultant, Scott Evangelista, who worked on Valtrex with one of my directors, Sean Cunliffe. Scott recalls one interaction.

"When I first met Sean," Scott said, "he was touting all the wonderful benefits of the drug. I said, 'Wow, that sounds amazing! Are there any issues with it?' Sean answered with, 'Well … the pill is slightly smaller than a college football.'

"Actually," Scott added, "A Valtrex was the size of a large vitamin pill. The size didn't hold back sales, but we learned it was mistaken a few times for a suppository."

In Valtrex, we had a better product than Famvir, a competitive SmithKline-Beecham drug for genital herpes. We needed doctors to switch from our Zovirax to next-generation Valtrex at a higher price, but we still wanted to take market share from Famvir.

How could we do this?

We pioneered a solution. My team looked at developing a television ad that targeted Famvir by name and touted the advantages Valtrex offered against it.

There was just one problem.

Back then, the United States Food and Drug Administration (FDA) did not allow TV ads that mentioned the actual name of a drug. No drug, in fact, had ever been advertised on TV by its name.

Why?

The FDA wanted fair balance in advertising. The agency didn't see how it was possible to include all the data needed to give fair balance to rival products in a sixty-second spot.

Tim Tyson and I, though, had an idea. We flew to Washington, DC, and met with Dr. Minnie Baylor-Henry, an FDA official who would eventually rise in status at the agency to head its Division of Drug Marketing, Advertising, and Communications.

We made a compelling pitch: What if GlaxoWellcome created a TV ad that named Valtrex and genital herpes and then gave the viewer a reference in a magazine for reading the full fair balance in the product label?

After some consideration, the FDA said yes. The deal satisfied the agency's need for fair balance, while it allowed

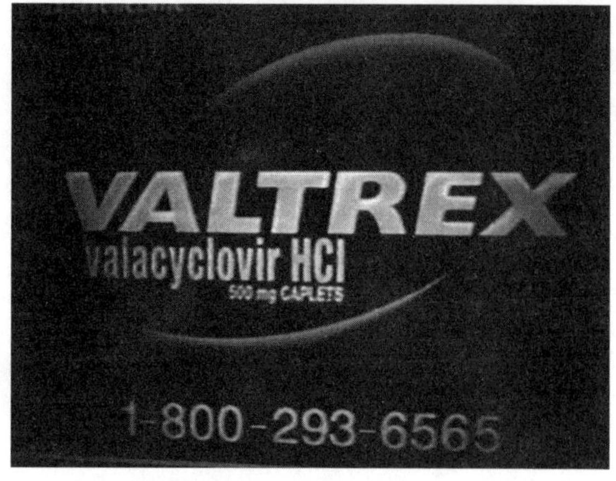

The Valtrex branded TV ad

GlaxoWellcome to name our powerful new drug and the disease it treated.

Within a week, we had our ad on TV. It was an amazing success. We converted most of our Zovirax business—and we also took half of Famvir's market share.

Today, the method of TV advertising we innovated with the FDA is standard industry practice.

Again, we changed the practice of pharmaceutical marketing.

From Marketing to Manufacturing

It's said that the only thing that doesn't change … is change.

Unexpectedly, GlaxoWellcome had come under major scrutiny with the FDA relating to the manufacture of sterile drugs in the United Kingdom (UK). The regulatory agency had issued a warning letter to our company for failure to comply with good manufacturing practices (GMP), mainly in the computer validation area.

An FDA warning letter is serious business. The reputation of a company comes into question. That's followed, worst case, by a legal order to shut down operations in question.

The problems in the UK had been brewing for some time. The company had ignored several past FDA inspections into its practices.

Impatient, the agency now threatened to ban all GlaxoWellcome drugs manufactured in the UK. This meant all imports to the United States, the world's largest pharma marketplace, would potentially be prohibited, including UK-made Imitrex, well on its way to becoming a billion-dollar franchise.

It was a massive crisis. Something close to panic spread throughout the company.

Bob Ingram, our CEO, needed a fixer. He called on Tim Tyson to move to the UK and get things right.

Always the good soldier, Tim accepted the assignment. He left his sales team and moved to London.

Within weeks of settling there, Tim picked up the phone—again—and called me.

Tim Tyson, the fixer, needed his own fixer.

"Wes took on the job," Tim said. "This project was another thing he'd never done before, but he's a quick study, a whatever-it-takes type of person. I knew it wouldn't be easy, but I knew even more that Wes would *get it done*.

"Anybody in pharma wants to be in commercial," Tim said. "That's where all the glory is. To get from engineering to commercial is relatively easy. But to go from commercial to manufacturing? That's not so easy.

"But I knew Wes had the leadership talent. He knew commercial. He knew restructuring. He knew multiple parts of the world. And he understood the pharma business."

I wasn't sure at first.

I was having a ball in marketing. I really didn't want to leave, and I still remember hearing our leader of commercial operations, George Abercrombie, say that if I left, "I would never see my way back to marketing again."

It was once common to think this way. Commercial operations and technical operations have always been like oil and water. They don't work well together. I can truthfully say that division still pervades the industry today.

Even tougher, I had my family to consider.

Erica, born in 1991 when I still worked out of construction trailers on the Glaxo R&D project, had turned age seven. Greg was

Our home, named "Fahrstede," in Denham Village

Erica and Greg at Fahrstede

nine. We all lived in a pleasant neighborhood with other young families, many becoming lifelong friends. I coached both kids' soccer teams and Greg's baseball team. Erica and Greg swam like fish, and both competed on a team at the University of North Carolina natatorium. I made good money. The family loved Chapel Hill.

It was a tough decision. But the company needed help, and it was Tim asking. I took the job and was promoted to senior vice president of GlaxoWellcome manufacturing strategy. My base would be in Stockley Park, near Heathrow Airport.

So the Wheelers moved again.

We sold our house and our cars. Marianne and I enrolled the kids in two different American schools in England. Within a month, all four of us lived in London, rooming in hotels while we searched for a rental.

We ended up in a 550-year-old cottage called Fahrstede, located in Denham Village outside London. Marianne managed to get Erica and Greg in the same school, and they commuted to daily classes in a small English bus.

Fahrstede was historic, and tourists sometimes stared into the windows. Our home stood next door to that of one of England's most popular and beloved actors, Sir John Mills. He was a wonderful gentleman. Now and then, Sir John's equally illustrious daughter, Disney actress Hayley Mills, would pop in.

We had left the comfort of North Carolina and successfully landed in jolly old England. We had kids in classes and a roof over our heads.

I had things figured out.

Everything, that is, except how to do the job Tim brought me over to do.

I had no idea how to develop a strategy for manufacturing. But by this time in my career, I knew I could figure it out.

A Second Assignment in England

At the time I took my desk down the hall from Tim in Stockley Park, GlaxoWellcome operated some sixty-five manufacturing sites in dozens of countries.

Its manufacturing was a complicated mess. The factories were not centralized. Each, in effect, marched to its own drummer. Those sixty-five facilities produced nearly forty thousand stock-keeping units, or SKUs, and paid more than thirty thousand employees all over the world to make and move this huge variety of products.

All the factories belonged to their respective local companies, which ran like separate little kingdoms. Many factories made the same products, sometimes with different formulations, trade names, and labels. The inefficiencies of this setup extended to independent central procurement operations that would duplicate purchases at times. Also, the sixty-five independent quality systems often set and enforced their own standards.

We had no leverage at all because every country was left to do what it wanted, however it wanted to do it, as long as it was produced according to Glaxo's specifications and made money.

As Tim busied himself politicking and resolving the FDA issues, I began to work out a global restructuring strategy for manufacturing.

I started by supporting the implementation of a single universal quality system. Janice Whitaker, then vice president of quality assurance, had been given needed global authority in the aftermath of the FDA warning letter.

I recruited senior staff and assigned them authority over particular therapeutic areas: respiratory, gastrointestinal, antivirals, antibiotics, and cancer. I tasked each director with designing a strategy for each product in his/her portfolio and had them create a launch strategy defining where to manufacture a product, how to launch it, the design of an initial supply chain, and so forth.

This process worked extremely well for the four years I held this position. I also appointed a leader named Mike Naylor to guide the overall strategy.

Naylor was my vice president of manufacturing strategy for a new global organization still to be created. The therapeutically aligned manufacturing directors all reported to me.

Compared to my next task, overlaying that universal quality system for sixty-five independent plants was a piece of cake.

Globalization: Bringing the Local Kingdoms Together

Tim Tyson planned a bold move to fix the manufacturing dysfunction at GlaxoWellcome once and for all. He wanted to bring all the plants under a single structure—to centralize the company's manufacturing.

The plan was as controversial as it was complicated.

Tim negotiated with CEO Bob Ingram to find a way to get all the regional and local leaders to give up control of their plants and allow us to manage them from a central headquarters. It took a lot of time and a lot of effort to convince them, and I supported Tim as he worked the leadership. He was very, very good at what he did—ultimately, we got Ingram's approval to proceed.

GlaxoWellcome launched its strategic master plan, or SMP, in 1998. As soon as it went live, Tim needed a ramrod for the project.

I guess by now he knew he could depend on me.

Leading the SMP would end up consuming the last four years of my time at GlaxoWellcome and its ultimate successor, GlaxoSmith-Kline. I set up shop. I built my team. I went to work.

I needed pros by my side on this huge assignment. I tapped Mike Naylor to lead things. He brought straight-shooting Bill Van on board. We recruited regional staff we could trust to work with local leaders, and eventually we also launched a new global logistics function to manage inventory positions and movements. We would ultimately make this a formal part of global GMS that would report to me.

I met Robert Blaha, leader of Human Capital Associates. Robert formed his company in the early 1990s as a leadership organization focused on deploying process improvement and Six Sigma and Lean practices throughout industry. Robert served as company president with two original partners, Charlie Johnson and Ken Somers (Charlie Johnson remains a partner today).

Robert introduced me to Ken, who became our on-the-ground leader as we launched the pharmaceutical industry's first-ever Lean Six Sigma effort, an internal curriculum we could apply to manufacturing operations everywhere in the company.

My style and Ken's fit like tongue and groove. The two of us would work together at GlaxoWellcome and on many projects at various companies in our careers.

"We had three objectives for this first project with Wes," said Ken. "And on every project after this one we ever tackled.

"Number one, we looked at ways to make the business more efficient, more customer focused. Two, we examined ways to take waste out of processes and save money. Three, we looked at ways to charge a premium for the premier products. That was the game plan."

Ken saw that I had a style distinctly different from my mentor.

"Tim Tyson would come to our informational meetings and sit on the front row, very visible, very conspicuous, lending authority to the program," Ken said. "Tim's presence was absolutely important for our effort to be accepted.

"But Wes sat in the back row. He's a working son of a gun, a hustler. He's laser-focused and was there to make sure we were choosing projects that got results and were aligned with GSK's strategy. That's how I saw Tim and Wes: strategy plus effective execution."

Ken could always count on my kind of leadership at decision time.

"Wes was always there for a business case analysis," Ken said. "Every time. We never had to come get him or get him ready for what we'd present. He would see it cold. Then he would turn to his staff and say, 'Here's how we're going to fix this ...'"

Ken had many opportunities to understand my still-evolving leadership style.

"To a certain level of management, Wes was very direct. But he was fair," Ken said. "He's all business, and he expects his team to be all business.

"I've seen him piss people off, but only because they resisted necessary change or didn't like being held accountable. Wes doesn't have that effect, though, with young and upcoming people. He really has a way with the next generation, the twenty-eight to thirty-year-olds. He's extremely motivating to them.

"The ones who understood that accountability and results matter have gone on to executive positions in the industry."

I tapped another trusted outside resource, Scott Evangelista. Scott had a background with Andersen Consulting, where he supported

Glaxo on the commercial side. We first met in the UK at a meeting called by Andrew Witty, the rising-star executive.

After the meeting, Scott and I met for dinner.

"Wes was still raw about the quality of recent consulting he'd seen," Scott said. "He explained how consultants were ruining the industry and had no real value to add.

"Now, remember, I'm a consultant. It was an auspicious beginning for a business relationship that would last for decades."

When Scott launched his own company, Swiftwater Consulting, I called him for help inventing a manufacturing strategy. Scott was still under a noncompete clause with Andersen, but he'd done such valuable work for me on Zantac, Ceftin, Raxar, Flonase, Relenza, and Valtrex that I contacted Andersen and got permission to work with him on the new manufacturing project.

"It was a crush of a project," Scott recalled. "We had data from 127 countries and every SKU at Glaxo and projections on ten-year demand and information on all the manufacturing lines, maybe sixty of those, all broken out by packaging and country, etcetera. We were trying to make sense of it all, looking at spreadsheets, pulling together a presentation for the board."

Tim Tyson had a board presentation on a Monday. I called Scott in on Thursday.

"It was unbelievably crazy," Scott remembered, laughing decades later.

"We needed a database, and we worked thirty-six hours straight to get information in it. We worked from Thursday morning to Monday morning without leaving the building. We brought in meals. We kept at it nonstop to get the project done, a mind-bending amount of work. And we got it done."

Scott noticed something about my work.

"Wes has in his DNA, probably from an early age, that you have to do what it takes to get a job done.

"Wes appreciates effort, but he's not always the most realistic about time. So, you work with Wes, you learn to get the job done. Whatever it takes."

The Power of One Meeting

The impetus for the SMP project, aside from fixing the FDA problem in the UK, was financial. Of course.

GlaxoWellcome's cost of goods (COGS) hovered near 20 percent of revenue at the time—unusually high and, over time, unsustainably so. Tim committed to GlaxoWellcome leadership that the new structure would reduce COGS to 17 percent, profiting the company with millions of euros annually.

Money talks. That kind of financial incentive won Tim project approval. So he handed me a hefty budget to manage restructuring, and tasked me to come up with the targeted amount of euros in savings.

Tim gave a name to the new centralized manufacturing organization: Global Manufacturing and Supply, or GMS. (Nearly a quarter century later, it still bears this name.)

I set up my team in a windowless London bunker. We needed lots of wall space to post data and visually compare sites and project design options. Though it was 1998, it felt like work during the Blitz in World War II must have felt, only with cell phones, flip charts, speakers, and wires—lots of wires—littering desks and tables. Chatter and speculation circulated constantly as my GMS team systematically met with regional strategy leaders to collect consistent information.

The team measured anything and everything—manufacturing capacities, volumes, performances, outputs, and other metrics. I developed a standard set of key performance indicators to objectively gauge how one facility compared to another.

Tim and I went on the road to sites. We probably, in all, went to forty of our sixty-five plants.

With our collected data, we then created a display for each of the sixty-five sites and posted these around our windowless room.

My team and I prowled those walls endlessly, asking tough questions: *Who will do what, and how much? Which sites had to close? Which sites would expand? How much money was needed to affect the expansion? How long would it take to shut a factory? What were the labor and legal hurdles?*

After a few months, we had a strategy.

Then came showtime.

Tim and team visited nearly every facility in the network

We called every factory manager from every country to join us in Lisbon for a first-ever meeting of the GMS organization. It was Tim Tyson's meeting, but my team and I put the whole thing together.

The Power of One was a three-day meeting with every factory chief who could wrangle a visa. (Leaders from Pakistan, Saudi Arabia, and wartime Sri Lanka missed out.)

We presented our strategy to each and all. We overviewed the new standards for quality, measurement and performance metrics, central procurement, reporting, organizational design, and Lean Six Sigma. We presented it as a balanced strategy, vetted and approved, good in the long run for everyone with strong performance and high standards.

Presenting at The Power of One meeting in Lisbon

We showed how the organization would produce 17 percent COGS and save millions of pounds in four years. Dartford, the company's largest facility in the UK, would close—the last plant to shut down before the entire project completed.

To end the Lisbon meeting, I gave each factory leader his or her own "site contract." This document outlined the products that plant would manufacture, which products it would transfer out, the performance metrics for the facility, how leaders would be bonused, their schedules to complete Lean Six Sigma training, who would supply their formulation excipients, the internal structures of their operations, and their reporting structures.

Each leader was asked to sign his or her contract before leaving Lisbon.

Nearly everyone did. Some signed reluctantly, but they faced a choice: do it—or leave the organization.

A few did leave. Those that remained would proudly be part of a new global organization and a leaner, more productive company.

Operationally Ready for the Future of Big Pharma

The SMP had been conceived, designed, and launched.

Now we had to operationalize it.

I appointed Mark Hembarsky, a colleague from back in my engineering days and a fellow graduate of the Exxon school of project management, to lead the SMP data management efforts. He would capture, analyze, and report key data from all the manufacturing sites and markets.

Mark relocated to London to join us. I was still in Stockley Park. We found a new place to centralize the team, at Taywood House, a few minutes away by car.

The biggest operational challenge? How would GlaxoWellcome move production of thirty thousand SKUs from one plant to another?

A quick tutorial in the requirements for regulatory transfer from one factory to another made the scope of the challenge even more daunting. Most product transfers take from nine months to two years each. With just four years to complete the SMP, we faced a regulatory nightmare.

I assigned solving the production transfer puzzle to a trusted colleague.

Bill Van came up with our answer. Like so much Bill touched, it was simple, but ingenious.

His plan worked this way.

For each product to be transferred, SMP set up a cardboard box. Each box contained every detail about the product to be transferred—its formulation, starting materials, analytical methods, donor site, and receiving site. A person at each end—at the former factory and at the new factory—would be in charge of the regulatory transfer. Monitoring made sure inventories at the donor site remained adequate, with enough shelf life, to supply existing customers.

When the box was full of the required paperwork, and inventories were deemed adequate to support near term sales demand, the donor site and the receiving site would start the product transfer. The receiving site had to manufacture three validation batches and produce sufficient data to support a regulatory filing. (In the United States, this procedure is known in FDA terms as a CBE-30.) After thirty days and with the FDA's approval, commercial batches could then be made and distributed.

We managed the regulatory transfers for each of our products worldwide. When transfers were complete or an alternative supply choice was qualified, we would then start shutting down a factory.

As this work proceeded, our crew monitored all other aspects of the SMP, keeping a close eye on performance metrics, then reporting to Tim Tyson.

Things looked good. The Lean Six Sigma methods created efficiencies up and down company processes. Now able to leverage the buying power of a centralized system for goods and services, we set up a central procurement function. Then we established the first global logistics function, responsible for managing inventory and distribution through the new network of manufacturing locations.

What I learned in that experience would prove invaluable in future roles.

I recruited Steve Blackledge from his role as site director of the Évreux plant in France to lead the new global logistics function out of London GMS headquarters.

In late 1999, Blackledge and I brought each of the world's site logistics leaders to Barcelona to introduce the new global logistics strategy and build a new sense of team and function.

For the first time in our company's history, as historic as our meeting in Lisbon, we had a global team focused purely on logistics. We knew what each manufacturing site was capable of producing, and now we had a global focus on optimizing how much inventory we would produce and hold at each site.

We were ready for the pharma future.

More Kingdoms to Merge: The Creation of GSK

The SMP project and the global logistics program appeared to be career-important successes for me—on the scale of experiences with the Glaxo R&D construction project in North Carolina and Exxon's Santa Ynez Unit project in California.

Then fate threw a curve.

GlaxoWellcome announced a merger. It would join with another big pharmaceutical firm, SmithKline-Beecham, to create a new entity, GlaxoSmithKline (GSK).

This powerhouse would enter business as the world's largest drugmaker, with $25 billion in annual sales, a market cap of $189 billion, and global operations.

SmithKline-Beecham would supplement our GlaxoWellcome pharma portfolio with a number of its own robust products, including household names like Augmentin, Paxil, and over-the-counter brands like their Lucozade nutrition drink and Aquafresh toothpaste. Much would change along with the product lines—for starters, the corporate logo, the corporate leaders, and our corporate initiatives.

For me, the merger meant suddenly managing the restructuring of a manufacturing system with 109 factories instead of 65. Symbolically, Tim and I renamed the SMP program the global supply chain (GSN), so we could make it new again and bring in our new SmithKline team members.

We moved operations to a bunker at SmithKline headquarters in Brentford. It was a post–World War II building with mold infestation—not a nice place but necessary for easily collecting SmithKline data. We also opened a second rented space at a building called Crescent Green in Cary, North Carolina, near RTP. I sent Mark

Hembarsky home to run the US team and recruited Max van Vessem to lead the UK team.

We still had Taywood House nearby. It remained our global headquarters for the restructuring of manufacturing operations.

Our financial target remained 17 percent COGS, even with the merger. Also, I now targeted reducing the number of factories from 109 to 70 worldwide.

Project implementation, though, was not the only thing that changed with the merger.

I changed.

Change in the Air

The stage felt overcrowded with the SmithKline-Beecham merger.

I sensed my ability to control events diminishing. Out of nowhere, new players and new leaders suddenly appeared on our team. Tim's staff was nineteen people, but meetings consisted of twenty-five people, and it felt like they had twenty-five different agendas.

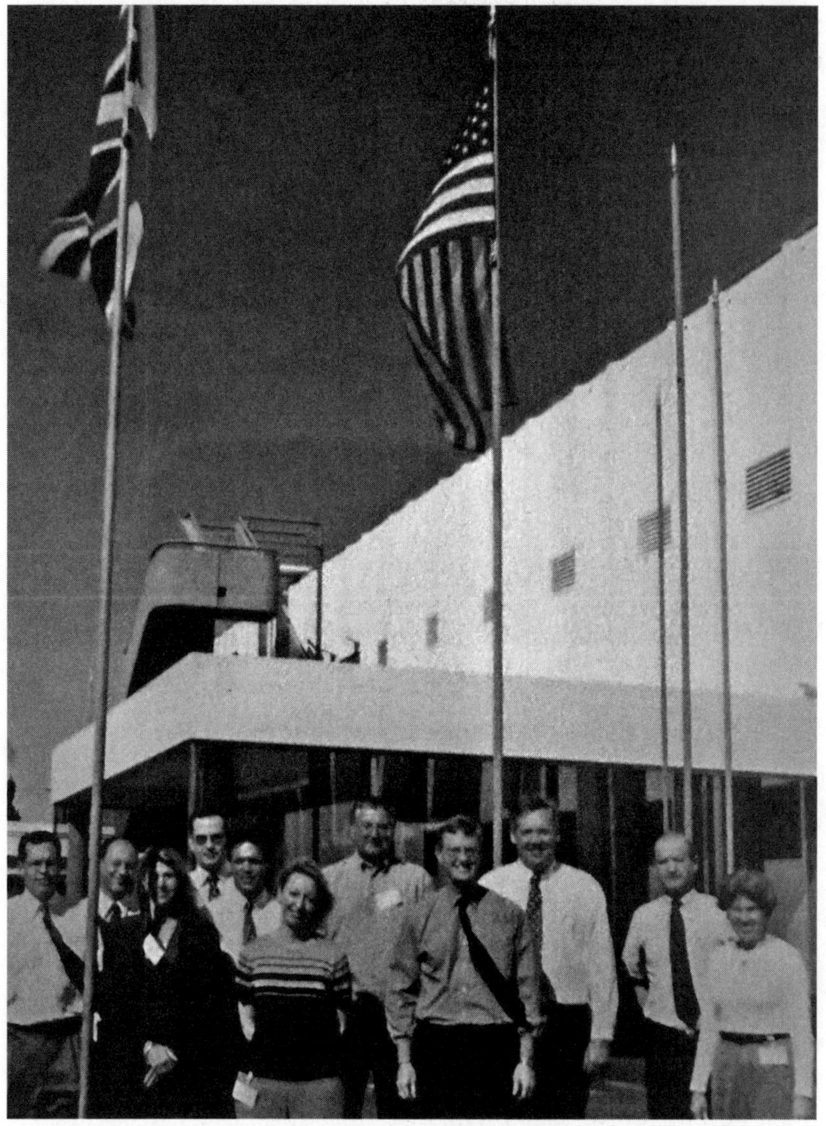

Tim's team started to expand

When J.P. Garnier replaced Bob Ingram as CEO, our new company, with its new name and brand, felt like the loser in a reverse takeover. Emboldened SmithKline leaders used their leverage whenever and however they chose.

The politics came at just the wrong moment for me.

We had the Stockley Park GMS headquarters humming like a machine. It was just perfect—and then Garnier decided that the manufacturing division would be directed out of the United States.

It was a political decision. It was based on no real logic. We were ordered to move the entire Stockley Park headquarters back to RTP in North Carolina.

Tim asked me to move first, and I agreed. I felt an urgency—this was the summer of 2000, and the kids needed to be enrolled in school before the term started in August.

Marianne and I scrambled back to Chapel Hill. We lived in a rented house for nine months while we built a new one, thinking long term.

But there wouldn't be a long term at GSK for me.

I was now reverse commuting from Chapel Hill to London, sometimes every week. Marianne and the kids watched me come and go, shuttling off to London to lead my team, then coming home, weary, trying to put the best face on a difficult situation.

"It was a terrible time for the family," Marianne confessed. "Wes has always said that moving the family back to RTP so early was a big mistake."

I regretted not having another year to shift the gravity of the SMP from London back to North Carolina. I regretted lost time with loved ones. I even grew to dislike Tim's staff meetings. Every week, in plain sight, I saw political backstabbing between the legacy Glaxo people and the legacy SmithKline people.

If anything, my disillusionment felt deeper than it had at the end of my Exxon service. I grew so frustrated that I began to brood over my next move.

Not even the return of Tim Tyson and other well-liked members of his team to North Carolina could lift my spirits. In my heart, I had already reached a decision.

It had become obvious to me that if you wore the wrong jersey, you were going to be left behind after this merger. At GlaxoSmith-Kline, I had reached the top of my ladder. I decided to move on.

But where?

Then something happened. Déjà vu, all over again.

My phone rang. Out of the blue.

I took the call. A recruiter. I listened.

I hung up the phone. I turned to Marianne.

"DSM?" I asked. "What's a DSM?"

LESSONS LEARNED

It is possible in a large company to make a real difference. Find a way to break out of the pack. Take on the tasks and the work that nobody else has the guts or energy to do. Do the hard stuff. The impossible stuff. Fill the voids. This is how you differentiate yourself from the others. And when you accomplish the impossible, you will leave a mark that stands the test of time.

N

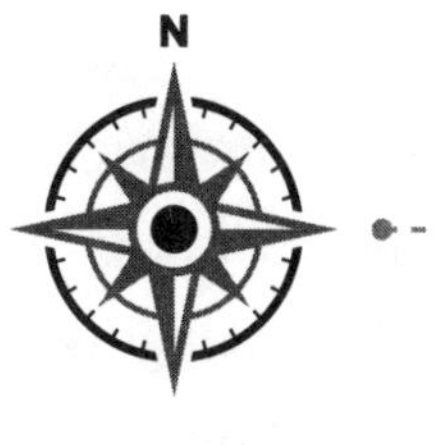

CHAPTER 4

DSM PHARMACEUTICALS, INC. (2002–2003)

A First-Time CEO Grapples with an FDA Warning Letter ... and Turns Around a Troubled Company

I accepted the job as CEO for the DSM Pharmaceuticals facility in Greenville, North Carolina, without ever setting foot inside the company.

I would become my own boss. I could freely apply all the ways I'd learned to get things done and create lasting value—on my own terms. With Tim Tyson's blessing, I felt free to reach for the highest rung on the corporate ladder: chief executive officer.

That next rung, though, came with splinters.

For starters, the Wheeler family had just completed construction of a fine, new North Carolina home in a fine, new development—our biggest house yet, nestled among trees on a two-acre lot with a pool, Jacuzzi, five bedrooms, and a well-stocked basement bar.

In the afternoons, I wore a whistle around my neck, coaching Erica's soccer team, a CEO on the sidelines. Greg starred for his Little League baseball team. Russell, our family's beloved golden retriever, had survived a lengthy quarantine after the move back from England. The family romped in the yard with a second puppy, Rex.

Family life, in short, was golden.

Now I faced a two-hour drive from our driveway in Chapel Hill to the factory in Greenville. Two hours was not exactly an easy commute—especially for a CEO whose presence and availability would be of great importance to my new staff at a troubled enterprise.

One evening, I screwed up my courage and asked Marianne if she would consider moving—for the ninth time in our marriage. I knew the answer before the question left my lips.

For the first time in our twenty years together, Marianne said no. We were finally settled, barely in our new house a year. Marianne had returned to full-time teaching, and the kids were thriving.

So I carefully drew up a commuter routine.

Each Monday, waking before the birds, I drove to Greenville, pulling into my parking spot at the facility before 7:00 a.m. to start each week. A new BMW made the trip comfortable, and I kept up on current events listening to all three cycles of National Public Radio's *Morning Edition*.

I'd slip out of the office late after my usual long days, heading back to my room of the week at the local Hilton for a few hours of sleep. On Thursday afternoons I raced back from Greenville in time to catch Erica's soccer practice. (Our team's assistant coach handled Tuesdays for the twice-weekly workouts.)

That commute would turn out to be the least of my troubles.

My welcome to the C suite would be nothing like I'd expected—or had ever experienced.

DSM Enters the Drug Manufacturing World with a Surprise

Things could have been rosy in Greenville.

Burroughs Wellcome originally built the plant and campus as its primary manufacturing center, a gorgeous, state-of-the-art facility producing the active ingredient for the blockbuster drug bupropion, marketed as Wellbutrin and Zyban. The plant also manufactured and packaged every other Burroughs Wellcome final-drug product distributed to United States wholesalers.

When Glaxo purchased Burroughs Wellcome (BW), it meant there were two redundant manufacturing facilities in the network—one in Zebulon, North Carolina, from the original GSK, and one in Greenville from BW. The Greenville site was superior, but GSK decided to sell it to Catalytica, Inc., and keep Zebulon.

Catalytica named a new CEO and transformed Greenville into a contract management organization (CMO), a company that manufactures drugs for other firms.

With a former Burroughs Wellcome CEO in place, GlaxoWellcome looked out for its previous operation. Business boomed on the strength of a solid contract, guaranteeing a five-year revenue stream for former BW products. Running full throttle, Catalytica in a short time attracted big-name clients.

The owners of Catalytica at this point gazed into a corporate crystal ball and smartly read the pharmaceutical industry's future: Pharma was evolving. More and more big players were realizing that biologics—large-molecule drugs made from organic sources with exquisitely precise standards for quality, storage, and transportation—would be the future. With smaller batch sizes and more complex processing requirements, biologics had already begun to replace small-molecule drugs.

Catalytica foresaw that it would prove more economical for companies to outsource certain parts of biologic processing to third parties and shed the costs. Biotech needs aseptic processing capabilities that will not harm the large biologic molecules. Huge plants that produce billions of mass-market tablets for generic and over-the-counter drugs would still be necessary, but the real blockbuster lay elsewhere: biologics. It was simply a matter of time.

In August 2000, Catalytica sold to the giant Heerlen, Netherlands, company DSM (previously Dutch State Mines) for $800 million in cash and debt (Appendix C4.1). My recollection is that the company sold at a previously unheard-of multiple of EBITDA, and the sale was, at that time, ranked as one of the most expensive CMO acquisitions of the day.

Catalytica was, at that time, one of just a few pioneers in the CMO market. It would also be one of the big winners in this early kind of industry disruption, the outsourcing of manufacturing.

The DSM site overview

In time, some big pharma companies would end up selling their manufacturing facilities for pennies on the dollar to relieve balance sheets. That frantic offloading of assets created a crowded CMO field that only added to drug-price pressures.

The FDA Warning Letter

After I became CEO, I could see why, on paper, the earlier motivation of DSM to pay so dearly for Catalytica made sense.

The Dutch firm had begun life as a European coal mining enterprise in 1902 before diversifying into chemicals and then pharmaceuticals, gradually leaving mining and growing big and important in making active ingredients for pharma clients. It lacked, however, a foothold in the world's most lucrative market—the United States. It also lacked a secondary manufacturing site capable of making finished goods.

So the purchase of Catalytica perfectly fit the Dutch parent company's growth strategy. Unfortunately, it also fell victim to Murphy's Law.

The reasons were completely predictable. First, the Dutch bought Catalytica under a tremendous misunderstanding. They thought their acquisition gave them a pharma company with the industry's famously high margins. They didn't grasp that a CMO is a completely different business.

Second, the new owners had no experience working in the United States, with our unique, freewheeling style of doing things.

Then, strike three, the Dutch similarly had no experience in secondary manufacturing, especially what it meant following FDA-regulated GMP (good manufacturing practice).

Some days after closing the deal to buy Catalytica, new owners in the Netherlands stared in surprise at a document, called a "warning letter," sternly stating that the Greenville site was in multiple violations of the US Code of Federal Regulations CFR 21, Part 11 (AC4.2).

DEPARTMENT OF HEALTH AND HUMAN SERVICES

Food and Drug Administration
Atlanta District Office

60 8th Street, N.E.
Atlanta, Georgia 30309

January 24, 2001

VIA FEDERAL EXPRESS

Peter A.W.F. Everding
Chairman
DSM N.V.
Het Overloon 1, Heerlen
P.O. Box 6500
6401 JH Heerlen, The Netherlands

WARNING LETTER
(01-ATL-25)

Dear Mr. Everding:

An inspection of your drug manufacturing facility, Catalytica Pharmaceuticals, Inc., located at US Hwy 264/Hwy 11 in Greenville, North Carolina, was conducted between September 19 and December 15, 2000, by Investigators Vicky C. Stoakes and Penny H. McCarver. The inspection revealed several significant deviations from the Current Good Manufacturing Practice for Finished Pharmaceuticals (CGMPs), as set forth in Title 21 of the Code of Federal Regulations (21 CFR), Part 211. These deviations cause your drug products to be adulterated within the meaning of Section 501(a)(2)(B) of the Federal Food, Drug, and Cosmetic Act (the Act).

You have failed to assure that each batch of drug product had appropriate laboratory determination of satisfactory conformance to final specifications for the drug product, including the identity and strength of each active ingredient, prior to release. The work performed by one of your analysts over a two-year period was found to have generated questionable data effecting [illegible] lots of product. [illegible] of these lots had data quality issues and the remaining lots had documentation issues associated with the analyses performed. Documentation issues included falsified data, discarding of data, failure to report original data, data substitution, and data manipulation. This analyst generated data to support finished product release and stability testing of finished dosage forms. Testing included dissolution, content uniformity, assay, and identity. These data quality issues were attributable predominantly to one analyst, however similar issues were noted in work performed by other analysts. The investigation into the extent of these problems continues at Catalytica.

1

This FDA warning letter appeared on the desk of DSM's Chairman soon after acquisition of the plant.

It wasn't good news.

In pharma, a warning letter is a somber precursor to the kiss of death—an FDA consent decree, which effectively puts the federal government in control of a site. To avoid the consent decree, the facility put itself under a *voluntary* consent decree, making a number of commitments equal to those the FDA would require. A crucial part of the commitment was an agreement to receive quality oversight from an external consultancy, KMI, a firm that hired many former FDA fellows and that the agency trusted.

The FDA had waited for a new owner to be in place before serving its warning letter, at which time the facility closed for two months to meet commitments it made as a response. Products in development were put on hold. Parts of the plant producing tablets and capsules still operated, as did the active pharmaceutical ingredient (API), operations that made valuable batches of bupropion. Still, naturally, volumes fell, and a proud company of $273 million in revenue began to hemorrhage cash (AC4.3).

It complicated matters greatly that the Dutch company had no experience running an American operation. Culture issues cropped up constantly. For the Dutch owners, this plant located in rural Pitt County, North Carolina, and ranking as one of the area's largest employers, might as well have been on the far side of Mars.

The Dutch were beside themselves, of course. They had expected a pharma gold mine. Instead, they had a failing acquisition, a company losing money and key people, in trouble with the FDA, and with an employee culture it didn't understand.

In something close to panic, the parent company airlifted to Greenville its corporate version of a SWAT unit and announced sweeping changes, including layoffs.

The Dutch simply cut people and salaries. Their customary techniques felt harsh and insensitive to American workers. They basically fired people in place, then demanded the employees remain in the workforce at reduced pay until the facility no longer needed them. The interim CEO, doing whatever he was told by the Dutch, proved ineffective. Soon he no longer had a job.

The Greenville factory was dying.

An Open Door Our Employees Needed

So in I walked in February 2002. Something like a corporate miracle would occur on my brief watch of one year and one month. It only happened, though, through the hardest work of my life so far.

My days in a single-wide trailer were long past. I was shown my office—palatial and huge, it had its own assistant's private office and a private bathroom—with a shower. Wow!

The Heerlen leaders were betting their euros on me as their white knight. Finally, they had come to believe a new style of leadership might turn things around.

Could I relate better to employees? Could I find a way to placate the FDA? Could I help the facility find some way out of its expensive predicament? As a first-time CEO, I stepped onstage to answer those questions—some of them for myself. Honestly, when I arrived, I did not fully appreciate how dire the situation was.

I knew about the warning letter. I knew the sterile unit had been temporarily shut down. I didn't realize, though, what a hard blow the intervention of the Dutch parent company had dealt our people. Morale was at its lowest, and employees were resigning every day. Drug manufacturing is a very labor-intensive, manual process. Without people, there's no factory—without a factory, there are no drugs and no revenues.

Terry Novak, my head of sales of marketing, remembers the situation this way.

"One meeting, the senior leadership team sat around a large table in the executive conference room," Terry said. "Wes passed around the long list of people, and their positions, that were to be laid off. He asked each of us to review the list and point out if there was anyone we felt was critical to our success.

"I listed four people, all operations management people, that I felt should stay and be reassigned to customer-facing roles," Terry added. "Why? Because these employees would be credible with customers we needed to keep, and they had relationships within the customer operations. Wes knew this was important. He was incredibly supportive and fought with the Dutch to be sure those people stayed, along with a few others that our management team deemed critical."

I saw that winning the hearts and minds of the Greenville site employees—at all levels of the factory—would become my biggest challenge. So I decided to do something very few CEOs in the corporate world ever do. I left the door of my fancy office standing wide open to one and all.

My office became a place for listening, understanding, and comfort. I welcomed employees to come and visit with me privately and tell their stories.

Pitt County people may not have been sophisticated by European standards, but they were proud, tough, and hardworking. Importantly, they were also willing and able to accept strong leadership.

The plant employed thirteen hundred people when I arrived. Along with the Pitt County Hospital System and Eastern Carolina University, it ranked among the county's three largest employers.

Factory work paid good wages. It offered many employees their first-ever health benefits. Some townspeople spent entire careers at the plant, mothers and fathers working alongside sons and daughters, nearly all of them hourly laborers with no union representation.

The Dutch management team lacked an intuitive understanding of this unique working-class culture. Its European-style treatment of people was at odds with basic US practices when it came to wages, severance, and especially termination.

Many of those selected to be fired by Heerlen were only given a vague date in the future when they would be allowed to leave. Until that time, they had to work with no prospects anywhere else in the pharma industry unless they wanted to move to Raleigh, Charlotte, or even further from their homes.

The merciless wheels of downsizing rolled on.

Heerlen decided to close the API (chemical) unit of the Greenville plant. A Dutch leader showed up to shut down that part of the operation. This counterpart of mine had an easy task—he simply posted an "out of business" notice and told Glaxo to start looking elsewhere for a source for its active ingredients.

As CEO, my job was to shoulder all these heavy problems and even more.

Commitments to the FDA to fix the plant's sterile unit required periodic shutdowns. The API unit had gone dark. Cash gushed like a financial artery had been cut. Every day, employees streamed through my open door in tears, brokenhearted, begging for their jobs. And the problems in quality assurance, a critical unit that initially triggered the FDA inspection and led to the warning letter, still hung over everything.

Just like a person's reputation, once a facility's quality is compromised—or even suffers the perception of compromise—it's difficult to recover the trust of customers and potential customers.

This was the hot mess I faced as we started the facility's turnaround.

General Colin Powell was one of my favorite speakers at Glaxo events. One of his quotes that's always stuck with me: "You can't fool the privates."

Quality Problems

My first act seemed natural, what any leader would do by instinct.

I listened to those I led.

Charlotte Bryant, my administrative assistant, had been at the plant for many years, working for all the site heads and CEOs since it was built. She knew everybody and their families—the mayor, the fire chief, every local newspaper reporter, every restaurant owner in town.

Nobody would prove to be more valuable than Charlotte in helping me understand the culture at the facility and in Greenville.

Hans Engels, the brilliant German-born head of our cloistered sterile manufacturing unit, became my trusted operations whisperer. Hans had a PhD and years of experience at the European pharma power Bayer. He knew his stuff. I also learned to lean on Terry Novak, the head of sales and marketing quoted earlier, along with select C suite team members. Hans and Terry had been hired just weeks before I arrived.

I really didn't know who I could trust at first. I had to rely on my intuition about people.

To get to know them, I walked the plant. I went over every inch of two million square feet of manufacturing, packaging, office, and utilities spaces. The facility was roughly the size of twenty city blocks. It took hours on foot. But I wanted to know the plant just the way the people who worked for me knew it.

I studied, firsthand, the troubled sterile unit. Far in back of the campus, it housed the world's largest lyophilizer, made by Edwards, Inc., one of three expensive freeze dryers off in a corner. Those dryers are used in the industry to stabilize sterile injectables by converting them from a liquid to a solid (powder) state.

The Edwards lyophilizer was three stories tall—and had never been used. Catalytica management didn't understand that in biotech huge batch sizes aren't practical, since the risk for financial loss is too high if a single batch fails.

A wasted investment like those dryers irked me, but I found something far more worrisome. On my walk-around, I got a bad feeling about our entire quality assurance unit.

In this poorly managed department lay a problem pinpointed by a vigilant FDA agent. The product at risk was a drug developed by a start-up company. The formulation of the drug was preventing its launch.

I reviewed quality assurance documents from the department—in dismay.

Months of outstanding reports were still in backlog. Sterile batch records weren't compiled in any timely way. The system hadn't been designed to urgently handle customer complaints, deviations, and other reportable events. In addition to our existing FDA troubles, I could see we were tremendously exposed to any new audits.

Our quality assurance practice at that time was simply to put everything on hold and then process a batch on a priority basis when the client needed inventory. Quality assurance staff would drop what they were doing and search for missing data in the batch record, then release the batch. This practice was not only inefficient but could lead to mistakes. In regulatory terms, our plant was a ticking time bomb.

The FDA never announces on-site audits in advance. We quickly needed a protocol to protect our company, our reputation, and our people. I moved managers around to install a trusted senior member of my team, Lindon Fellows, at the helm of quality assurance. We installed an industry standard system to tighten things up.

When an FDA inspector arrived, a security guard would notify me immediately. The guard then put an official identification on the inspector before he or she came on-site. Security would usher the inspector into a designated conference room near the plant entrance, while a select team of quality assurance and various other subject matter experts (SMEs) scrambled to a nearby room we called the data center. A runner brought in information requests from the FDA inspector on a special form. Our brain trust then hustled to hand over any requested information, accurate and official, as fast as possible. If the FDA visitor requested a physical tour, I provided an official escort.

It was very strict, but very necessary. We were operating under a warning letter; we had to be ultracareful. We faced an unwanted side effect too—our best SMEs were often tied down in audits instead of improving our systems.

During my thirteen-month tenure, the facility would be inspected or audited more than fifty times, including thirty-four customer audits and two surprise FDA inspections. We had additional audits from Great Britain, the European Union, Italy, and other international bodies. These events placed tremendous pressure on team members that handled them while they simultaneously did their best to keep the plant running.

Building a Winning Team

My family needed time too.

I was commuting from Chapel Hill to Greenville almost every day, two hours each way, four hours a day in all. Cell phone technology and the improved availability of signal towers gave me adequate coverage coming and going, and I conducted much company business on the road. With good weather, I could leave Greenville on Tuesdays and Thursdays at 3:00 p.m. to get to Erica's soccer practices on time. I changed into my coach's gear as I drove and did my practice planning on the dashboard, while answering calls on my cell phone.

That routine brought me home every night too—a loss to the Hilton, but an improvement on the domestic front.

I could now focus more fully on the turnaround.

I convened a trusted team at a special off-site meeting. Familiar faces filled the room, many from my previous assignments at Glaxo.

I had Bill Van, my go-to problem solver with the construction and SMP projects at the company that became GSK. Bill brought a few of his own crew. Ken Somers, the Lean Six Sigma pioneer, held a seat. Robert Blaha too. I brought in Jim Scandura, the Johnson Controls contractor I met during construction of the Glaxo campus. Jim had started his own consulting company.

Over steaks in a Greenville hotel, I laid out our situation.

I opened up the financials, listed the operating problems, laid bare the facts. I hoped my talk would fire up my colleagues at the table with a sense of urgency in the way I'd seen Tim Tyson fire up Glaxo's leaders years before, when the R&D construction project deadline looked impossible.

"We cannot fail," I told the room, in so many words. "I have twelve months to fix this. I need a plan. I want to show it to the FDA and monitor and measure its progress every month until we're out of the woods and growing again."

I won the room. My team of superheroes took up the challenge.

Bill Van would exorcise our quality assurance demons. Ken Somers would run a facility-wide Lean Six Sigma effort, following notable good results with efficiency and productivity work at GSK. Jim Scandura would take charge of overall program management.

The internal name of the turnaround effort?

Project Phoenix.

Project Phoenix and Rising from the Ashes

My turnaround team flew into action, most urgently with Bill's work in quality assurance, where he and Lindon Fellows uncovered a little shop of horrors. They dug out thousands of deviations and complaints in Greenville's quality processes that had never been addressed.

The transgressions went beyond the jurisdictions of products consumed only by US citizens and regulated by FDA. Because our products went out to the whole world, authorities from around the globe brought their own observations.

My DSM Staff: Dr. Hans Engels (bottom left), Terry Novak (center row, left), Lindon Fellows (center row, third from left), and Dr. Terry Tipple (third row, third from left)

Earlier, as part of the voluntary consent decree to the FDA's warning letter, the Dutch had chosen to throw swarms of consultants—especially KMI consultants—at their quality system problems, but without any real structure.

"It was chaotic," Bill said. "Those consultants were good at identifying things, but not so good at correcting them."

At speed, I assigned department leads (engineering, quality, logistics, etc.) to go after the issues. Bill started by bringing a trusted person from the ranks to start a database for quality assurance. Despite obfuscations and impediments that initially kept him from getting a grip on all that was happening, Bill soon generated an organized database that brought our quality turnaround efforts into clear focus, almost like on a construction project.

Bill found that during the year that had lapsed since the facility's turnaround commitment to the FDA, not much had actually been done. And of the $100 million pledged to correct problems, 70 percent of the money was gone (AC4.4).

We would stop that waste.

By the second week of Project Phoenix, Lindon Fellows had dismissed half the consulting resources. Not long after, the other consultants were shown the door. Bill's database did what all those hired guns failed to do—it captured nearly three thousand observations that required formal closure and, in many cases, some form of corrective action.

The difference between Bill's work and the work of dozens of consultants came from Bill's blue-collar instincts. He trusted the shop floor employees, not their bosses. The managers had titles and positions, but all too often they didn't really understand the floor of the pharma industry.

"I come from the world of construction," Bill said. "I have always respected those who actually *do* the work."

Bill made lightning-quick changes where he saw people in the wrong jobs.

"Some needed to be in another business," he said. "I politely gave them an option to go find another house to haunt."

We learned that identifying—and removing—those who block improvement creates a huge energy boost for the vast majority of workers who know how things should operate and who take pride in getting things right.

Lean and Six Sigma

As Bill worked the quality front, Ken Somers pinpointed areas systemwide where waste and inefficiency could be rooted out. Using Lean Six Sigma initiatives—a blending of two proven efficiency programs, Lean and Six Sigma—he aggressively targeted the institutional plaque buildup that slowed internal processes, looking at every step in a process and culling out any that were unnecessary. Every eliminated step reduced a chance of error—and the possibilities of lost time and money. The Six Sigma system examined root causes of variations that led to errors.

"In simple terms," Ken said, "Lean makes you faster, and Six Sigma makes you better."

Ken and I selected a small pool of high-potential young managers from the workforce—"leaders of the future," Ken termed them. He trained them to become black belts, a position of achievement gained through mastery of techniques and tools used in Six Sigma.

It worked like this: Ken took a dozen young people and tutored them for a week in Six Sigma ways. That squad carried out a business case analysis, examining the facility's organic structure, support systems, engineering, R&D, and how systems ideally supported operations. They investigated how managers used their time, and how many people were optimal to get successful results. Finally, it followed the money.

This all went on in a small room with no computers—flip charts on the walls, magic markers in hand. "It was old school as hell," Ken said.

Next came business unit analyses.

"Wes wanted us to do a baseline assessment of everything," Ken said. "The areas that made tablets, the area that made capsules, those that made lotions and sterile injectables, and all our product lines. Wes knew we could make an impact."

With baselines set, next came show and tell.

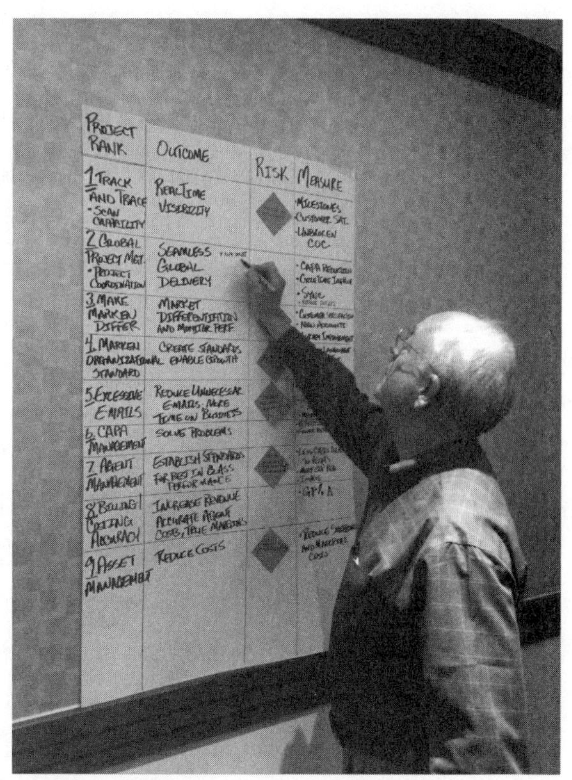

Dr. Ken Somers, the LeanSixSigma master at work

"We brought in the whole executive team for a presentation," Ken said. "No chairs. No debate allowed on data. It took one hour."

It was revelatory.

The siloed HR director stared at the analysis of his department. The siloed head of engineering saw for the first time how his department articulated with the work of others. All the management heads got a real-world view of roles, responsibilities, ramifications.

They learned how their business actually *ran*.

After a few more days of absorbing information from floor-to-ceiling charts and diagrams, every facility leader stepped forward to sign a contract for change.

I was the first to pick up a pen.

"Wes loves this work," Ken said. "He loves coming in to find out what's been discovered. He loves a call to action. And he knows if the process goes off the rails, it's his responsibility. He's the turnaround guy."

Ken's work targeted two particular operational areas.

First, production of the Shire Pharmaceuticals future blockbuster, Adderall XR, had lagged. Getting the drug through the facility required constant overtime and a three-shift-a-day, seven-day work schedule. Employees burned out.

Second, the laboratory's turnaround time needed improvement. Lab scheduling ran into constant problems. Throughput kinked, then kinked again. No one seemed very concerned.

The Lean Six Sigma process was a model of focused efficiency itself. Using it to assess production for any one drug could generally reveal how production worked for others. Identifying delays in one line usually revealed similar snafus and hitches elsewhere.

One of Ken's newly minted black belts, Navnit Patel, came up with an ingenious demonstration that illustrated our paperwork flow-through problems. After gathering system and flow data, Navnit took a cardboard box the size of a doll house and threaded colored knitting yarns all through it—on two levels, like the factory. It graphically showed the overly complicated, meandering path that documentation essential to drug movement traveled in our facility.

The astonishing yarn tangle vividly demonstrated where paper delays happened, where siloed managers didn't move quickly enough, where hiccups or bureaucracy or inattention halted our vital flow. The bewildering snarl symbolized the whole company transition from Glaxo to GlaxoWellcome to Catalytica and, finally, to a muddled Dutch DSM governance.

Ken and Navnit brought the box to a meeting, where Navnit made a dramatic presentation. In his closing remarks, the young black belt triumphantly pointed at his yarn rat nest and delivered a verdict: "A piece of paper moves through our plant slower than the speed of a garden snail."

I stared wordlessly at Navnit's masterpiece. After a long moment, I rose from my seat.

I said just two words.

"Fix it!"

With that blank-check endorsement, Ken and the management team went to work overhauling the flow system for paperwork and for plant production.

They consolidated where products arrived on loading docks. They adjusted the manufacturing rhythms that produced different dosages of drugs, making them more efficient. With these and other fixes, the overtime and seven-day workweeks ended, saving us tens of thousands of dollars each week.

Fifteen years later, long after Navnit Patel unveiled his preposterous colored-yarn science project as a lower-level manager in our quality assurance group, he applied for a C suite position as head of quality assurance at Marken, another company I would lead.

I had not seen Navnit since I'd left Greenville, but I never forgot his presentation.

I hired him on the spot.

Solving the Sterile Unit

I assigned Hans Engels to solve the problems that plagued the sterile plant. The main FDA concern involved the unreliability of data (data integrity issues) that invited the chance that sterility and safety of products might be compromised.

Hans dug into the sterile unit's processes, piece by piece, component by component, to find answers, then solutions.

Hans came in as a vice president just before I arrived. He had previously finished three years of work successfully resolving severe compliance issues for a Japanese-owned blood plasma company in California.

Hans found that the Dutch in Greenville, like the Japanese in Pasadena, had little experience working with US companies and regulators. In both cases, foreign owners of US companies had a tendency to aggravate problems instead of solve them.

"Wes came in as CEO and put me over all technical aspects of the plant," Hans recalled. "Watching the situation, I saw two complete misunderstandings.

"The Dutch at headquarters misunderstood the business they had acquired. And Wes Wheeler misunderstood the expectations of the Dutch."

"Wes came from big pharma," Hans explained. "He felt he could make the operation a pharma company, not just a manufacturing company."

Hans knew the cold reality—the Dutch had no intention of acquiring products. Heerlen only wanted better margins on existing services, despite the fact that services have notoriously low margins. At the same time, our facility soberly recognized how much risk came with products—one bad batch, one sliver of glass in a vial, and a patient could die. Hans was right. We had to focus on quality.

"As soon as the Dutch became aware of this completely different risk profile and the damage that would be reported to the stock community and shareholders," Hans said, "it wanted to get rid of products as soon as possible."

We had other reasons to fret.

The FDA warning letter had zoomed in on data integrity issues—and to the FDA, issues with data integrity are pretty much the worst of all things in a drug manufacturing facility. They'd found contradictions in reporting records, and then Hans found records that hadn't been filled out. He also found contradictory dates on records, a batch produced one day but with someone's signature confirming it on another day. The majority of problems had bubbled up in the lab, the worst of all places from the FDA's point of view.

I also learned of issues in quality assurance, human resources, operations, and finances. The big, gorgeous Greenville facility—a "beautiful site built with the ambition to be the manufacturing showcase to the rest of the world," in Hans's words—was ten years behind, its management systems fractured, nothing tied together internally, its quality systems inappropriate.

Before I arrived, Hans had watched a swarm of consultants from KMI oversee the commitment the facility made to its remediation program. Without them, the company would have gotten the dreaded consent decree. These consultants fulfilled functions outside the operations purview of the Lean Six Sigma program.

With all this going on, I had to shout like a soccer coach in my new role as the man in charge, urging deep remediation, faster growth, and new business.

My efforts, aided by Lean Six Sigma, worked—we increased production by 15 percent. The plant reduced cycle times for all batches by an impressive 35 percent, and the warehouse saw inventory decrease by 15 percent (AC4.5).

Perhaps most importantly of all, from a reputational standpoint we improved product quality by 70 percent, as measured by the number of deviations per batch.

Momentum with Morale

As we tackled the quality issues, I turned to another troubled feature—factory morale.

A sense of failure hung in the air. The plant had lost $8 million in profit in the year prior to my arrival. When I took on the job, we continued to gush red ink and gobble cash. Employees had shell shock. Many had shown up for work, only to be told they would soon be fired (AC4.6).

Conspicuous signs of distress made matters worse. The company gift shop shut down. The cafeteria cut back service and open hours. Building and equipment repairs had been curtailed. Lights were shut off in many parts of the plant to preserve energy.

I had lunch in the cafeteria one day. In a friendly talk with an hourly worker at the next table, he told me the cafeteria had stopped serving hot breakfast in the morning. That was a blow, the worker said, because the first shift workers came in super early, and they didn't have time at home to fix something to eat. A hot breakfast was an important but simple perk.

I instantly fixed that. Hot breakfast returned to the cafeteria, one of many adjustments I made to restore morale.

I also addressed the elephant in the room; I started a relationship with the office chief of the FDA's Atlanta District, which had jurisdiction in the Carolinas.

On regular calls, I talked through the steps Greenville was taking toward quality remediation. I developed a data integrity plan unique to our facility, a master plan that covered every observation and every citation listed in the FDA's inspection reports, known as "483s." (The agency recorded violations on its Form 483.) All the 483 observations and all the customer complaints had been entered into our quality system, along with even more deviations Bill Van and his team had discovered and logged.

We now had one giant database that I could use to show our genuine progress to the FDA.

I worked with a special task force to formalize a new remediation plan. The Atlanta FDA liked what it saw, and invited me and the crew to present it in person—a consequential moment in the Greenville turnaround. We flew five people down to Atlanta on a private King Air turboprop. It went well enough so that this became almost a monthly event. The FDA was warming to us.

Something equally important happened with my leaders too. Our team bonded. People came together around the purpose of launching new products and moving the company toward a brighter destiny.

Launches Lead to Revenues

Other issues kept me up at night. We needed more revenue. And we needed to win the confidence of our major customers and find some new ones.

A first win, I quickly saw, would be Amgen's new launch of a product called Enbrel, a biologic used to treat autoimmune diseases, including rheumatoid arthritis. Enbrel was the first drug to receive FDA approval for that form of arthritis, and later for ankylosing spondylitis, a debilitating inflammation of joints and the spine.

Amgen designated Greenville's plant as its global launch site.

Fabrizio Bonanni, Amgen's senior vice president of quality and compliance and a member of the executive committee, labored under great pressure to get his projected blockbuster on the market. Amgen's CEO had asked Fabrizio to oversee the relaunch of Enbrel following Amgen's acquisition of Immunex, the company that developed the drug but ran into manufacturing difficulties with it. Fabrizio would later become Amgen's head of manufacturing and then executive vice president of operations.

I discovered from Hans Engel that the manufacturing process for Enbrel had not been optimized. Even as Hans worked neck-deep to smooth the overly complicated and even sloppy procedural and production practices, we teamed up to personally focus our production, marketing, and systems experience on the crucial Enbrel launch.

"Amgen had decided to go with Catalytica years earlier," Hans said. "But they got a first shock when the new Dutch owners took over and nobody seemed to give them the time of day. Then they got a second—and bigger—shock—the FDA warning letter."

Hans continued. "Enbrel was the most important launch in young Amgen's history. The company needed to feel Greenville gave them proper attention. Wes worked hard on that."

The drug went out to the world on July 24, 2003.

Our newly certified sterile unit redeemed itself. Enbrel went on to peak at $7.2 billion in sales in 2019 (AC4.7) and is still not widely available as a generic. (The formulation changed later from vials to prefilled syringes, which Greenville didn't provide. But our initial launch work was critical to the ultimate success of Enbrel, and we supported substantial peak early sales.)

The same thing happened with Shire PLC's Adderall XR, another potential blockbuster. I made personal contact with John Lee, Shire's senior vice president of manufacturing. John and I became close during those months. He watched how we made the launch successful with grit and close attention to detail.

The Shire story also had a happy ending. Adderall XR launched from Greenville, then went into full production there and at two other sites. By 2021, prescriptions had hit 41.4 million (AC4.8).

Our facility turnaround would ultimately be quantified by these two major product launches, a growing revenue base, and the increased output from operational improvements.

A Warehouse Reckoning

One big stone remained in our turnaround path—getting finished goods out of the warehouse.

We were not able to release batches of finished product due to severe problems getting paperwork, of all things, through the quality assurance process. Finished goods piled up in the warehouse, at peak representing millions of dollars of revenue we were unable to realize.

Those process issues and the mushrooming number of quality assurance deviations had been backlogged in our plant systems. It was a classic bottleneck.

A sardonic bon mot came into use. Instead of the acronym GMP standing for Good Management Practices, it came to mean Great Mounds of Paper.

One day, I took a tape measure to check a batch record, a stack of paperwork for one sterile batch of twenty-one thousand vials. It measured nearly a foot thick.

That was just *one* single batch record. And we were trying to release dozens of new batches each month, on top of all the warehoused batches in the backlog. Our quality assurance offices smelled like cardboard.

I toured the place, and I was astonished at the number of pallets of boxes in there, stacked three high with barely room to move among them. I had been asking for weeks to find a solution, but nothing yet had relieved the backlog.

We could point to lots of causes. An important one lay in the fact that the FDA warning letter situation made customers nervous. They came on-site to do an assessment and asked for more protocols, reports, and oversights. In a weak position and with prior weak leadership, the facility couldn't fight the demands and just gave in. Those on-the-spot visits and newly demanded documents replaced systematic quality assurance and created a real risk for quality and compliance. Our line quality assurance workers didn't know how to diligently fulfill their jobs without holding everything up.

To fix this, I took a calculated risk with my team.

I decided to hold my next staff meeting in the warehouse.

The clutter lay so deep that we had to move boxes to make room for a conference table and bring in a phone line.

Later that same day, I had a meeting scheduled at the plant with the world headquarters leaders—the big bosses. The meeting took place at that very same warehouse table, with my team present.

Having the Dutch masters on-site at Greenville was a win in itself. Gradually, patiently, I had improved the relationships with Heerlen, shuttling back and forth to the Netherlands when I wasn't shuttling back and forth to Chapel Hill or shuttling back and forth to Atlanta.

Near Maastricht, I met the parent company's new managing director, Feike Sijbesma. We dined and earned one another's trust. I assured the Dutch their situation in Greenville was under control. The Dutch, in turn, gave me extra latitude.

I didn't necessarily want the brass to see a warehouse so out of control, but I did want them to understand that our team knew what was causing revenue issues of the past. Showing them a root cause was, in effect, asking them for patience.

Some of my own team didn't much like the meeting in the warehouse either—they had never before set foot in that vital part of their own factory.

Entering, my staff stared in disbelief at towers of finished product, labeled and ready to ship, but at a dead standstill due to clogged paperwork. So much product waited, in fact, that no more could be brought in—expensive rental space elsewhere would soon be required as new batches rolled out.

Boxes towered over the conference table. I let my team gawk for a minute. Then I started the meeting.

I said, "We're not leaving this warehouse today until we come up with a solution for this."

By noon, two batches of products had been released. Cheese pizza arrived for lunch. That afternoon, two more batches left the warehouse.

Product moved again.

Our warehouse staff meeting became folklore, the stuff of company legend. Word came back to me from the brass in Heerlen …

Wes forced the staff to meet in the warehouse!

Within days of the gathering, boxes flew from storage into the waiting world, on the way at last to patients and clinics and pharmacies.

Our revenues started to grow.

Trust and Confidence with the FDA

Like the first flowers of spring, signs of progress now popped up everywhere.

Ken and Hans and the Project Phoenix team were solving major problems with the way our whole factory worked. Employees breathed again, their hours more humane, more manageable.

Progress also showed on the regulatory front.

We continued meeting almost monthly with the FDA in Atlanta. We built trust and confidence with the agency. We were honest about what we uncovered, and at the same time we showed we had ways to resolve every issue.

Each meeting, I saw the FDA grow more and more confident in our recovery measures. I dialed our Atlanta contact now and then just to keep him up on things. In a sign of growing confidence as we completed all the FDA requirements noted and developed during the post-warning-letter negotiations, the FDA waived twenty preapproval inspections. When the agency is comfortable with a plant's regulatory adherence, it can exercise the option to waive such inspections.

We stayed on their radar, and we kept prepared. When we got hit by two surprise FDA inspections, we followed our protocol. They had observations, of course, but we had already reported those in our regular meetings in Atlanta.

The good ship Greenville began to break out of the dark clouds.

More product left the docks. The sterile unit began producing regularly at high capacity, and we could acquire new projects. Suddenly, our name showed up more frequently on banners and booths at sales conferences.

Pfizer became a major client, and we even sold its over-the-counter drugs in our company gift shop. Shire and Amgen couldn't have been happier, with their new launches selling like gangbusters.

Jim Scandura sums up why things turned out right.

"The Greenville story shows the way a leader can be successful at this kind of thing," Jim said.

"All the things that worked there are things Wes did again and again. You gather a cadre of people you respect, who are competent, and who will work hard to help you. Then you do that over and over. Wes is really good at it."

A Remarkable One-Year Turnaround

Our energetic people drove turnaround at every level. There was good yin and yang among us all.

I gave Hans leadership of all the manufacturing operations. As he focused on cleaning us up internally, I could see that our vice president of commercial operations, Terry Novak, was a master at sales, supporting existing customers, and bringing in new business from outside.

While Hans and his team were busy fixing the business operations, Terry worked the phones and managed relationships.

"Winning back customer trust was just as important as everything we did in quality and operations," Terry said.

"After the warning letter hit and we had our plan in place," he continued, "I flew to every customer and explained the plan and that we would have the highest quality, operations, and customer management system in place, to ensure product delivery on time and in full."

Terry added, "In the end, no customer left us and, in fact, new products from these customers were added. We also brought very profitable biotech customers to the sterile business, the primary profit driver of our CMO business. Our communication to customers after we received the warning letter was another success factor. The fact that Wes and the senior leadership team were the communicators instilled trust."

Operations improved. The first eight high-potential Lean Six Sigma black belts flexed their new management muscle with excellent results on separate projects.

Thanks to all these efforts, an amazing thing happened. The plant turned a profit.

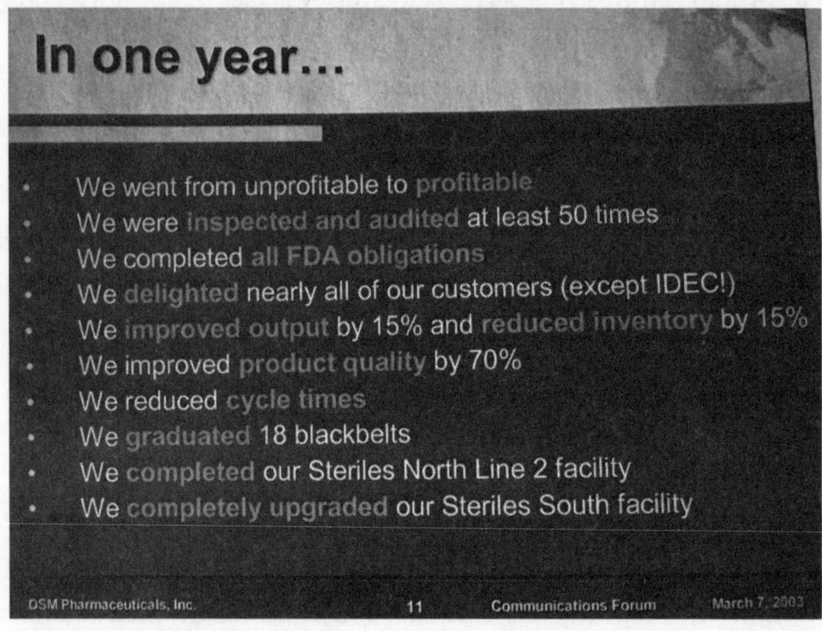

In one year...
We went from unprofitable to profitable
We were inspected and audited at least 50 times
We completed all FDA obligations
We delighted nearly all of our customers (except IDEC!)
We improved output by 15% and reduced inventory by 15%
We improved product quality by 70%
We reduced cycle times
We graduated 18 blackbelts
We completed our Steriles North Line 2 facility
We completely upgraded our Steriles South facility
DSM Pharmaceuticals, Inc.
11
Communications Forum
March 7, 2003

Accomplishments presented to DSM senior management in March 2003

Buoyed partly by products from earlier years, the facility in Greenville reverted from losses in profit of $8 million to gains in profit of $13.6 million, an improvement of nearly $22 million—in just one year (AC4.9).

A delighted leadership team in Heerlen stood back in amazement, now giving us even more space to continue the transformation.

Raised Spirits and Revenues

Still, morale remained a work in progress. The blue-collar Joes and Janes left after layoffs and pay cuts in the hard times gave Greenville a kind of collective PTSD.

I couldn't be at peace with this situation.

I took up free time just wandering, walking the factory floor. Later, I would learn a term for these walks—*gemba*. That Japanese word means, loosely translated, *the place where value is created.* For me, it meant being part of the activity where actual work is done, like a shop floor or a construction site.

I never knew it had a name. It just seemed to me to make sense wandering, stopping, talking to my people.

One whole afternoon, I visited our central control room, chatting with operators. They had hands-on oversight of all the plant's utilities, cold chambers, air flows, chilled water and purified water manufacturing, compressed air operations, and vacuum systems. Their cameras watched every move at the plant.

They were the behind-the-scenes heroes of our facility. I learned a lot talking with them, practical things. I took their ideas back to staff meetings.

One walk-around took me through an office area with a musty smell. The carpeting there held years of dust, spores, and who knew what.

I would not want to work in a place that smelled that way. So, we had crews come in over a weekend and replace all the carpets in the entire plant—thousands of square yards that cost nearly $100,000 that hadn't been budgeted in our cash-constrained business.

But what a difference a simple sprucing up made. You could just see it on people's faces.

We rallied spirits in other ways. As part of a Together We're Better campaign, I hosted town halls so our factory workers could see their leaders. Reporters came on-site to write about the plant and our people. We hosted community events in Greenville. I met the mayor. I got to know the chancellor of East Carolina University. I befriended the CEO of Pitt County Hospitals.

We restored Family Day, when employees could bring their families to the factory for a barbecue. Those were really popular.

We also launched a continuing education program. And a new Diversity Council sought to strengthen human bonds in the workforce.

We also, finally, stopped the demoralizing corporate programs. We upgraded the company benefits program. Money went to improvements in the looks of the site, the environment inside it, even the parking areas and security features for the twelve hundred remaining plant employees—the twelve hundred *right* employees, after Lean Six Sigma processes—who spent much of an average week on premises.

Things felt great. Our negotiations with the FDA would soon release us from all our commitments made to answer the agency's warning letter. Enbrel had launched, with much fanfare and industry buzz, and so had six other pharmaceutical products. Our plant would boomerang amazingly from that $8 million loss to that profit of $13.6 million in just twelve months under my leadership.

I could have spent the rest of my life steering this company into the destiny it deserved after our remarkable turnaround.

But then the phone rang. Once again. Out of the blue.

And here I was, a successful and ambitious CEO at just age forty-six, suddenly again hearing a siren song.

A New Horizon?

Tim Tyson called.

He lived now in Newport Beach, California. My longtime mentor had indeed said goodbye to GlaxoSmithKline, as my hunch told me might happen.

Tim had landed something new, something enticing. His title was initially chief operating officer, with a promise to succeed to CEO in two years. He had joined Rob O'Leary, a former chair and CEO of the Sagamore Group, an enterprise specializing in corporate restructurings, in an ambitious turnaround of their own.

The new outpost was a company called ICN Pharmaceuticals, based in Costa Mesa, California. My brother Jon, a successful obstetrician at Hoag Hospital, lived not far away in Newport Beach.

"You can have any job here you want," Tim told me.

The Irish writer Oscar Wilde once famously wrote, "I can resist anything but temptation" (AC4.10).

I studied the ICN data. My spider senses tingled.

This would be new. I could be president of ICN North America. I could have responsibility for global marketing. I could lead corporate mergers and acquisitions. I could move back into running a pharma company instead of a contract service company. I could create my own products with no remote corporate oversight.

After a lot of hard thinking, I decided to go for it.

A Farewell to Friends

The day I resigned from leading the facility in Greenville was one of the saddest of my career.

We had turned around this huge operation. The plant would receive a notice from the FDA in a few days that the Warning Letter would be lifted.

The impact this job had has never left me.

My life lesson from thirteen months as a first-time CEO was simple and clear: *take care of the people, and the people will take care of you.*

I delivered the farewell news to my staff. I still remember their downcast faces. The parent company didn't take the news well either.

I almost felt selfish, making a decision for myself and my family in the face of such success, and such promise, at the plant.

I arranged a formal goodbye, almost a ceremony, for my final day. The main hall of the plant only held four hundred seats, so television monitors went up everywhere, allowing the workforce to watch. My leadership team and the eighteen new black belts who came through the Lean Six Sigma ranks looked on.

Heerlen flew in the top brass from Holland, a gesture of respect, and I arranged front-row seats for them.

That's where the Dutch were waiting when I stood up to give my farewell remarks. And that's where they sat during my final words, as four hundred of our best and brightest rose to their feet and applauded until their hands hurt in an emotional, tearful, triumphant goodbye.

It's honest to feel that I helped save their jobs—and maybe even their town, in the long run.

I was very moved. I was emotional. The Dutch leadership team didn't expect such a powerful reaction. It caught them sitting down, surprised, everyone else standing.

I will cherish that moment all my life.

DSM chief Wheeler leaving for Calif.

■ Community leaders praise Wesley P. Wheeler, departing president and chief executive officer of DSM Pharmaceuticals, for re-energizing the company's community spirit.

By Ginger Livingston
The Daily Reflector

The top executive at DSM Pharmaceuticals has accepted the presidency of a California-based pharmaceutical company.

Wesley P. Wheeler, president and chief executive officer of DSM Pharmaceuticals, announced Tuesday he is resigning to become president of North American Operations for ICN Pharmaceuticals based in Costa Mesa, Calif. Wheeler leaves DSM on March 15. His successor has not been announced.

Greenville business leaders reacted to the announcement with disappointment, saying Wheeler re-energized the company's community spirit.

"It's a major disappointment because we found Wes Wheeler to be an excellent, energetic, visionary partner," said Tom Feldbush, East Carolina University vice chancellor for research, economic development and community engagement.

WHEELER

"Timing is never perfect. I hadn't planned on this," Wheeler said. "It was a nice opportunity professionally and a nice opportunity for my family."

The job returns him to his roots in marketing specific brands of drugs. It also moves his family closer to relatives living on the West Coast.

See WHEELER, B3

It was sad leaving DSM

LESSONS LEARNED

Dying companies can be saved. It takes grit, determination, good people, and a steady hand. Whatever the situation, you must win the hearts and fire the enthusiasm of others around you. Set a clear path for success, repeat it often, and the people will follow.

I also became a believer in the concepts of Lean. When a complex problem seems too big to understand, the only way to tackle it is in detail. Solve each element one at a time, then work your way back up until all the elements work together more efficiently.

N

CHAPTER 5

VALEANT PHARMACEUTICALS INTERNATIONAL, INC. (2003-2007)

An SEC Consent Decree ... and Fixing a Broken Company

My next company came to life in a garage in Los Angeles in 1959 when a young graduate of Tulane University's biochemistry program borrowed $200 to buy equipment to synthesize chemicals he could sell to research labs.

Milan Panić would, eventually, grow his little endeavor into a global company named ICN Pharmaceuticals, later Valeant, while also finding the time to serve as Prime Minister of the Federal Republic of Yugoslavia (1992–1993), and to run unsuccessfully for president of that nation (1993).

The acronym, ICN, was a sign of the times. It stood for International Chemical and Nuclear Corporation, a somewhat foreboding name for a pharma firm. The company's first logo even resembled the alarming, though widely recognized, radiation warning symbol posted at fallout shelters by the US government during the Cold War.

At the height of ICN's success, it produced six hundred drugs and operated in ninety countries. Our US Securities and Trade Commission (SEC) Form 10-K filing for the fiscal year ending December 31, 2002, showed annual sales of $737.1 million ($466.8 million in product sales and $270.3 million in royalties) at the time Panić stepped down as CEO in 2002 (Appendix C5.1).

Despite his lustrous international profile, Panić had run into troubles in the pharma world. A September 30, 2002, *Forbes* magazine article (AC5.2) told the tale:

> *After enduring multiple proxy battles, accusations of sexual harassment, a paternity lawsuit and legal scrapes with the Food & Drug Administration, the Department of Justice and the Securities & Exchange Commission, Milan Panić, 72, finally conceded defeat in June. Ending one of the more colorful and controversial careers in business history, he promised to retire as chairman and chief executive of ICN Pharmaceuticals, the Costa Mesa, Calif. drug company he founded and lorded over for 42 years.*

Panić left one year before I arrived—and with ICN still under the stigma of a stiff SEC Consent Decree—though he remained a board member until his term expired.

LITIGATION RELEASES

ICN Pharmaceuticals, Inc., Milan Panic, Nils O. Johannesson, and David C. Watt

SECURITIES AND EXCHANGE COMMISSION

Litigation Release No. 16249 / August 11, 1999

SECURITIES AND EXCHANGE COMMISSION v. ICN PHARMACEUTICALS, INC., MILAN PANIC, NILS O. JOHANNESSON, AND DAVID C. WATT,

Civil Action No. 99-1016DOC (ANX) (C.D. Cal. August 11, 1999)

SEC Sues ICN Pharmaceuticals, Milan Panic, and Other Top Officials for Fraud

The Securities and Exchange Commission filed a complaint today in federal district court in Los Angeles against ICN Pharmaceuticals, Inc. ("ICN"), a Southern California-based manufacturer and distributor of pharmaceutical products, Milan Panic, ICN's President and Chairman of the Board of Directors, Nils O. Johannesson, a former Executive Vice-President of Research and Development at ICN, and David C. Watt, ICN's General Counsel. The Commission has charged the defendants with

SEC sues ICN for fraud

Robert O'Leary, an ICN chair and the new CEO, came to ICN with deep experience in managed care and hospital administration, having made a name in the industry as a specialist in spinoffs and corporate restructurings. At the time of his hiring, he led Sagamore Group, a well-regarded spinoff/reorganizational consultancy with one employee: Rob.

ICN Pharmaceuticals, Inc.

This was the ICN logo before we rebranded the company

Before that, he served as CEO of American Medical International, which merged in the 1990s with another company to form Tenet Healthcare Corporation. Rob had also merged several companies to form Premier, at that time the largest healthcare group purchasing organization (GPO) in the country. After Premier, he was recruited as president and CEO by PacifiCare Health Systems, then America's biggest Medicare health maintenance operation (HMO).

Rob stepped into ICN's C suite under the dark cloud of the Consent Decree. That edict, in effect a gag order, placed severe restrictions on how ICN would disclose its financial statements to the public and the investment community. The SEC and FDA required a review and approval of all press releases and public financial statements before ICN could send them out.

No ingenue, Rob knew his ICN mission.

"He came in to replace Milan Panić and make something out of a troubled company," said Tim Tyson, who would soon himself play an important role at ICN. "In my opinion, Panić was just one of those different guys, favoring those who would support his thinking and execute his directives. It seemed to me the rules didn't matter to him."

Rob spent his first six months evaluating just what he'd inherited. He found an extremely complex business with scores of offices and factories operated by sixteen thousand employees around the world.

The ICN of 2002 manufactured many of its own products, some very old, acquired through the years from large pharma companies divesting off-patent products. The ICN arsenal included well-known brand names like Efudex, Mestinon, Virazole, Librax, Bedoyecta, and hundreds of others created by Roche, Novartis, and other companies.

Rob wanted good and able help to handle such a complicated enterprise.

In November 2002, he wooed Tim Tyson away from GlaxoSmithKline in North Carolina and made him chief operating officer—with an asterisk. Tim was guaranteed to be the CEO within two years, Rob promised.

That would indeed happen in January 2005, but first Tim left the merger battlefield at GSK and moved to Newport Beach, California, close to ICN's headquarters at Costa Mesa.

He leaned into a company that might be easily restructured for near-term profits and that had a possible pot of gold at the end of the rainbow—a pipeline hopeful, Viramidine, a drug that appeared able to be safely converted by the liver into an effective hepatitis C treatment.

It wouldn't be long before Tim asked me in to help him.

Neither of us, however, would be completely prepared for the corporate chaos we would enter.

Sizing Up the Problems—and the Opportunity

Tim's first impression of the ICN corporate offices remains indelible.

"It was pure Eastern European bloc," he said. "It looked straight out of central casting—the executive suite was literally walled off, with twelve offices behind locked doors."

Deciding to tackle that particular problem later, Tim moved into an office on the second floor and began a deep dive into ICN's financials. He found discouraging numbers.

The 2002 United States Securities and Exchange Commission (SEC) Form 10-K stated that ICN "had revenues of $737 million and a net loss of $135 million. Based on the closing price of the Company's common stock on the New York Stock Exchange on March 17, 2003, the Company had an equity market capitalization of approximately $751 million" (AC5.3).

The lion's share of income came from the royalty stream for Ribavirin, the hepatitis C drug at the center of the company's SEC problem. Licensed by Schering Plough as Rebetol, Ribavirin represented 37 percent of ICN's total revenue, some $270 million in royalty revenue, according to the 2002 SEC 10-K filing (AC5.4).

Royalty revenues flow straight to a company's bottom line at a 100 percent margin. Such a healthy jet can mask other problems, and that's what Tim found. One single drug's royalty overshadowed the poor performance of products everywhere else in ICN's portfolio.

As per ICN's 2002 annual report (AC5.5), all the products at ICN not named Ribavirin brought in just $467 million in annual revenues in 2002—less than the cost of operations to make them. The share price of ICN in December 2002 was $6.40 per share, a loss of 80 percent from its high and a loss of 80 percent of its top market capitalization. That plunge, entirely due to investor lack of confidence in the company's operating base business, came over the course of a mere twelve months. Investors could clearly see that the royalty stream would eventually disappear.

Simply put, Ribavirin *was* ICN.

"We had ten different business streams not making any money," Tim said. "We clearly needed to reinvent ICN as a real pharma company. And we had to innovate. In pharma, if you don't innovate, you end up with nothing to sell."

As this became clear, Tim and Rob grappled with a fundamental business decision. Should ICN shut down scores of offices and plants to live on Ribavirin royalties alone? Or would ICN see a more prosperous future if the leaders aggressively restructured to build a profitable company across the board?

Tim, as CEO-in-waiting, was gung ho. *Build and grow! Of course!*

Rob, who knew a thing or two about restructuring, agreed.

The two men began to implement a long-term Tim Tyson strategy to reinvent—and revive—nearly every feature of ICN Pharmaceuticals, right down to a new corporate name and a modernized logo with no hint of geopolitical baggage.

Two Steps Forward

Two significant moments followed.

First, after years of meetings and ongoing resolutions of issues, Tim, Rob, and the Valeant board of directors convinced the SEC and the FDA that Valeant was wholeheartedly committed to cleaning up the books and building a new company based on a foundation of quality, regulatory compliance, transparency, and trust.

The SEC would later lift its consent decree in January 2004.

The commitment we made to the federal government was an audacious goal. Tim and Rob made sure that we backed up our promises with sincere efforts, honesty, reportable action, and tangible results.

A second critical act for Valeant? Milan Panić disappeared from the board of directors in 2003.

"He was barred from being a director at a public company due to litigation, and Valeant was a public company," Tim pointed out. "The board of directors did not put him up for reelection, and it began trying to take away assets, raise cash, and assume full control."

Now Rob O'Leary, CEO, and Tim Tyson, heir apparent, could turn to face the fierce pharmaceutical future on their own.

Three Strategies for Change

Tim's reinvention of Valeant would be based on three strategies: Restructure. Transform. Innovate and grow.

To restructure, Valeant would slough off the parts of its business that didn't make money. Simple. In time, many facilities would be closed, and the company would reduce the number of products it sold from four hundred to two hundred—but with only twenty or so being the earnest focus of marketing and promotion efforts.

To transform, Valeant would prioritize efficiency and operational excellence.

To innovate and grow, Tim and Rob knew the real key to a turnaround—they needed to fill the Valeant pipeline with new products that would create fresh sources of revenue.

They began with a quick move to reacquire the outstanding 20 percent of Ribapharm, a R&D subsidiary of ICN. Panić had been forced to sell ICN's stake just before Rob arrived. This acquisition created an innovation platform with a few promising pipeline products for the company. It had good scientists and represented much-needed underlying value going forward—the $208 million buyback yielded a newly functioning R&D unit with two new and potentially special products under development, Viramidine (later rebranded taribavirin), a drug for hepatitis C, and Remofivir, a small-molecule drug then in early stage development that targeted hepatitis B.

To further guide Valeant's turnaround, Tim and Rob also knew they needed a capable operating team and strong new leadership.

For his chief financial officer, Rob brought in a longtime industry colleague, Bary Bailey, who had a background in hospital services and pharmacy benefit management (PBM). On Tim's recommendation, Rob also hired a lawyer who had worked previously with Tim (and me) at Glaxo as executive vice president and general counsel.

Tim also wanted me. Again.

We first talked in February 2003. We had—and still have—the greatest respect for one another, our brotherhood first forged in a decade of accomplishments together serving various Glaxo incarnations.

Still in North Carolina at the helm of DSM, I felt satisfaction with a remarkable turnaround there. Even so, something deep inside told me I'd proven all I could to myself at that particular time and place.

I still commuted from Chapel Hill to the plant in Greenville nearly every day, a drive that increasingly wore me out. Still, I could see the potential of DSM and, for the moment, had no intention of taking my foot off the accelerator.

But Tim knew me through and through. He knew my passions and ambitions. Craftily, he placed a recruitment call one day as I walked the noisy factory floor in my North Carolina plant.

"Wes," Tim said, "you wouldn't believe what I'm seeing right now!"

"What's that?" I shouted.

"I'm on the Pacific Coast Highway in a rented convertible with the top down. I see the ocean breaking on my right and the San Joaquin Hills on my left. Wes, I know how much you love California. Where are you now?"

Suddenly, I was thinking more about my family than my career.

I recalled the joyful early years of marriage with Marianne there, before the kids. I remembered the wonder years with Greg, and the next ones with beautiful Erica. During those happy times, every day seemed like a golden coin.

An added allure lay in the fact that my brother, Jon, a prominent obstetrician at Hoag Hospital in Newport Beach, lived nearby. Jon and I had lost touch through the years, with so much physical distance between us. If I moved, our two families would live close by, and the kids in both families would grow up knowing their cousins. To me, family bonds mean more than most people could possibly understand.

Tim then delivered a recruiting coup de grâce. He topped his California memory-lane call with a professional appeal that touched my heart.

The leader and professional whom I respected more than any other on earth, simply said, "Wes, I need you here. We can fix this company together."

That night, Marianne and I held a family meeting in our nice new home in Chapel Hill.

Greg, then age fourteen, and Erica, twelve, listened and chimed in as we went through a point-by-point assessment of the pros and cons of our current life in North Carolina versus a new life in California.

The Wheelers made a family decision.

California, here we come.

From Manufacturing Back to Commercial Operations

I asked Tim for a role leading the North American business unit. I also asked to lead their global marketing team. Furthermore, I asked to lead mergers and acquisitions.

Tim said yes to all.

"Wes was the right man," Tim said. "He had morale, leadership talent, knew commercial ops, knew restructuring, knew multiple parts of the world, and he understood the pharmaceutical business.

"My biggest challenge was to get him to come and join a terrible company and turn it into something great. Somehow, I sold him on my vision. Luckily, Wes saw the same things I did. He was always willing to bet on himself."

No one else at ICN had a hybrid role like mine, and only Rob and Tim had more responsibility than I had. Together with the CFO, who had control of the purse strings, I knew I would be a critical part of any turnaround.

I walked onto the job in March 2003.

"I had no question that Wes would succeed, no question about his ability to manage complex issues," Tim said. "He's a quick study, and Wes was part of my cadre. I knew I could trust him. I learned in the military that you don't have time to figure out who to trust after bullets start flying."

After I signed on, Tim next recruited Chuck Bramlage, my outstanding Glaxo colleague and Erica Wheeler's godfather, to run Europe operations. Tim also added John Cooper, a key executive from his Glaxo England team, to oversee manufacturing.

Eyeing transition stability, Tim temporarily left the heads of some regions in place, though he would eventually hire Martin Mercer, a GSK veteran like Chuck and me, to run Latin America. Tim also later hired Geoff Glass from Capgemini, formerly known as Ernst & Young Consulting. Geoff would become the company's chief information officer.

Thus, the CEO's strategic plan roared to life.

The European Theater

Chuck Bramlage had stayed in touch after I left GlaxoSmithKline. Now we were teamed up again, Chuck running Europe and me North America.

Chuck could define his job in three words: *Clean it up*.

"I went over and visited the operations in Europe," Chuck said. "I fired fourteen of sixteen direct reports within months. They appeared to me to be either stealing or incompetent."

Examples?

Chuck couldn't understand why profit margins were lower in Italy than in other European countries. He put a little pressure on the commercial leader there, who abruptly quit. Chuck brought in a forensics expert to search the left-behind computer.

"I felt like I was in the middle of a movie," Chuck said. "I'd never seen a smoking gun like that one. The emails confirmed that two of the key managers put a percentage of ICN sales right into their bank accounts."

When Chuck visited a factory in Russia, he literally feared for his life.

"It was my first time in Russia," he told me. "At dinner, I told a manager that we'd been looking at the numbers, the margins were too low, we couldn't understand why. Basically, I was saying, 'You're cheating us.'

"That night was scary. I honestly thought he was going to off me in my hotel. We quickly fired him the next day, and I got out of there."

Valeant was "one of the craziest companies I've ever seen," Chuck said.

Chuck began to rip out the rot, replacing it with well-trained professionals for his European leadership roles. He and I also began to triage the confusing hodgepodge of drugs that ICN seemed to have simply bought willy-nilly, without strategy or synergy.

"We got rid of businesses losing money," Chuck says. "And we did some normal business stuff that should have been done already."

One product for skin cancer sold in Spain for just $2 a unit. Chuck put a sensible price tag on such a valuable drug and sold it for $30 a unit all over Europe, despite loud outcries from several governments. In Europe, every country establishes a standard price for drugs. Price increases are allowed by law, though, and Chuck simply pushed for a fair market charge.

Europe turned a profit in a short time.

New Branding, New Attitudes

With agency help, I initiated a project to change the company's brand. In 2003 ICN became Valeant Pharmaceuticals International, Inc. The stock ticker changed to VRX. A commanding purple—the historic color of royalty—animated our Valeant logo and all our branded materials.

The leadership team was enthusiastic. Valeant was ready to shed the past and build a strong new image.

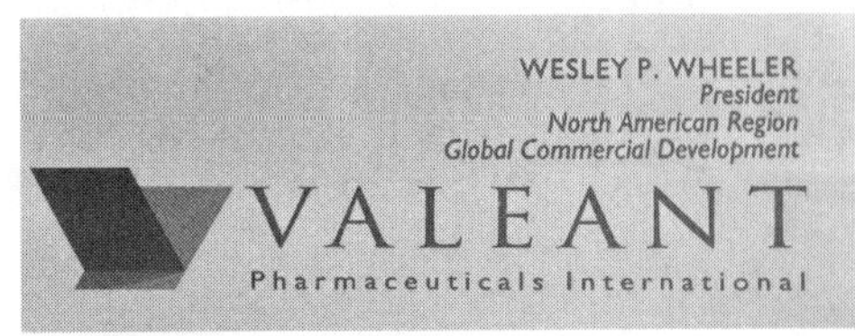

A new name and a brand to go with it

As reported in the *Los Angeles Times* (AC5.6), Tim and Rob divested the Russia business in June 2003, reducing costs and adding millions in new cash for investment. By the year's end, as documented by another *Los Angeles Times* story (AC5.7), we also sold our Personal Radiation Dosimetry Service Division. In addition, as reported in the SEC 10-K for 2002 (AC5.8), we had divested our plants in Hungary and Czech Republic and our Circe unit.

In total, Tim's grand design would reduce our number of factories from thirty-three to just five in three years. I would lose one of my two plants in Canada, holding on to Montreal but shedding the one in Quebec. With that operating burden also went labor and benefits costs for about one thousand employees.

To fill the product pipeline, our R&D team accelerated dual Viramidine phase 3 studies, known in the clinical trials community as VISER 1 and VISER 2. Those studies were beginning as I came aboard. Viramidine (later rebranded taribavirin) would treat hepatitis C, a leading cause of liver cancer and liver disease.

I remember a private meeting I arranged with our R&D leadership. They told me in confidence that they had already decided on the Viramidine dosage for the two trials. I couldn't question the logic at the time, nor was it my place to do so. But, as we would later learn, that dose could—and should—have been higher.

Meanwhile, back in my office, I was looking for my own team of people to trust. I had responsibility for $90 million in commercial business in the US, Canada, and Puerto Rico, which represented only 14 percent of the entire company's revenue. But I also had responsibility for marketing and for M&A, which as mentioned was to become the growth engine for our company. That degree of responsibility was more than plenty for me at the time, and I needed a competent team around me to make our growth goals a reality.

I recruited another GSK veteran to run our US business, and I promoted Thomas Schlater, a native Canadian, to run Canada. With another promotion, I gave Logistics and Distribution over to a longtime local ICN veteran.

Inorganic revenue, through acquisitions, was critical to the turnaround strategy. I hired a young woman who had worked for Amgen to temporarily lead mergers and acquisitions. I would later recruit an executive from Abbott in Chicago to permanently head M&A.

Confident from successfully leading a marketing unit at GlaxoWellcome, I ran Valeant's marketing myself, helped by local advertising agencies. I hired a loyal, efficient, and intuitive woman named Marcella Quinonez to be my executive assistant, and I promoted Jeff Cole, a local ICN finance manager, as my divisional CFO.

In less than six months, I had my full team ready for action.

The Grow Light Comes On

A clear sign of the underlying weakness of Valeant's business model glared through in our 2003 SEC Form 10-K filing (AC5.9):

North America	$ 99 million
Latin America	$136 million
Europe	$232 million
Asia / Africa	$ 52 million
Royalty	$167 million
Total Revenue	$686 million

What's clear in those SEC 10-K annual report numbers is just how far Valeant had fallen. Ribavirin royalties from Schering Plough plunged total revenue of $737 million in 2002 to $686 million in 2003. Net income went blood red, with a reported net loss of $56 million. The share price had risen through the year, from a low of about $7 per share at the beginning of the year to a high of $25.85 per share on the basis of growing investor confidence with new leadership and performance expectations for Viramidine. Results were public, of course, but despite the net income loss our share price held at $25, giving leadership time to breathe.

But investors stayed skittish. The bottom line? Organic growth wasn't happening fast enough to cover the drop in royalty income from Schering Plough, at a time when the Viramidine phase 3 VISER trials were still only just starting.

Rob, Tim, and our CFO spent a great deal of time with investors and analysts, highlighting the potential of Viramidine and pointing to the organic growth starting to materialize.

Those efforts were working, but in the meantime, Chuck and I felt intense pressure. My North American business unit brought in less revenue than the two other major regions, Latin America and Europe, but it represented by far the company's largest growth opportunity, and I also held the keys to new revenue streams that could instantly flow in from mergers and acquisitions. Viramidine was in the R&D camp and held incredible potential, but most of the rest of our growth would have to come from the North American team and new acquisitions while our company waited on VISER results.

Our CFO spent the better part of the year unwinding the complex web of debt instruments that had previously been in place. With cash coming in from ongoing product divestments and with fresh funds raised through the issue of new convertible notes, we had grown cash reserves from $245 million in December 2002 to a healthy $872 million at the end of 2003, as reported in the SEC 10-K annual report for that year (AC5.10).

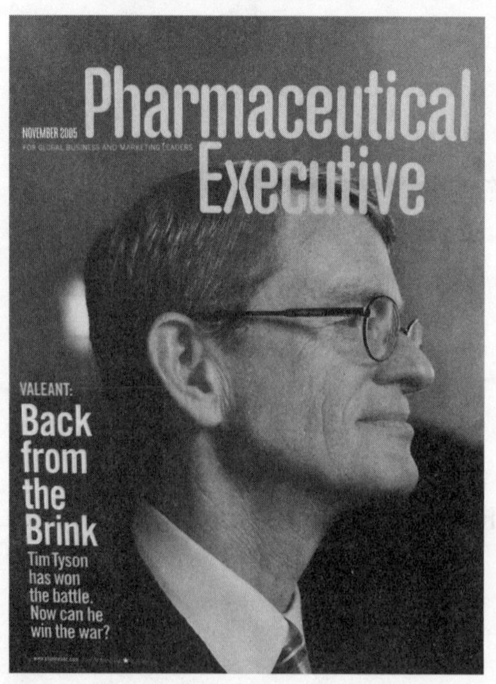

The SEC filing also showed we still carried more than $1 billion in long-term debt, but the terms were now more manageable. Some of our cash would be used in 2004 to reduce debt to $800 million.

In surveying portfolio and pipeline assets and assessing opportunities in North America in conjunction with the rest of the team's efforts to improve financials, I reaffirmed that we would do best to focus on three therapeutic areas: dermatology, virology, and neurology.

Tim turned on the green grow light.

In February 2004, as recorded in *The Pharma Letter*, I immediately acquired a small, but promising, company called Amarin Pharmaceuticals (AC5.11) with the help of Swiftwater Consulting's Scott Evangelista. The $40 million buyout brought in a few older products, plus some still in the pipeline.

Fierce Pharma covered our purchase of a pipeline product that would launch in 2006, Zelapar (AC5.12), developed for the treatment of Parkinson's disease, and two months later, as *Parkinson's News Today* documented, we acquired a Roche drug, Tasmar (AC5.13), that also treated Parkinson's, for $13.5 million. (These transactions are also detailed in the Valeant Pharmaceuticals SEC Form 10-K for the fiscal year ending December 31, 2004.)

I knew that boosting the inorganic growth of the company would be crucial to our turnaround. Those purchases early in 2004 gave us a good start.

Over the next year, my M&A team brought many individual products to the executive team for approval. Annoyingly, very few made the cut, due to conservative modeling and numerous cautionary scenarios that would require us to pass on the opportunities. My team surveyed more than one hundred products and small companies in that time, but did not get approval to buy one until we purchased Xcel Pharmaceuticals more than a year after acquiring Tasmar from Roche.

At the same time, internally, we put more energy into our organic growth, finding ways to stimulate sales of brands we'd inherited.

The biggest opportunity, Efudex, one of many ICN products in our portfolio, had become (and still remains) the gold standard for treatment of actinic keratosis (sun-damaged skin). The topical cream penetrated the epidermis and killed precancerous cells before they turned malignant.

Invented by Roche, 5-Flourouracil, or 5-FU as Efudex was generically known, yielded remarkable—and potentially lifesaving—results with just two weeks of application.

Efudex had lost patent exclusivity but, because of a gap in the FDA approval process, generic companies couldn't produce a similar cream formulation of 5-FU without conducting their own expensive, full-scale phase 3 clinical trials to prove bioequivalence. No generic company was willing to invest to compete against Efudex. As a result, the drug stood alone as a dermatology market leader.

My team decided to kick marketing efforts for Efudex into a higher gear. It worked like a charm. The drug would ultimately generate the highest revenue in the corporate portfolio.

A completely unpromoted cosmetic, Kinerase (named for its active ingredient Kinetin, a natural substance with benefits to human skin), proved to be another diamond in the rough. I learned, to my surprise, that customers could only find Kinerase online. I also learned, to my delight, that two international cinema heartthrobs, the married (at that time) celebrity couple Brad Pitt and Jennifer Aniston, loved Kinerase. They bought lots of it.

Was Kinerase the real thing? I went online and ordered some for Marianne. I shared it with women in the Valeant offices too.

They all loved it. Marianne used Kinerase for years.

That was all the valid sample I needed. We put serious marketing money behind the beauty cream, deciding that Kinerase needed a celebrity spokesperson. Our search led to another iconic "it girl" of the early 2000s—Courteney Cox, a star of the popular TV series *Friends*.

She was perfect. Courteney was forty years old, brunette, had that girl-next-door look, and was a household name. She was A-list but also affordable. And, it turned out, Cox loved Kinerase too. She knew about it from Aniston, her TV castmate, not only a *Friend* on the show, but a friend in personal life.

As covered by *American Spa* (AC5.14), Courteney Cox became the appealing face of Kinerase for two years, and the sales financials we carefully monitored inside Valeant took off nicely, with revenue growing 125 percent, from $12 million to $29 million in the two years Cox was under contract.

Courteney Cox and I

We found yet another hidden gem in Cesamet, also in the original ICN portfolio. This drug is used to prevent chemotherapy-induced nausea and vomiting. The cannabinoid (a synthetic THC, the active ingredient in marijuana) had been discontinued in the United States, its sales stunted by the stigma of being associated with weed. Canada, though, had opened its arms wide to cannabinoids.

Cesamet already had Canadian government approval. It could easily be marketed and sold there. In fact, I learned from my Canada-born colleague, Thomas Schlater, that a growing number of oncologists north of the border prescribed Cesamet for cancer pain relief. The drug was used off-label without company promotion, and it was administered at the discretion of doctors.

We decided to discreetly support Cesamet in Canada by gathering a number of oncologists who believed in the drug. That paid off. As I recall from memory, Cesamet ended up as our best-selling product in Canada, producing more than $50 million in Canadian dollars in its best year.

Building the R&D Pipeline

Still, all the new growth wasn't happening quite fast enough for investors.

Tim called for patience with Valeant's restructuring. He, Chuck, and I had good things in the works, our CEO told investors, even though 2004 net results were worse than in 2003.

Valeant posted a 2004 net loss of $170 million, as reported in our SEC 10-K annual report for 2004. But the filing also reported sales on the rise—a bump from $467 million in 2002 to $606 million in 2004, a healthy increase of 30 percent in two years.

Those millions helped. But gains in organic revenue and efforts to save costs still couldn't make up for the loss of royalties from Ribavirin, the company's fatted calf for so many years. As the SEC filing for 2004 showed, Ribavirin royalty revenue had now fallen to just $76 million in 2004—another $100 million in lost revenue that came right off the bottom line (AC5.15).

Valeant's soft underbelly was exposed again.

Tim and our team, though, convinced shareholders to look forward. We showcased the growth of the rest of the business, especially from fresh revenues and profits in my North America unit.

Also, Chuck's Europe region was improving its operating profit through cost savings and closures. The promise of ongoing VISER 1 and VISER 2 phase 2 clinical trials added confidence too. So, despite bottom-line losses, Valeant shares remained relatively stable at the end of 2004, ranging from $22 to $27 per share (AC5.16).

Our key products: Turning lemons into lemonade

In March 2005, the *New York Times* (AC5.17) reported on our acquisition of the San Diego–based biotech company Xcel Pharmaceuticals for $280 million, bringing an important new product to the US portfolio—Diastat, a rescue drug for epileptic seizures. Rectally administered, it proved best for infants and young children who could not take oral seizure medication or use inhalants. It was a gold standard drug; Diastat eventually rose to be the second-ranked product in Valeant's global portfolio.

Xcel also added one other important product to the R&D pipeline.

Retigabine, its working name, was developed as a novel potassium channel blocker for epilepsy patients. When Valeant bought Xcel, the drug had already entered phase 2 clinical trials, and early results looked promising.

A one-two punch of a powerful epilepsy treatment already at hand and another equally powerful one in clinical trials perfectly aligned with our Valeant turnaround strategy.

The investment firm Bear Stearns, at the height of its influence in 2005, went on record saying it considered the Xcel buyout one of the best of that year based purely on the pipeline value of Retigabine.

Our R&D team led Retigabine's phase 2 trials, and those had shown impressive results, appearing safe and effective for healthy adults. The team had even selected appropriate dosage as Valeant began preparations for the phase 3 trials.

Valeant would eventually sell Retigabine to GlaxoSmithKline for nearly $900 million.

These potential blockbusters, along with the fresh cash, the burgeoning pipeline, the ongoing VISER trials, and the growth of smartly marketed portfolio products—Efudex, Casamet, Kinerase, Diastat, Mestinon—plus a Latin American region drug, Bedoyecta, a novel vitamin B product popular in Mexico, made 2005 a pivotal year in Valeant's turnaround.

Revenue from Valeant's portfolio of drugs had grown to $732 million, as reported in the SEC 10-K annual report for the fiscal year ending December 31, 2005 (AC5.18). The royalty stream remained stable at $92 million for the year, bringing total Valeant revenues to $824 million. Net income, however, remained well below water, with a loss of $188 million, and we were still investing in the business.

The United States' generally accepted accounting principles (GAAP) required the reporting of already sunken costs of acquisitions as "paid-in R&D expenses." This was killing our P&L statements on paper.

Cash flow was strong, though. Investors understood, but we couldn't risk losing their patience going into 2006. The share price dipped in 2005, but recovered by the time we announced 2005 annual results in March 2006.

Tim and our new leadership had the big train rolling.

And then came 2006—the year the wheels came off.

VALEANT PHARMACEUTICALS

	Revenue ($M)				
	2002	2003	2004	2005	2006
Product	467	519	606	732	826
Royalty	**270**	**168**	**76**	**92**	**81**
Total Revenue	737	687	682	824	907
Net Profit/Loss	+84	-65	-170	-188	-56

Valeant's Achilles Heel was declining royalties

A Promising Trial

New hope. New brand. New building.

Tim and our team sold the old ICN building in Costa Mesa and took on a lease to upgrade to a beautiful new campus in Aliso Viejo, California, a dozen miles away.

"My objective was to get out of that third-world building and into one more fitting for a first-world pharmaceutical headquarters," Tim Tyson said. "We took away the doors. We took away the walls."

It was a fresh start for the whole company.

In November 2005, my team announced Valeant would acquire from InterMune, Inc. a promising product called Infergen, an interferon Alfacon-1 for hepatitis C.

Amgen, the product developer, found Infergen difficult to manufacture at its Thousand Oaks, California, plant and divested it. We picked it up for $113 million, and R&D took over development. We soon found a way to reduce Infergen's production costs by transferring its tricky manufacturing to Boehringer Ingelheim, a German pharma company specializing in biologic drugs.

The Infergen purchase looked like a winner. The novel interferon, a protein that inhibited virus replication, would nicely complement Valeant's proven hepatitis C fighter Viramidine, now freshly under development with its new FDA-approved name, taribavirin.

Much depended on the Viramidine/taribavirin trial. Our team understood the stakes. This showed in the enrollment time for the phase 3 trials. Big trials normally average a year to eighteen months to complete enrollment. Tim sent some of Valeant's employees trained in Lean Six Sigma to troubleshoot and work around typical delays.

I watched them get the VISER 1 study up and running in record time—seven months. The second study completed enrollment even sooner, a full month faster.

Tim and our whole team knew what was riding on these studies. Some in the industry speculated long-term revenues for Viramidine would be in the billions of dollars.

"The most critical thing to our company right now is Viramidine," Tim said in a November 1, 2005, interview with *Pharmaceutical Executive* (AC5.19). "It's a significant improvement for treatment of hepatitis, and it will be an overall less costly treatment regimen for those paying for medicines. It is a huge financial opportunity for Valeant."

Tim, though, also knew the gamble. Phase 3 clinical trial results could not yet be unblinded. A clinical trial requires that data coming in from the trial be blinded from the company in order to minimize bias while the trial is in progress. The "unblinding" happens later, when the data are analyzed. Tim and I and the rest of the team waited and watched.

In the meantime, Infergen had brought healthy new revenues—$43 million, as noted in the 2006 SEC 10-K filing (AC5.20)—which would have prepared us well for a new hepatitis portfolio. But synergistic value would go up in smoke without a taribavirin launch. Valeant did not have a fully marketable portfolio for hepatitis C with Infergen alone.

A blow came when former CEO and deeply trusted chair Rob O'Leary died suddenly in August at the age of sixty-two.

Rob was a smart, good-hearted leader. We lost a great friend and a great businessman.

Now having to search for a new chair, Tim relied on his network once again. He introduced Valeant's directors to Robert Ingram, a longtime associate who had served as CEO at GlaxoWellcome. The board appointed Ingram as the new chair.

Despite the seriously sour notes, Valeant's organic turnaround continued to show progress.

We had achieved a major streamlining of the labor base in three short years, shedding more than 8,000 employees. In all, we reduced payroll from 11,625 employees in 2002 to 3,440 in 2006, as documented in the 2006 SEC 10-K annual report (AC5.21).

As we continued to close or sell unprofitable businesses and factories, Europe and Latin America profited. My team also produced great results in North America—revenue grew from $90 million in 2002 (restated) to $307 million by 2006—with a 40 percent operating margin. (These are figures from a combination of our 2006 SEC 10-K filing and internal notes from our Infergen sale.)

Tim had these surging revenues, a new management team, and a new board of directors. Valeant was his now. He yearned to make a bold move that would leave his mark on the pharma industry forever.

Our CEO turned his attention to other options to grow. We looked at Shire Pharmaceuticals, an important company focused in neurology, the third therapeutic focus of the Valeant strategy.

Moving some strategic chess pieces, Tim quietly initiated a potential acquisition of Shire through a planned unsolicited bid for the larger company. The deal would require about $7 billion in cash, or cash and equity.

Tim enlisted big-league help. Two of the world's largest private equity firms and two of the world's largest investment banks at the time were brought in to assist with the offer and an ultimate transaction.

McKinsey & Company would be brought into the process to provide due diligence on the potential deal.

The involvement of that fabled consultancy would soon spell trouble for Tim and for all of Valeant.

A Failed Drug and a Failed Deal

No one ever got fired for hiring McKinsey, goes an old saying in corporate America.

The global management firm started in the 1920s in Chicago, and grew by opening offices in major cities and cultivating its expertise and reputation through top-line hiring. By the 1950s, McKinsey had differentiated itself as one of the premier management firms in the world. The firm has long been a default call for corporate boards and investment bankers.

The investment bankers wanted McKinsey's valuation of Valeant as a way to confirm the proper valuation of each company, Valeant and Shire. The Valeant pipeline was a key component of the valuation.

To our surprise, McKinsey came back with a wholly different range of value for our corporation, notably based on its risk and future value assessments of our two pipeline drugs, taribavirin (previously Viramidine) and Retigabine. In disappointing final meetings, this reveal of McKinsey's assessment, compounded by differing expectations, regretfully killed the deal.

A Bear Stearns executive told me privately that the Shire acquisition was the best deal that never happened.

What now?

Valeant was at a crossroad. The taribavirin data were scheduled to be unblinded, and the fate of our gamble disclosed. We placed all our focus on market development and preparation for a taribavirin launch.

When the data were disclosed, the trials *marginally* failed to meet the primary end points. It was clear that the dose selection was too low. But it would cost many millions of dollars and take years of work to redo the trials at a higher, weight-based dose.

And to make the decision clearer, Gilead Sciences was working on a novel drug for hepatitis C that would likely launch ahead of a new taribavirin product.

"Our R&D team made the protocol development decisions, including dose and phenotype selection, during very challenging times," Tim said.

"In pharmaceutical drug development, the most important aspect is how you design the clinical trial protocol. In selecting the dosage we used for taribavirin and the demographics of the patients enrolled, some mistakes were made that biased the results. We weren't aware of them, but they led to a failed study."

Why didn't Tim see the problem sooner?

It's complicated.

"The SEC rules in public companies mean you have to be incredibly cautious with data," Tim said. "I was talking to public markets all the time—doctors, financial analysts, and such. I didn't want to give any inference about results, so I didn't ever look at interim data during the conduct of the two trials. Our R&D team was strong, and I trusted it.

"In the end, it came down to one thing. The protocol requirements—the reasons for putting people in the study—ended up not being the right criteria. It skewed the data, and it made a very good drug look very average.

"With the right protocols, we would have had a most successful hepatitis drug. But the taribavirin study came out about the same as others—not better, as a lot of people had hoped.

"The trial was seen as a failure. And Valeant took a terrific hit."

At this pivotal moment, Tim made a change.

He asked me to take charge of Valeant R&D.

Of course, I accepted, and there I was, a guy who once thought of myself simply as a "project manager," stepping into one of the most challenging positions of my career.

I had something to prove.

VALEANT PHARMACEUTICALS

	Revenue ($M)		
	2003	2006	2007
North America	99	307	330[1]
Europe	232	277	308
International	187	241	201
	519	826	785
Royalty	168	81	86
	686	907	872

[1] Revenue reduced to $277 after Infergen divestment.

North America revenue tripled under my leadership at Valeant

Learning to Lead R&D

I took on the R&D leadership while still leading the North American business, global marketing, and mergers and acquisitions. And, not long after I absorbed R&D, Tim gave me even more responsibility, as head of manufacturing.

At that moment, I had responsibility for about 80 percent of Valeant's operating expenses.

"It's a testament to Wes Wheeler's intellect and drive," said Dr. Terry Tipple, the organizational psychologist I hired again as my professional coach.

"The nerdy engineer was now in charge of marketing groups and business groups because his interest in things was broad and always went far beyond any job he was doing at the time," Terry said.

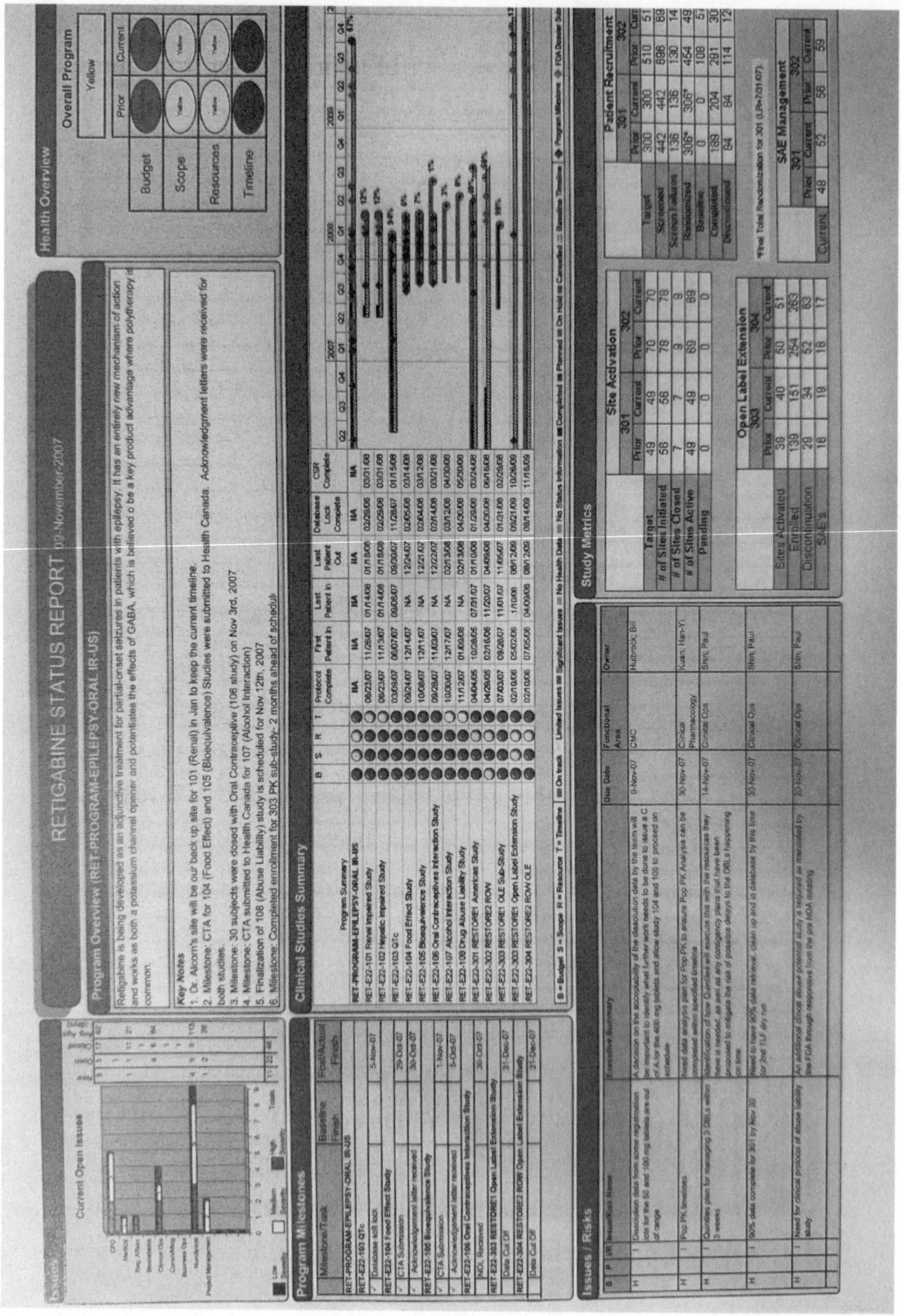

RETIGABINE STATUS REPORT 09-November-2007

Issues

Current Open Issues

Low Severity | Medium Severity | High Severity | Totals 11 | 22 | 46

Program Overview (RET-PROGRAM-EPILEPSY-ORAL IR-US)

Retigabine is being developed as an adjunctive treatment for partial-onset seizures in patients with epilepsy. It has an entirely new mechanism of action and works as both a potassium channel opener and potentiates the effects of GABA, which is believed o be a key product advantage where polytherapy is common.

Key Notes

1. Dr. Alcorn's site will be our back up site for 101 (Renal) in Jan to keep the current timeline.
2. Milestone: CTA for 104 (Food Effect) and 105 (Bioequivalence) Studies were submitted to Health Canada. Acknowledgment letters were received for both studies.
3. Milestone: 30 subjects were dosed with Oral Contraceptive (106 study) on Nov 3rd, 2007
4. Milestone: CTA submitted to Health Canada for 107 (Alcohol Interaction)
5. Finalization of 108 (Abuse Liability) study is scheduled for Nov 12th, 2007
6. Milestone: Completed enrollment for 303 PK sub-study- 2 months ahead of schedul

Health Overview

Overall Program	Yellow	
	Prior	Current
Budget		
Scope	Yellow	Yellow
Resources	Yellow	Yellow
Timeline		

Program Milestones

	Milestone/Task	Baseline Finish	Fcst/Actual Finish
RET-PROGRAM-EPILEPSY-ORAL IR-US			
RET-E22-103 QTc			
✓	Database soft lock		5-Nov-07
RET-E22-104 Food Effect Study			
✓	CTA Submission		29-Oct-07
✓	Acknowledgement letter received		30-Oct-07
RET-E22-105 Bioequivalence Study			
✓	CTA Submission		1-Nov-07
✓	Acknowledgement letter received		5-Oct-07
RET-E22-106 Oral Contraceptives Interaction Study			
	NOL Received		30-Oct-07
RET-E22-303 RESTORE1 Open Label Extension Study			
	Data Cut Off		31-Dec-07
RET-E22-304 RESTORE2 ROW Open Label Extension Study			
	Data Cut Off		31-Dec-07

Clinical Studies Summary

Program Summary	B	S	R	T	Protocol Complete	First Patient In	Last Patient In	Last Patient Out	Database Lock Complete	CSR Complete
RET-PROGRAM-EPILEPSY-ORAL IR-US					NA	NA	NA	NA	NA	NA
RET-E22-101 Renal Impaired Study					08/23/07	11/26/07	01/14/08	01/18/08	02/29/08	03/31/08
RET-E22-102 Hepatic Impaired Study					08/23/07	11/13/07	01/14/08	01/18/08	02/29/08	03/31/08
RET-E22-103 QTc					03/09/07	06/07/07	09/06/07	09/30/07	11/28/07	01/15/08
RET-E22-104 Food Effect Study					09/24/07	12/14/07	NA	12/24/07	02/05/08	03/14/08
RET-E22-105 Bioequivalence Study					10/08/07	12/11/07	NA	12/21/07	02/04/08	03/12/08
RET-E22-106 Oral Contraceptives Interaction Study					09/28/07	11/03/07	NA	12/22/07	02/14/08	03/21/08
RET-E22-107 Alcohol Interaction Study					10/30/07	12/17/07	NA	02/13/08	03/12/08	04/30/08
RET-E22-108 Drug Abuse Liability Study					11/12/07	01/09/08	NA	02/13/08	04/30/08	05/30/08
RET-E22-301 RESTORE1 Americas Study					04/04/05	10/28/05	07/31/07	01/10/08	01/29/08	03/24/08
RET-E22-302 RESTORE2 ROW					04/29/05	02/16/06	11/20/07	04/09/08	04/30/08	06/16/08
RET-E22-303 RESTORE1 OLE Sub-Study					07/03/07	09/28/07	11/01/07	11/05/07	01/31/08	02/29/08
RET-E22-303 RESTORE1 Open Label Extension Study					02/10/06	05/02/06	1/10/08	08/12/09	09/21/09	10/26/09
RET-E22-304 RESTORE2 ROW OLE					02/10/06	07/05/06	04/09/08	08/12/09	09/14/09	11/16/09

2007 | 2008 | 2009 — Q2 Q3 Q4 Q1 Q2 Q3 Q4 Q1 Q2 Q3 Q4 Q1 Q2 Q3 Q4

B = Budget S = Scope R = Resource T = Timeline | On track | Limited Issues | Significant Issues | No Health Data | No Status Information | Completed | Planned | On Hold | Cancelled | Baseline Timeline | Program Milestone | FDA Dossier Sub

Issues / Risks

S	P	I/R	Issue/Risk Name	Executive Summary	Due Date	Functional Area	Owner
H		I	Dissolution data from some registration lots for the 50 and 100 mg tablets are out of range	A decision on the acceptability of the dissolution data by the team will be important to identify what further work needs to be done to issue a C of A for the 400 mg tablets and allow study 104 and 105 to proceed on schedule	9-Nov-07	CMC	Hulbrock; Bill
H		I	Pop PK timelines	Need data analysis plan for Pop PK to ensure Pop PK Analysis can be completed within specified timeline	30-Nov-07	Clinical Pharmacology	Kuan; Han-Yi
H		I	Quintiles plan for managing 3 DBLs within 3 weeks	Identification of how Quintiles will execute this with the resources they have is needed, as well as any contigency plans that have been proposed to mitigate the risk of possible delays to the DBLs happening on time	14-Nov-07	Clinical Ops	Shin; Paul
H		I	90% data complete for 301 by Nov 30	Need to have 90% data retrieval, clean up and in database by this time for 2nd TLF dry run	30-Nov-07	Clinical Ops	Shin; Paul
H		I	Need for clinical protocol of abuse liability study	An additional clinical abuse potential study is required as mandated by the FDA through responsive from the pre NDA meeting	20-Nov-07	Clinical Ops	Shin; Paul

Study Metrics

Site Activation	301 Prior	301 Current	302 Prior	302 Current
Target	49	49	70	70
# of Sites Initiated	56	56	78	78
# of Sites Closed	7	7	9	9
# of Sites Active	49	49	69	69
Pending	0	0	0	0

Open Label Extension	303 Prior	303 Current	304 Prior	304 Current
Sites Activated	39	40	50	51
Enrolled	139	151	254	263
Discontinuation	29	34	52	63
SAE's	16	19	16	17

Patient Recruitment	301 Prior	301 Current	302 Prior	302 Current
Target	300	300	510	51
Screened	442	442	696	69
Screen Failures	136	136	130	14
Randomized	306*	306*	454	49
Baseline	0	0	108	57
Completed	189	204	291	30
Discontinued	84	84	114	12

*Final Total Randomization for 301 (LPI=7/31/07).

SAE Management	301 Prior	301 Current	302 Prior	302 Current
Current	48	52	56	59

We tracked every drug candidate in detail

"A lot of people think Wes traced his success from his mentor, Tim. Sure, there was a certain amount of political cover from above that allowed Wes to do his job. But above all that, Wes had tremendous self-confidence. He honestly believed he had what it took to be a success in business at any level. He combined that with a tremendous ability to reflect and absorb and learn. Wes Wheeler always carried his weight."

At that exact moment, I needed to carry R&D. I had to get the product pipeline flowing again.

But it wasn't the best of times for Valeant R&D.

Now taribavirin would never come to market, after losing many millions in investment. That event gave Valeant's value on Wall Street a hard blow. I found that the only products left in the pipeline were Retigabine and a handful of product line extensions for Efudex, Librax, Cesamet, Bedoyecta, and Kinerase.

I would waste no time turning on the floodgates, but Valeant's healthy share price at the start of 2006 had dropped by midyear.

There was one really bright spot. Just after taking the reins of R&D, I made an important contact in the legal department, a kindred spirit who would be a key ally for the rest of my corporate career.

Doaa Fathallah was born in Egypt and raised in Los Angeles. A bright, engaging lawyer, she shared my no-nonsense, tell-it-like-it-is personality. She was also the best corporate lawyer I ever met.

Doaa joined Valeant as vice president, assistant general counsel, reporting to the corporate general counsel, with a dual reporting line to R&D. She had legal responsibility for global research and development, working at an office not far from mine, though we barely knew each other until I took over R&D.

Doaa watched me try to master R&D leadership before her eyes.

"As soon as he was appointed," she said, "Wes set up full-day meetings, at first twice a week. He had thirty people in the room and a thick pad. He filled it up with notes. Next meeting, he'd have a new notebook.

"Wes was studying at night, learning R&D from the ground up, asking everybody everything he could think to ask."

Doaa knew that some of those in the room didn't care for me.

"Everybody seemed shocked to find out that Wes wanted to do what was logical, what was best for Valeant," she said. "He wanted to put the right eggs in the right baskets, so he needed data to make tough decisions, to prove viability, to show the board what it would take to succeed.

"Wes gradually turned around nearly every person who didn't think highly of him. A person may not have liked him, but he certainly had respect.

"You were either on the Wes train, or you weren't. He could come across as bulldoggish and abrupt, but he wasn't mean—he was on a mission.

"If you didn't like that, you didn't like Wes Wheeler."

Consultants Come Back for a Second Look

Meanwhile, still stinging from the collapse of the Shire deal and now a failed taribavirin trial, Tim made a significant—and perplexing—decision.

He contacted McKinsey & Company about a reevaluation of the Valeant R&D pipeline.

Tim strongly felt McKinsey had low-balled the potential worth of Retigabine, and he felt even more strongly that the consultancy's near-zero valuation of Viramidine/taribavirin had been a mistake.

He also knew that McKinsey would now see a whole new Valeant pipeline.

As head of R&D, I now had oversight for Retigabine's phase 3 trials that had launched in December 2005. Two pivotal studies, known as Restore 1 and Restore 2, offered treatment for partial onset refractory epilepsy seizures.

Things looked promising again—recruitment was going well, and phase 2 results had been excellent. The drug was safe, with potentially better efficacy than the current gold standard treatment.

My team had also jump-started a new indication for Cesamet's pain treatment in the US market, and line extensions for other Valeant products moved briskly. The pipeline flowed. The R&D team was suddenly solid and the team was motivated.

Now Tim wanted to right an old wrong by bringing McKinsey back for a second look. That firm's analysis had soured the Shire deal. Our Valeant CEO simply could not believe the fabled McKinsey & Co. could have gotten things so wrong.

Tim boarded a jet with Chuck Bramlage and me, and we flew to New York City to engage McKinsey again.

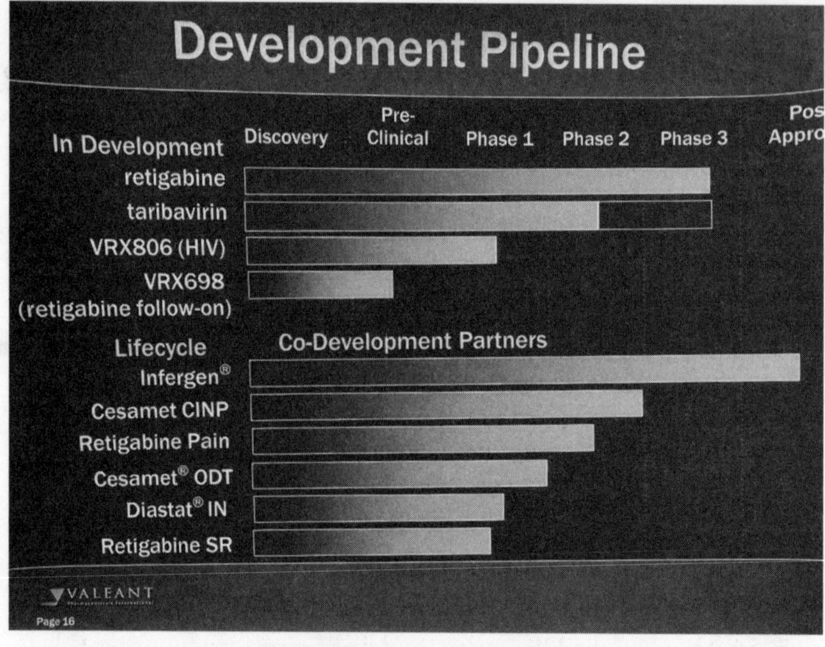

Our Valeant pipeline in 2005

It started about the same way it would end.

A McKinsey executive kept us waiting for thirty minutes. When he finally walked through the door, he looked like he'd just come out of the shower without looking in a mirror.

Valeant thus encountered a McKinsey managing director who would throw a long shadow over the future of our company.

The moment previewed what would turn out to be one of the strangest and most unsettling consulting relationships I've witnessed.

Tim, as planned, invited McKinsey to reevaluate our drug pipeline. The managing director smiled. The managing director said yes and quoted a reasonably low fee.

In no time, Valeant's California offices swarmed with McKinsey staffers. Boxes upon boxes of material were provided to them—many of the same boxes provided for the Shire evaluation.

Chuck and I soon got this very weird feeling. McKinsey was poking around in places and asking questions that had nothing to do with our pipeline.

Something seemed wrong.

I look back on those events now, and I can't help but feel some bitterness.

No one ever got fired for hiring McKinsey. Right?

An Activist Investor Enters the Scene

Something *was* wrong at Valeant.

All during 2006, an activist private equity firm had been quietly accumulating shares of Valeant stock at its lowest valuations. Chuck and I hadn't been dozing—we first noticed the new player with a disclosure of 5 percent of Valeant shares.

That position climbed fast. Too fast.

Chuck and I did some homework.

We found that the activist private equity firm's bread-and-butter business model involved a hostile takeover beginning with staking out a minority position in a troubled company at 5 percent. It would then increase its ownership to 15 percent, grab a board seat, do some maneuvering—and ultimately overthrow the existing management team.

The 5 percent position was a red flag. And, sure enough, the firm grew its ownership stake to just under 15 percent of Valeant and held a board seat.

And then things happened that simply mystified Chuck and me.

The first involved an effort by my M&A team to acquire Bradley Pharmaceuticals, a significant New Jersey-based dermatology company with an easily affordable $400 million price tag. The deal should have been a slam dunk. Valeant now had a reinforced cash position and an equally solid debt capacity.

Bradley had other suitors, but Valeant emerged as a frontrunner in the auction process, and we appeared well positioned to take ownership of the prize. I had Tim's approval to proceed to the board.

I presented the pending Bradley deal at a special board meeting—but, to my amazement, the directors voted down the purchase.

I now sensed something surely was rotten in the state of California.

Bob Ingram, the new chair and an old business friend of Tim's, had voted no. The private equity firm director had voted no. At least one of the other independent directors blackballed the deal.

Heavyhearted, I withdrew Valeant from the auction process. Bradley Pharma sold to the Swiss company, Nycomed, the next year, and I would rue the missed opportunity to make Valeant an industry leader in dermatology.

I knew enough about corporate life to sense that all this meant something was brewing beneath the surface.

Why? What? Where was the explanation? Why did the board vote no to a perfectly good acquisition? What were the McKinsey people up to?

An even darker thought crossed my mind: Was it possible that Tim could be forced out? My mentor and great champion?

And that led to another question. Should I wait around for that to happen and be left vulnerable to a similar fate?

An Offer Out of Nowhere

The phone rang.

Throughout my career, a phone always rang.

Spencer Stuart, the executive recruitment firm, called me.

Would I consider a CEO position? Would I simply have a conversation with a company that really, really wanted me?

Given all, I decided to at least kick the tires on a new opportunity.

I flew to New York City and met with a company called JLL Partners that wanted a new CEO for a Canadian contract manufacturing organization (CMO) called Patheon. Headquartered in Toronto, Patheon was a public company traded on the Toronto Stock Exchange.

Back home, with time to think about it, I gave JLL my answer.

No.

Tim's words from long ago, his recruiting call from the Pacific Coast Highway, came back to my thoughts.

Wes, we can fix this company together.

I couldn't help but believe that still was true. In fact, we *had* fixed the company, and now it was time to grow it.

Corporate Intrigues

I dug back into the work at Valeant.

I stayed professional, stayed focused on the Valeant mission, and stayed resolute as McKinsey consultants crawled in and out of offices and collected information for some end none of us could perceive.

I confided in Chuck Bramlage. Our trust had been formed at two companies and as close friends in England.

As Valeant leaders of North America and Europe, we racked our brains trying to figure out what was going on.

When I mustered the courage to ask Tim directly, he reassured me. *Everything is fine, everything is fine.* But I detected a distant, noncommittal tone that made me even more suspicious.

The activist private equity firm was taking a larger role on the board. New directors smiled and acted friendly at dinners and in formal meetings. I sensed something superficial, though.

In my bones, I knew something heavy was happening behind the scenes.

I was dead right.

Entering the fall of 2006, in September, the Valeant board of directors convened a special session.

The man running it?

The same McKinsey managing director who had met us in the New York offices, and who had spearheaded the long, aggravating review and assessment of Valeant.

Never in my career, before or after, would I take part in a board meeting presided over by a consultant from outside my company.

Our general counsel and I presented, offering our versions of the Valeant valuation process. I found the faces of board members unreadable.

It didn't feel right.

I left after my presentation, but Tim sat through the whole meeting. Afterward, he would not tell me what transpired, though I heard things through the grapevine.

The McKinsey managing director had proposed a radically different Valeant strategy than the one Tim and I had used to reverse the fortunes of ICN and then make Valeant profitable in 2006.

Although I was not in the room, I assumed that the McKinsey team discounted the future, global value of Retigabine. It gave little to no value to taribavirin, and the team urged Valeant to divest its dermatology business.

I don't know for sure but I would later suspect that the McKinsey managing director had thrown Tim under the bus behind the scenes and in that board meeting.

I would also ask myself later, in light of all that happened, if this McKinsey consultant, who'd been brought on by Tim simply to evaluate the organization, hadn't somehow led the board to believe he'd do a better job as CEO of Valeant.

Trouble at the Top

It hardly seemed possible, but McKinsey now became even *more* present at Valeant. The board expanded the assessment mandate.

Tim grew more distant. When Chuck and I pressed him for insight, our friend and CEO held his peace.

"I knew the private equity firm wanted to drive change," Tim said, "but I thought we had support. Our whole intent was to find valuable products, build our company around pharma. We were not into buying garbage and propping it up like a house of cards waiting for the wind to blow it down.

"I thought we had the board's support—until they told me we were not going to continue with the course we'd set.

"Wes and Chuck were strong professional colleagues and highly valued friends. If I could have told them anything, I would have."

Tim may have deceived himself.

Something was obvious to anyone who really wanted to see.

Tim Tyson may be in trouble.

A Momentous Career Decision

My phone rang. Again.

Spencer Stuart, the recruiter, repeated its offer. JLL Partners wanted to talk with me—again—about the CEO position at Patheon.

I accepted a second invitation to travel to New York City. I met with JLL, Patheon's minority owner, a second time. And this time, I listened more thoughtfully.

I would need to decide for a second time if I would leave Tim, my lion of a friend, and step into a second C suite as CEO on my own—this time leading a public company.

It would be another family decision too.

The Wheelers had put down deep roots in Newport Beach. Erica celebrated her senior year in high school anchoring a water polo team that finished second in the 2005 state finals. Greg looked forward to trips home from college at Miami University of Ohio. Marianne had a close group of friends. We had a boat at the yacht club.

The Wheeler family had a lot of fun in California

This go-around, I didn't even bother to ask the family if they'd be willing to move. I simply accepted that I'd be a commuter, just like in North Carolina. Only this time, I'd fly back and forth from Los Angeles to Toronto every week.

I said yes to the top job at Patheon.

For the second time, I'd leave Tim for my own greener pastures.

It was a painful decision. We'd had so much success with the Valeant turnaround. We really *had* fixed the company, despite all the noise around us.

Our North American business unit had metamorphosed from an operation with a paltry $90 million in annual revenues before I started to one with $330 million a year—and a fat 45 percent contribution margin. I had sold Infergen to Three Rivers Pharmaceuticals for $91 million, letting go of the drug after two years of good profit for the portfolio (AC5.22).

The hepatitis franchise dream had vaporized with the VISER results. Still, we had moved Retigabine well into phase 3 trials. The first Restore study recruitment finished, and the second had begun, with studies hinting at good results with few adverse events. Valeant's R&D portfolio had muscle. The company sat on more than $400 million in cash (AC5.23).

I could leave a job well done.

My work at Patheon started in November 2007.

Dr. Terry Tipple believes my departure and its timing were absolutely the right career moves. He feels something else important happened in that moment too.

"For fifteen years of their work together," he said, "Wes Wheeler wanted to be like Tim. When this break came to move to Patheon, he decided, 'Now I've got to be me.'

"That was when Wes Wheeler really became his own man, at last, leaving on his own terms, headed in his own direction."

A Corporate Coup Is Consummated

After I departed, the sad end of the Valeant story took only the blink of an eye in corporate time.

Tim explained it all with a few carefully chosen words.

"The activist private equity firm had a specific desire to cut costs, and it first wanted to stop R&D," he said. "They felt 'buy and build,' the McKinsey recommendation, was a great way to go instead. They chose to move forward with an acquisitive strategy.

"I wasn't in those discussions. I thought our value proposition was the right one. It seemed clear that buying things with giant debt would turn out to be a problem. But the board made a decision to execute on that strategy."

Tim feels that a change at the top must have been coldly easy for the private equity firm.

"Remember," he said, "this is an activist shareholder. Its whole object is to make money. For themselves. They had a playbook, and they followed it—get some company ownership, get seats on the board, make friendships and create alignments, and restructure.

"In the end, the firm made a lot of money on the Valeant deal. All the rest of the investors were left badly damaged by what happened—and so was the reputation of the entire pharma industry."

That McKinsey managing director? He replaced Tim as Valeant CEO in 2008.

The activist private equity firm had its man.

Tim would move on to Aptuit LLC, a contract research organization based in Greenwich, Connecticut, as CEO. He and I remain close friends.

Tim is unusually blunt about his dismissal from Valeant and the private equity takeover.

"The wolf was in the henhouse," Tim said. "They had aligned the directors and found a CEO to do what they wanted. The activist shareholders knew I wasn't a patsy who would go along with them. Money wasn't my objective. Doing the right thing was."

Chuck Bramlage and Martin Mercer followed Tim out the door. Doaa Fathallah left too.

Chuck Bramlage is a man of faith.

"For me," Chuck said, "I'll never know why all that happened. I'll never know why we were not there to finish the job, as Wes and I and Tim wanted to do.

"I believe we just weren't meant to be there."

Tim also holds a definite view of destiny.

"I think we were doing a phenomenal job, taking a bad company from where it was to world-class, best-in-class performance. We were on the path to do phenomenal things. Then a few people with bad objectives took control of a place with a really good group of people doing good things and turned it into a poster child for the worst of the pharma industry.

"Honestly, the industry has struggled with its reputation ever since. What happened at Valeant put the pharma industry in a bad light, and I'm not sure it has ever really recovered."

Prescription for Disaster

The downfall began innocuously. Instead of divesting dermatology and exorcising the drug products he and McKinsey found so objectionable in its two assessments, the new CEO and his team initially followed the Tyson/Wheeler game plan to the letter—with one exception.

They sold the drug Retigabine that McKinsey had low-balled for the Shire deal. That scoffed-at product brought the new CEO and

Valeant a cool $670 million—plus future milestone payments, which could bring the total to $900 million, as reported by *Fierce Biotech* in August 2008 (AC5.24). GlaxoSmithKline paid for it in cash, and cut Valeant in on profits in some countries and royalties in others.

They took that cash windfall, plus the $400 million war chest Tim and I had built, and started buying companies—including a major dermatology player.

Rather than divesting dermatology under the new ex-McKinsey CEO, they *expanded* it.

The new CEO would come to a sad end.

He brought in a buy-and-cut business model he championed at McKinsey, purchasing more than fifty companies, ballooning Valeant debt, and ratcheting the stock price astronomically. He raised prices for certain drugs preposterously.

Examples?

A *Forbes* magazine article (AC5.25) on May 9, 2016, stated, "Valeant boosted the price of its diabetes drug Glumetza by about 800% in 2015, the year Valeant bought it. The company acquired Carac cream in 2011, and the price for the treatment of cancerous skin conditions rose by 1,700% in six years …"

Wall Street at first seemed all-too-eager to climb aboard the CEO's huffing and puffing train to glory. A few big-time players saw huge gains—on paper. Indeed, the CEO himself—on paper—became a billionaire.

The *Forbes* reporting gave some idea of the immensity of the Valeant bubble.

"Wall Street analysts, whose investment banking colleagues thirsted for Valeant's fees, issued bullish reports, and big hedge funds rushed into the stock," wrote *Forbes* (AC5.26). "Valeant's shares soared by 2,450% in seven years, affording it a market cap of nearly $90 billion by 2015. Investment banks like Goldman Sachs and Deutsche

Bank made $750 million in fees. [The activist shareholder] realized $1.15 billion in gains—and still retained a 4.4% stake in the company. Everybody got rich—at least on paper …"

But what goes up, must come down.

In March 2016, Valeant surprised Wall Street—and the Street doesn't like surprises.

The company told investors that projections for earnings and revenues would fall far short of expectations. *Reuters* (AC5.27) also revealed that ongoing problems in filing an annual financial report might mean defaulting on $30 billion of debt. (Covenants on leases are legally enforceable.)

Valeant also announced that its CEO would be leaving the company. Directors' faith in him had come to a screeching halt.

By August of that year, as *Forbes* later reported (AC5.28), Valeant had lost a soul-crushing $80 billion in shareholder value. Market cap fell by 87 percent.

The regulatory and political sharks also attacked.

A new name, Philidor Rx Services, popped up out of nowhere. This mail-order pharmacy controlled by Valeant had allegedly used controversial tactics to coerce doctors, patients, insurers, and other customers into buying higher-price Valeant products instead of drugs at a lower cost.

The SEC started looking. Class action lawsuits brought lawyers running. In Washington, DC, saber-rattling about contempt proceedings began at the Senate Special Committee on Aging, a group watching over the interests of elderly people who most need drugs. Other politicians loudly declaimed against drug-price gouging. As CNBC later reported, a Valeant executive and the head of the mail-order pharmacy would ultimately be sentenced to prison for illegal activities involving Philidor Rx (AC5.29).

The same high rollers that loved Valeant so much once upon a time now watched their investments circle the drain.

The May 9, 2016, *Forbes* article (AC5.30) reported, "Bill Ackman, who famously compared [the Valeant CEO] to [Warren] Buffett, was forced to join Valeant's board in an effort to shore up billions of dollars that his Pershing Square has lost so far on investment."

That same *Forbes* article also quoted pharma expert Eric Gordon, at the University of Michigan's Ross School of Business.

"Their [Valeant's] business model was: borrow money, buy companies, and boost prices," Gordon told *Forbes*. "That's a lousy business model, and it's a business model which you should know obviously comes to an abrupt end."

Salvaging bits of investment and reputation, a new collection of leaders decided the ex-CEO's leadership had left Valeant with so much scar tissue that it had to be completely rebranded.

Again.

They hid their sins under protective cover of a still-respected eye care and lens maker, Bausch & Lomb, one of the dozens of companies bought in the spree after Tim's departure.

Bausch Health Companies was announced in July 2018. Valeant no longer existed—except in bad memories.

The public outrage the CEO who had worked at McKinsey drew to the brand assured that the Valeant name would rest in infamy.

And me?

I never looked back as the flames rose over Sodom and Gomorrah.

Instead, as a newly minted CEO, I watched maple leaves change colors outside Patheon's Toronto headquarters.

Weekends back home, I savored the fragrance of eucalyptus trees shading the Pacific Coast Highway, the same trees that lined the road when Tim called me about the Valeant job five memorable years earlier.

I shuttled back and forth across a continent until Erica graduated from high school and went off to college at the University of Michigan.

Then I brought my family east to join me in my new chapter.

LESSONS LEARNED

There are good people and bad people in business, as in all of life. We must learn to identify the bad actors as early as possible. If the bad actors work for you, you must remove them. If the bad actors have control over you, there is a choice to be made. Either learn to trust them ... or watch your back. But trust must be earned through deeds and actions. If the bad actors are left unchecked, they can and will destroy you.

N

CHAPTER 6

PATHEON, INC. (2007-2010)

Building a Quality Reputation during a Corporate Takeover

I look back on three tumultuous years at Patheon with mixed feelings.

The opportunity for me to run a public company on my own for the first time was awesome. But that stint also stands among the toughest professional and personal times in my life.

As Patheon's new CEO, I led a company turnaround that positioned it for tremendous future success. I achieved this goal despite factions at war in a corporate takeover, and in spite of the Great Recession, chilling the global economy like a new Ice Age. It would not be a growth story, but one of repair and survival, leaving the growth to my successor.

On the home front, I faced a weekly commute back and forth from Newport Beach, California, to Toronto, Canada, four days a week the whole year of 2008. I scrambled to catch important moments of Erica's senior year in high school—a time she competed on her high school water polo team. (Greg was already away at college.)

Even with its challenges, my tenure at Patheon would stand out as an undeniable success story.

By the time I unwillingly departed at the end of 2010, I had stabilized the fragile and disorganized company I'd first walked into. The organization had skirted financial collapse, and by 2010 all the Patheon financial vectors were pointed up.

It's my opinion that had our management team not kept Patheon from almost certain bankruptcy in 2009, that company would not exist today. (It's now a successful subsidiary of ThermoFisher Scientific Inc). Things might have been very different.

Good Bones

As I considered taking the CEO position at Patheon, I saw a company with problems but with good bones.

Patheon had seen its share price get in trouble after a 2004 acquisition of Mova Pharmaceutical Corp., a drug manufacturer based in Puerto Rico with three active plants on the island, management issues, and debt. An inexperienced former general counsel had somehow wound up as CEO, overseeing three additional facilities that one board observer later simply called "lemons."

Patheon had the right instincts—its contracts had begun to expire, and it needed new volume to fill capacity. But the price tag of $350 million for Mova in cash, debt, and newly issued shares, as reported in November 2004 by Canada's newspaper of record, the *Globe and Mail* (Appendix C6.1), raised eyebrows. The CEO of Mova cashed out but rolled enough of his proceeds into the new deal to retain 20 percent of Patheon equity. (We refer to him in this chapter as the "former CEO" or "ex-CEO" of Mova.)

Even though Patheon grew from nine to fourteen sites, as the *Globe and Mail* reported, and raked in $677 million in 2007 revenue with a healthy $90.3 million in profit, investors perceived the company's high level of debt and its untested leadership team as simply too big a risk.

One group, though, smelled opportunity.

In March, *Fierce Biotech* reported that a New York private equity firm, JLL Partners (JLL), invested $150 million in Patheon (TSX:PTI) in convertible preferred shares on March 2, 2007 (AC6.2). A *Reuters* news story (AC6.3) added that the new JLL team procured 25 percent of the voting rights on all Patheon's corporate decisions and got three board directors ... and that those JLL preferred shares could be converted at any time to common shares at $5.55 each.

The JLL infusion paid down $138 million of Patheon's existing debt of $238 million, as *Reuters* noted. Even so, company financials that I would later see but that were not public confirmed that the investment did not help the company's heavy cash flow burden. Its stock price remained in the tank.

Patheon shares had hit a high of C$12 per share in 2004 when it acquired Mova, but it became clear over the next three years that investors lacked confidence. In that time, Patheon slid rapidly to about C$3.75 per share, losing more than 60 percent market value. All stock values were available on the Toronto Stock Exchange (AC6.4).

This is what attracted JLL to the investment. And this is why Patheon immediately started its search for a new CEO.

I was drawn to the job, in one sense, because of its troubles. Turning around troubled organizations seemed to be something I did well. Maybe I had a knack for it. And here was a new opportunity.

On November 21, 2007, Patheon's board announced me (AC6.5). I succeeded an interim "office of the chief executive officer," in place while a selection committee of the board of directors found a replacement for former CEO, Robert Tedford.

On December 10, three weeks after my announcement, I walked through the doors of Patheon's Toronto headquarters to start work.

During my first week, I contacted Doaa Fathallah, the attorney I most trusted back at Valeant. Doaa would prove to be an essential ally in a place where allies would be sorely needed.

Turnaround Experience in Demand

The masters of the universe at that moment worked at JLL Partners.

The investment firm effectively controlled Patheon's nine-member board of directors with its three directors, plus me and an ex-CEO of Mova. As with a partisan Supreme Court, this 5–4 majority could control all key decisions.

My reputation for turnarounds had earned me Patheon's top job, and JLL desperately needed such expertise. The company currently reported operating losses every quarter, mostly from interest and dividend expenses, Canadian taxes, and capital expenditures for operations in five countries.

A month after taking the job, on January 9, 2008, I made my first presentation to Patheon's board. I handled it the old-fashioned way—by myself, with no pricey consultant on hand to usurp a CEO's duty.

I laid out the facts. According to our internal data, which the company used in promotion, Patheon employed some fifty-three hundred people, among them fourteen hundred degreed scientists, ninety-two with PhDs. The company's fourteen global sites made about 750 products for more than two hundred customers.

I told the board I believed Patheon had a strong foundation, but it could be better. To improve it, I proposed a new strategy to:

Increase CMO market share from 5 percent to 6 percent.

Maintain the number-one position in outsourced pharmaceutical development.

Form strategic partnerships where necessary.

Find alternate revenue streams through joint ventures and new intellectual property.

Develop a full suite of key performance indicators (KPIs).

Improve EBITDA margin from 12 percent to 18 percent.

Develop a sustainable corporate culture.

The board agreed to all seven strategic goals. I was in my honeymoon period.

Later, I proposed more immediate short-term tactical objectives:

- Shut down one Canadian facility.
- Shutter and sell the Carolina, Puerto Rico, facility.
- Install new leadership in Puerto Rico.
- Expand hormone production capacity in Toronto.
- Install a prefilled syringe line in Swindon.
- Install a pilot scale unit at the Ferentino, Italy, facility.
- Expand lyophilization facility at Monza, Italy.
- Develop a site in the UK for new drug development.
- Launch a global Lean Six Sigma (L6S) program.

We got things moving. A crackling new current of positive energy shot through Patheon.

Halfway through 2008, I gave my second major board presentation. Directors got a comprehensive review of our new strategic plan's first six months.

We had forward motion. I had moved to replace the chief financial officer. Shortly after that, we let go of the head of North American operations after I learned that he had been occasionally attending my staff meetings from his sailboat in the Caribbean.

A new chief information officer would soon come in. A Lean Six Sigma program had been launched, overseen by my tried-and-true efficiency/quality stalwart Ken Somers.

Bill Van, another trusted consultant, was put on notice to bring in his expertise at solving manufacturing problems, as he'd done so well for me at Glaxo and DSM.

Doaa was hired as senior vice president, general counsel, Europe and Global Pharmaceutical Development Services. She started work the day after she left Valeant in May 2008.

Things percolated nicely during those first six months.

For starters, revenue stabilized and began to increase. We had also already sold the Niagara operations, as reported by *Reuters* in April 2007 (AC6.6), and I'd begun to consolidate Canadian volume from York Mills to Whitby, as noted by *BioSpace* (AC6.7) in February 2008. It took some cash to make these changes—the repositioning costs topped $16 million, a figure we reported only internally—but I assured the board those outlays were a reasonable price for fixing a global business.

I also cautioned that Patheon still needed a lot of work.

Internal reporting that I saw and remember showed that the balance sheet remained upside down. Capital spending stayed stubbornly high, especially in the ex-Mova operations in Puerto Rico, which was burning a $30 million hole in our cash reserves.

PATHEON'S CHALLENGING JOURNEY

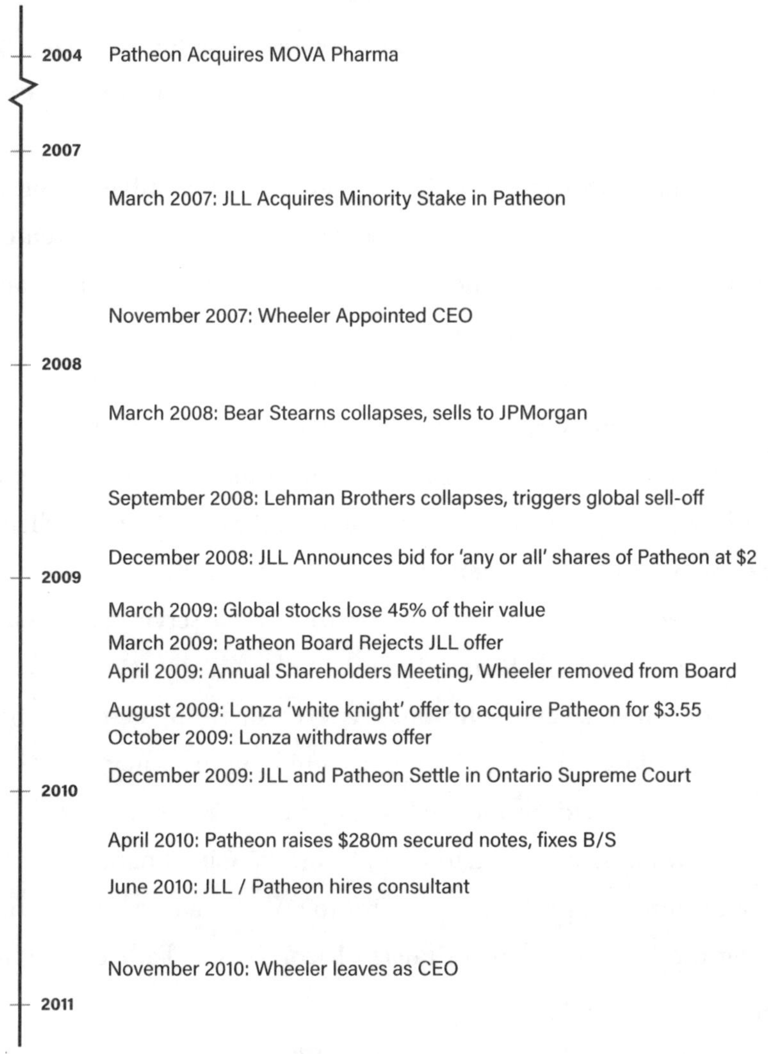
2004
Patheon Acquires MOVA Pharma
2007
March 2007: JLL Acquires Minority Stake in Patheon
November 2007: Wheeler Appointed CEO
2008
March 2008: Bear Stearns collapses, sells to JPMorgan
September 2008: Lehman Brothers collapses, triggers global sell-off
December 2008: JLL Announces bid for 'any or all' shares of Patheon at $2
2009
March 2009: Global stocks lose 45% of their value
March 2009: Patheon Board Rejects JLL offer
April 2009: Annual Shareholders Meeting, Wheeler removed from Board
August 2009: Lonza 'white knight' offer to acquire Patheon for $3.55
October 2009: Lonza withdraws offer
December 2009: JLL and Patheon Settle in Ontario Supreme Court
2010
April 2010: Patheon raises $280m secured notes, fixes B/S
June 2010: JLL / Patheon hires consultant
November 2010: Wheeler leaves as CEO
2011

Taxes took big bites from Patheon too. Internal reports, available only to me and my team, showed that in Italy, one of our most profitable businesses, our effective tax rate hit 56 percent, and the US business in Cincinnati was taxed at 35 percent. Depreciation ran hot at $50 million, while SG&A (selling, general, and administrative) expenses had risen despite flat volumes.

Perhaps most concerning of all, crucial clients had grown fed up with Patheon's sketchy customer service.

I showed the board some ugly performance metrics, available only to that internal audience but clearly in my memory all these years later.

Batches right first time (BRFT) stood at an embarrassing 86 percent. On-time performance was only at 87 percent. Inventory turns stood at 3.3, about the industry average, but that metric would need to improve to differentiate Patheon.

Tired of such an unreliable partnership, dependable customers—Watson, Novartis, Centocor, Gilead, Sanofi, and Merck—had begun to pull volume. I stressed to directors in the June 2008 board meeting that I'd been spending important time with those disgruntled clients, offering price incentives and making new service commitments.

Patheon, I said, urgently needed to solve its service and quality problems as well as its financial ones.

I outlined several solutions. As I recall from memory, these actions would yield $50 million to $70 million in savings.

Already, I had announced hiring freezes at some sites. I had reduced workforces in Puerto Rico, Swindon, Cincinnati, and at the Mississauga headquarters near Toronto. Work had begun on shuttering the Carolina plant in Puerto Rico. We cut Patheon's capital expenditures by 20 percent.

To address our lackluster service issues, I was counting on Ken's Lean Six Sigma Operational Excellence initiative, projected to save $15 million to $20 million a year when fully implemented.

Critically, I had also established a new quality management system, and I'd installed a new management incentive program to reward and retain the right people.

Operational metrics had been overhauled to address the real issues troubling customers. We created a customer survey to assess their needs and then to design our metrics around them.

The push now, I summarized, *is to hold on to as much revenue as possible, focus on quality, and pay better attention to our customers.*

Transformation in Progress

As a public company, I was obligated to host quarterly earnings calls with investors and analysts. That important audience seemed to like what it heard, but buyers remained cautious. Still, the stock price on the Toronto Stock Exchange began rising above C$4 per share in the first half of 2008, showing progress.

The month of my second board meeting, June 2008, we opened the turnaround floodgates.

In a momentous thirty days, our team proudly unveiled a new brand image, new color palette, and new slogan: "Performance the World Over." *BioSpace* (AC6.8) reported on that, and on our announcement of the formation of a Japanese subsidiary in Tokyo, a sales office focused on serving pharmaceutical companies in that region (AC6.9).

We also applied a first tourniquet to our Puerto Rico problem by revealing plans to introduce high-potency manufacturing capacity in Manati, on the island's north coast. That was our first step toward consolidating all Puerto Rico operations into one plant in Manati, a site originally built by Roche at a beautiful island location. It would ultimately save us millions of dollars and make our Puerto Rico operations profitable.

The summer of 2008 saw further transformation.

In July, as reported by *BioSpace* (AC6.10), Patheon announced a partnership with BSP Pharmaceuticals in Italy.

Some years earlier, Patheon had invested to help build BSP's new plant in Latina, south of Rome, and it now owned 18 percent of that company. Under the partnership agreement, BSP would supplement Patheon's sterile capacity by adding cytotoxic cancer drug production. The Italian plant was a model facility and stands today as a best-in-class operation under Aldo Braca's leadership.

To mitigate the whopping tax bite, we got creative.

"Wes asked me to set up a more tax-efficient structure," said Doaa, our Europe general counsel. "That meant creating a whole new team and finding a place for it."

In November 2008, we opened an office in Zug, Switzerland, establishing it as European operations headquarters. We conducted business there with our European customers.

The strategy was to reduce our tax burden by operating in more tax-efficient Switzerland, globally known as an international tax haven. *BioSpace* covered that move (AC6.11).

By February 2009, I could point to more cost reductions.

That month, Patheon announced the promised closing of the Carolina plant in Puerto Rico. Another part of the Puerto Rico fix was also in motion—a project to move all volume from Caguas to Manati, with the ultimate goal of also shutting down Caguas and selling the site. *BioSpace* also covered these events (AC6.12).

In Canada, the York Mills plant closed, with all volume moving to Whitby.

Now Patheon could bank on these streamlining moves.

Our 2008 results looked OK. Revenue grew by $40 million, and profit after restructuring expenses was healthy at $82.6 million. We still had a problem, though, with negative cash flow due to a heavy balance sheet.

Even with our problems, Patheon had rolling momentum—until it didn't.

The Great Recession changed everything.

Global Financial Collapse (Didn't See *That* Coming!)

Patheon wasn't alone in facing headwinds in 2008.

In March 2008, the *New York Times* (AC6.13) reported that Bear Stearns, a leading global investment bank, failed and sold itself to JPMorgan at $2 per share, a fire-sale price. Six months later, September 15, 2008, *TheStreet* (AC6.14) reported that Lehman Brothers filed for bankruptcy, the largest ever in US history, and that Lehman held more than $600 billion in assets.

When those two icons of the global financial system went down the drain, they sucked a lot of wealth with them. *Reuters* reported that the Standard & Poor's 500 stock index lost more than one-third of its value, 38.49 percent, by the end of 2008 (AC6.15). That's about the same amount (35 percent) lost on the Toronto Stock Exchange in that same time, as noted by *The Canadian Press* (AC6.16).

At Patheon, the impact of the financial meltdown hit hard. The company's share price had been growing nicely, but by the third quarter of 2008, due to forced selling by traditional investors, any trader could pick up a share for as little as $1.07 Canadian on the Toronto Stock Exchange (AC6.17).

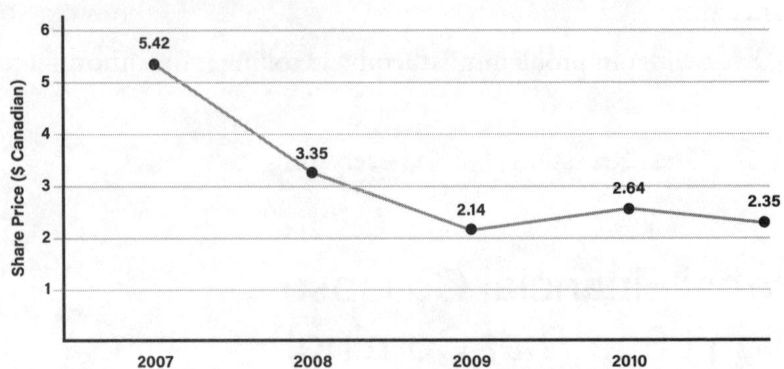

Patheon was valued at over C$5.00 / share before the global recession, and was externally valued at that price through the JLL process, but market forces out of our control suppressed the share price until it started to recover in 2011.

Action was needed.

In June 2008, I announced we would move Patheon headquarters into a growing US biotech hub, the Research Triangle Park, near Raleigh in North Carolina.

We planned to relocate all overhead positions from Toronto to North Carolina to be more strategically situated for the long term. We could also reduce the US tax burden this way, moving more of our overhead costs to the US legal entity, thus offsetting the profits generated at our Cincinnati facility and reducing our US tax basis.

Only a few Toronto executives made the move to our new HQ in Research Triangle Park, near Raleigh. We ultimately hired nearly eighty headquarters staff from North Carolina's talented local labor pool.

I also brought my family from California back to familiar ground in the Tarheel State. This time, we would stick.

We always loved life in North Carolina. And my commute to Canada was over.

By December 2008, Patheon was headquartered in North Carolina but still publicly traded on the Toronto Stock Exchange.

The advantage was that our US cost base would neutralize the profits made in Cincinnati and reduce our US tax burden. I, however, still lived in California and commuted, which took a toll on the family.

An Unsolicited Takeover Bid

Even as we made these moves, an unforeseen development stopped the presses in the pharma world and kept the presses running overtime in financial media.

On December 8, 2008, minority shareowners JLL Partners announced an unsolicited offer to buy "any and all" shares of Patheon stock for $2 a share, news recorded by *PE Hub* (AC6.18). We were still trading below $2 per share, as the financial markets were still suffering. The former CEO of Mova, a member of our board, made it clear that he did not intend to sell his shares, but he seemed supportive of JLL's move—at least for the time being.

The market was a mess. Patheon shares stubbornly remained below C$2 per share. The "any and all" JLL offer at US $2 per share basically cemented that price on the Toronto Stock Exchange, and it stayed there through much financial maneuvering to come.

The JLL rationale was simple. The private equity firm felt before making its offer that the offer represented a very significant premium over the low share price.

An old saying in business goes: *never waste a good recession.*

I sensed that some company leaders felt JLL's offer was an aggressive and unfair attempt to take advantage of the financial crisis and Patheon's shareholders. The board of directors seemed to consider JLL's move a hostile takeover attempt, though shareholders were never forced to sell their shares.

We conducted an independent valuation that concluded the company was worth between $4.20 and $5 per share. By that assessment, the $2 per share offer by JLL fell far short.

The board of directors was obligated to take action to protect the shareholders.

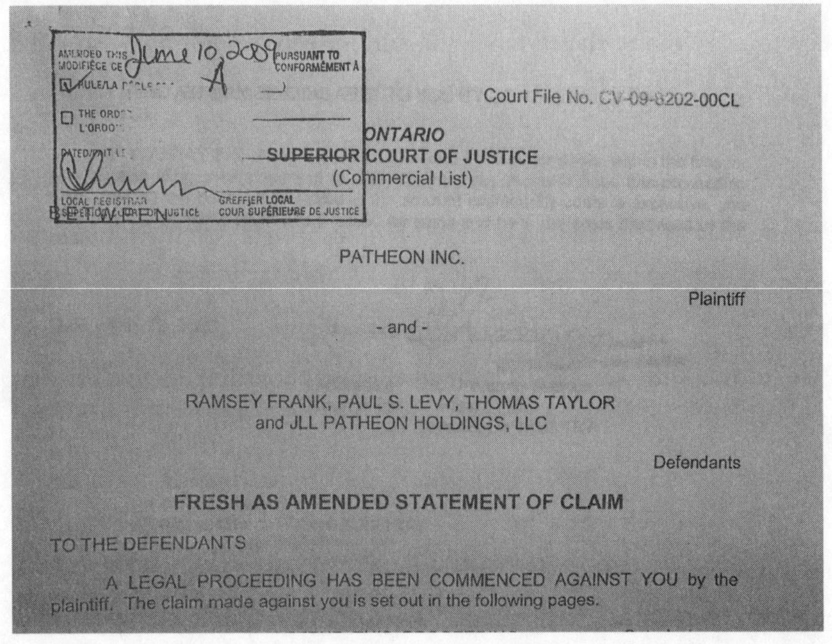

AMENDED THIS June 10, 2009 PURSUANT TO
MODIFIÉ CE CONFORMÉMENT À
RULE/LA RÈGLE A

THE ORDER
L'ORDONNANCE

DATED/FAIT LE

LOCAL REGISTRAR GREFFIER LOCAL
SUPERIOR COURT OF JUSTICE COUR SUPÉRIEURE DE JUSTICE

Court File No. CV-09-8202-00CL

ONTARIO
SUPERIOR COURT OF JUSTICE
(Commercial List)

BETWEEN:

PATHEON INC.

Plaintiff

- and -

RAMSEY FRANK, PAUL S. LEVY, THOMAS TAYLOR
and JLL PATHEON HOLDINGS, LLC

Defendants

FRESH AS AMENDED STATEMENT OF CLAIM

TO THE DEFENDANTS

A LEGAL PROCEEDING HAS BEEN COMMENCED AGAINST YOU by the plaintiff. The claim made against you is set out in the following pages.

First lawsuit against JLL

Eleven days after JLL's offer went public, Patheon's board formed a new Special Committee of Independent Directors, a select team of four board members based in Canada with a specific mandate that heavily restricted Patheon's ability to operate.

Somehow, amid the turmoil, I managed to guide my leadership team's 2009 budget to approval.

On March 25, 2009, Patheon's directors advised shareholders in a press release published the next day by *Contract Pharma* (AC6.19) to reject JLL's offer. Especially vocal was the former Mova CEO (and board director) who still owned 20 percent of all Patheon shares. He reversed his position and stated that the JLL offer was unacceptable. On April 24, the Patheon Special Committee lined up behind him, reaffirming its opposition to a $2 per share buyout.

Patheon's Special Committee separately asked the Ontario Securities Commission to stop JLL's takeover bid. When JLL dropped some contentious terms, the OSC allowed the bid to go ahead.

That's when the knives came out.

On April 29, as the annual meeting began, two brand-new, independent directors were voted onto the board, replacing me, the company's CEO, and the former Mova CEO. The power play gave the Canadian investors added control of the board.

Though I have to this day no more information than the facts presented in this chapter, one would have to ask if the Special Committee had somehow accumulated enough votes among the Canadian investors ahead of the annual meeting to make this happen.

It was a shock to everyone—especially to me and JLL.

Ontario Securities Commission	Commission des valeurs mobilières de l'Ontario	P.O. Box 55, 19th Floor 20 Queen Street West Toronto ON M5H 3S8	CP 55, 19e étage 20, rue queen ouest Toronto ON M5H 3S8

IN THE MATTER OF THE SECURITIES ACT
R.S.O. 1990, c. S.5, AS AMENDED

- and -

IN THE MATTER OF PATHEON INC.

- and -

IN THE MATTER OF AN OFFER TO PURCHASE FOR CASH ANY AND ALL OF THE RESTRICTED VOTING SHARES OF PATHEON INC. BY JLL PATHEON HOLDINGS, LLC

- and -

IN THE MATTER OF AN APPLICATION BY THE SPECIAL COMMITTEE OF THE BOARD OF DIRECTORS OF PATHEON INC. FOR CERTAIN RELIEF UNDER SECTIONS 104(1) and 127

REASONS FOR DECISION
(Sections 104(1) and 127 of the Act)

The Ontario Securities Commission Decision (AC6.26)

A Drama Unfolds ... and Gets Personal

On May 12, 2009, the revamped board with its newest members held an initial meeting.

A first order of business? Restrict even more tightly the operations of our company.

Now off the board, I had no say-so in that decision. It had the practical effect of tying one arm behind me while leading the company. I was invited to board meetings and still ran the company, but I was not a voting member.

"It was insulting," Doaa said in my defense. "When they removed Wes from the board at the shareholder meeting, he just couldn't fathom it. It was a shock."

More knives flashed.

On May 15, JLL Partners filed a motion in the Superior Court of Justice in Ontario. It alleged improper behavior by the two newly elected independent directors. The new board, of course, had excluded JLL directors from its actions, igniting JLL's legal action.

Meanwhile, somebody had to pay the bills. They had begun to exceed our available cash. My team and I struggled to continue the Patheon turnaround amid the uncivil civil war.

Remarkably, we made progress.

A new multicoated tablet operation came online in Cincinnati. I had recruited a new chief science officer. Canada looked stronger. The Toronto expansion went live, giving Patheon the means to produce more high-potency volume. Whitby's additions came online, and Swindon overhauled its sterile suite. We now had new capacity to sell.

In Puerto Rico, Bill Van and my engineering team, led by Ray Guidotti, had solved a mystery of how to manufacture an important new drug developed by Merck that was scheduled to launch from the Manati site. The relocation of Caguas production to Manati had begun, making it even more complicated as demand for the Merck drug was rapidly growing.

Further abroad, a new pilot plant in Bourgoin-Jallieu, France, hummed to life. In India, a partnership with Kemwell stretched our footprint to the East.

All this happened against the headwinds of the recession and as Patheon's board waged war. I simply kept my head down and stayed the course.

It was no easy task.

The bickering board fell into camps—JLL Partners on one side, the Special Committee of the Board, consisting of the Canadian directors, on the other. I was left in the middle.

The former Mova CEO immediately requested a new shareholder vote to regain his seat and oust the rest of the board.

In late May, JLL Partners sued Patheon to overturn the April board election.

Patheon countersued JLL Partners, asking a court to stop the bid and award more than $100 million in damages to Patheon.

By that same month, May 2009, JLL had already accumulated more than a third (36 percent) of all common shares of Patheon. On May 8, JLL had again extended its offer to buy "any and all" shares of Patheon at $2 per share. The offer stretched until August.

Then the vortex finally sucked me in.

On May 27, I received a letter from Davies, Ward, Phillips, and Vineberg, the law firm hired by the Patheon Special Committee. The firm had begun discovery of all internal documents that would be used to defend against JLL's lawsuit.

The Special Committee, in early June, made a statement of claim about my role as a director. The legal document did not accuse me directly of indiscretion, but it alleged that JLL had coerced me and members of my team to act in its favor during the offering period. These assertions were untrue, and they were also distracting. Worst of all, they could have been damaging to my reputation.

I drafted a lengthy paper addressing, and debunking, the claims. Working with Doaa, I vigorously defended myself. I even hired a personal lawyer from Lenczner Slaght LLP, a Toronto-based law firm. My personal attorney did a masterful job of defending my position.

The suspicions that certain management team members had sided with JLL—especially that I, Doaa, and my CFO had picked sides—arose from the Special Committee.

"The management team in a situation like this one must stay neutral," Doaa stressed. "Sharing information is not appropriate."

Who did the Special Committee suspect?

On June 26, I got called in for a meeting. I received a letter from Patheon's lawyers addressed to my lawyer. It declared that I was to be deposed in Toronto on the statement of claim issues. I was forced to hand over my laptop. I was under investigation. I was placed under severe restrictions. The basic question to me was: Why are you siding with JLL?

Well, I wasn't siding with JLL. I was remaining neutral and trying to keep the business running in the worst economic crisis in nearly a century.

Still, the negative press about all this turmoil was not helping me find new customers or retain old ones. But we soldiered on. What choice did we have?

Finally, I was cleared. Even so, in July the Special Committee and Patheon's lawyers sent further instructions to me and my management team warning us not to provide any nonpublic information to JLL Partners while its takeover bid continued. One can only imagine the irony of this situation—still not being able to share financial or any nonpublic information with the company's largest shareholder. But this is what we legally had to do.

Later that month, the court threw out JLL's attempt to overturn the board election approved by Patheon shareholders. That gave a perceived win to the Special Committee.

The internal fighting went on. In the summer of 2009, board meetings were intolerable. It got to the point where Directors and Officers (D&O) Insurance was reviewed to protect all the directors from external lawsuits. I hired another attorney just to represent my management team.

It should be no surprise, too, that investors by this time were appalled by extensive media coverage of the hostile behavior on both sides. From the outside, it looked like a cage match.

Even at this point, there were still enough outstanding shares to keep control of the company and out of JLL's hands.

But the drama took its toll.

"Here's Wes trying to run a company, get the Puerto Rico sites fixed, trying to convince pharma companies in the public domain to stick with Patheon," recalled Doaa. "But every day you've got directors suing each other.

"Patheon was nothing but noise every day."

As the year went on, our company reputation wasn't the only thing scraping bottom.

We were running out of cash to operate the company. We had money in several bank accounts, including the United States, Canada, United Kingdom, Italy, and France. We were moving money around from bank to bank just to make payroll.

I asked the board to approve a new, lower threshold of working capital to have on hand for operations. At the lowest point, we were running the entire company, a global enterprise, with just $2 million in cash on hand. We scrupulously sorted supplier invoices to keep critical materials flowing. I also tried to defer all legal expenses until after the circus left town, though my attempt failed.

Patheon had to pay law firms their supersized invoices. And I also had to find money to pay fees to Special Committee members. They all wanted their payment in real time, knowing that someday this whole thing would be over, and they might never be paid.

The fractures at the top widened and deepened, eventually showing up at the production level.

We put our Cincinnati plant on a two-week furlough to get through September 2009. In various other plants, we had to continue paying construction contractors to complete work and keep critical projects on schedule. We moved cash from Canada and Italy to make payroll in the US.

It was a challenging time.

A White Knight?

The long legal delays held a silver lining for the Special Committee.

Those board members from the Canada side of Patheon prayed feverishly, searching high and low, for a white knight to ride in with an offer better than JLL's $2 a share.

Their would-be Lancelot appeared in the form of the Lonza Group, a Swiss contract manufacturing company. In August 2009, *Industry-Week* (AC6.20) reported that Lonza came forward with an offer of $3.55 per share, higher than JLL's $2 per share offer but still below the company's true valuation. The share price rose to $3.00 on the news.

The Special Committee jumped at the Lonza opportunity. They encouraged shareholders to approve the buyout offer.

The *IndustryWeek* article also reported that Lonza's offer would buy 67 percent of the company but presumably exclude the shares JLL had already accumulated. The JLL stake now stood at 57 percent of all outstanding common stock shares. To give Lonzo majority ownership, JLL would have to agree to sell some or all its shares at $3.55.

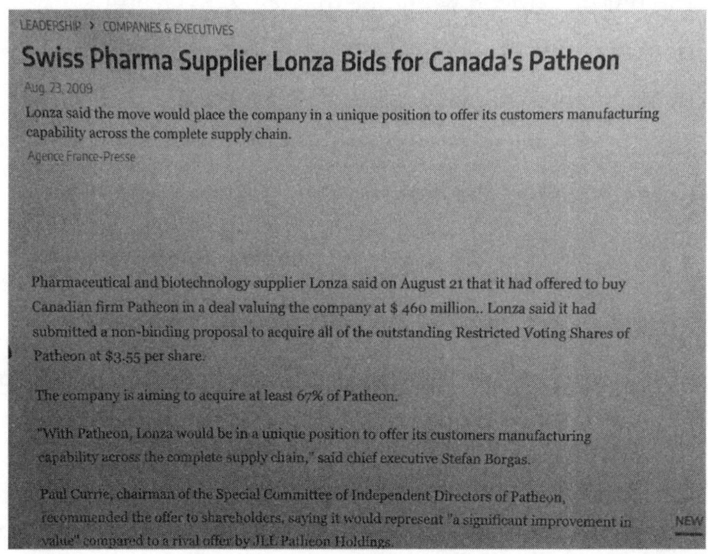

LEADERSHIP > COMPANIES & EXECUTIVES

Swiss Pharma Supplier Lonza Bids for Canada's Patheon

Aug. 23, 2009

Lonza said the move would place the company in a unique position to offer its customers manufacturing capability across the complete supply chain.

Agence France-Presse

Pharmaceutical and biotechnology supplier Lonza said on August 21 that it had offered to buy Canadian firm Patheon in a deal valuing the company at $ 460 million.. Lonza said it had submitted a non-binding proposal to acquire all of the outstanding Restricted Voting Shares of Patheon at $3.55 per share.

The company is aiming to acquire at least 67% of Patheon.

"With Patheon, Lonza would be in a unique position to offer its customers manufacturing capability across the complete supply chain," said chief executive Stefan Borgas.

Paul Currie, chairman of the Special Committee of Independent Directors of Patheon, recommended the offer to shareholders, saying it would represent "a significant improvement in value" compared to a rival offer by JLL Patheon Holdings.

NEW

Lonza's White Knight offer

Due diligence began. My leadership team and I were directed to work with Lonza on that process. Meetings took place in London. Our Patheon team and the Lonza teams were actually getting along very well. I thought to myself that this would be an efficient way to get out of the mess.

On August 7, *CBC News* (AC6.21) and other services announced that JLL ended its outstanding offer of $2 per share, making it clear it would not tender to the Lonza offer at $3.55.

Things rocked along, all positive vibes for Lonza's activities. I attended lots of meetings and became close to the Lonza CEO.

There was just one sticking point—but it got more and more sticky over time.

Lonza could not get comfortable with Patheon's assets outside of Italy because they were generally nonsterile and did not dovetail with its business. The Lonza CEO and his team wanted the sterile facilities only. The rest of Patheon would be incidental to them.

Still, talks went on.

On September 28, Lonza and Patheon announced in *BioSpace* an extension of the Swiss offer, with exclusivity (AC6.22). The $3.55 per share price remained. The deal was extended to October 15, though JLL continued to say that it would not tender any portion of the 57 percent of shares it had accumulated.

Finally, though, the weight of assets not essential to Lonza's model—and the relentless refusal of JLL to sell its majority block of shares—simply proved too much.

On October 20, *OutsourcingPharma* (AC6.23) reported that Lonza withdrew the $3.55 per share offer and walked away from the deal.

That was a crushing embarrassment to the Special Committee.

JLL Partners got what it wanted all along.

On December 4, 2009, JLL and Patheon reached an agreement approved by Canada's Supreme Court, effectively ending all disputes. The independent board of directors and the Special Committee were instantly dissolved.

Now JLL had full control of the company.

I was reappointed to the board of directors. All the onerous mandates placed on me, my team, and the operations were reversed.

Work finally got back to normal, but normal had a short shelf life at Patheon.

Ramsey Frank of JLL became the company's new chairman. A new leader from JLL Partners also joined the board.

With this executive's arrival, what might have been the smooth turning of a page instead became a loud ripping noise.

The new JLL leader did not show a lot of respect to the management team—including me. I was confused as to why.

Given the state of the world economy in 2009, and the hostile environment which we had just endured, financial results in the Patheon Annual Report to Shareholders for that year (AC6.24) looked quite respectable, and full-year EBITDA stood at a presentable $83 million on revenue of $655 million.

Revenues and profits, though, had slipped that year, mainly due to clients preserving their own cash flows during the severe economic downturn. The main hit came from Patheon's pharmaceutical development (R&D) revenues, as clients cut back on pipeline activities. Currency fluctuations in 2009 didn't play well for us either.

The new leader from JLL wasn't happy, regardless of the numbers. In a meeting with me and my team at his New York office just after JLL took over, he questioned what we had accomplished, despite all we'd done to stabilize the company under my leadership.

Had he been asleep through the whole previous year?

Overall, I knew that the moves we made as a management team, despite the chaos all around us, showed conspicuous positive results.

The calendar turned. I kept our team motoring. We had already implemented Salesforce.com as our new customer relationship management (CRM) system, and the sales team was well staffed and well led. Customer service metrics looked much better.

By April 2010, Patheon felt it was time to find some financing. Media, including *BioSpace* (AC6.25), covered our offer of a placement of $280 million of senior secured notes. Money poured in. The very successful round of financing finished on April 27.

We used those proceeds to pay off all existing debt and restate the revolving debt, plus place cash on the balance sheet. We badly needed cash, especially after paying all the legal expenses from the previous year.

Operationally, it now looked like Patheon had turned a corner.

Our team finished building a soft gel capsule facility in Cincinnati; the plant was becoming a company jewel and had started manufacturing a five-layer coated tablet for a new product launch. The Toronto facility and the two Italian facilities turned major profits. In Puerto Rico, the full-scale expansion at Manati had reached a point where costly Caguas could be shut down and sold in a few more months. The Caguas site was located in a commercial shopping area, which bode well for potential, nonpharmaceutical, buyers.

Looking back, given the economic meltdown outside and the year of takeover fratricide inside, our accomplishments could easily be considered remarkable.

But JLL Partners had triumphantly taken the battlefield, and now they wanted even more.

The new JLL leader now on the board had not been involved in operations before the takeover. But with JLL in full control, he felt the need to force management to hire a consulting firm.

I couldn't believe it.

The new owners wanted a fabled consultancy to waltz in, as at Valeant, to "reevaluate the Patheon strategy."

That's exactly what started to happen.

I was cooperative to a point. But it seemed entirely possible to me that this consultancy would cost a ton of money only to come up with many, if not all, of the same decisions we'd already made.

My numbers are approximate and from my recollection, but I believe that in the end Patheon ended up paying the consultant more than $20 million.

Most of that spending, though, would come on someone else's watch.

Sometime in the late fall of 2010, I had a difficult meeting with JLL. I told them perhaps they had the wrong CEO if they wanted to continue paying an expensive consulting firm to "take our watch and tell us the time," instead of listening to its own management team.

I had survived many painful consultancy meetings and had simply been harassed too long. I wanted time to settle the company in the aftermath of the takeover bid process. My team was anxious too—the environment was difficult in this new ownership structure, and JLL had begun to behave differently toward us.

I left Patheon on November 30, 2010.

I negotiated a two-year continuance while the company searched for its next CEO. That person, James McMullen, arrived in early 2011. Doaa Fathallah and my CFO hit the door soon after I did.

An Insider's View

Ramsey Frank, the JLL Partners board chair who delivered the news that I would no longer be CEO at Patheon, offered his own perspective from the private equity side of these events.

"Wes is one of the toughest, most resilient people I've ever seen," Frank said. "I give him a lot of credit for what he was able to accomplish at Patheon under the most difficult circumstances. At times like those, you get to know what a person is really like. Wes is a very high-quality individual."

Frank had joined JLL Partners after tenures with multinational investment bank Drexel Burnham and with US investment bank Donaldson, Lufkin & Jenrette. He was no novice to corporate fracases, but he looks back with particular fascination at the complexity and challenge of the Patheon takeover.

"When we first looked at Patheon, the general counsel was effectively serving as the CEO. The company was overleveraged, and the acquisition of the Puerto Rico assets nearly killed them. The leadership issues were obvious—the entrepreneurial founder had been thrown out. The general counsel had never even been to Puerto Rico to see what was there.

"Our JLL offer put in $150 million to pay down the company's debt and restructure it. We got convertible preferred stock and became the largest shareholder in March 2007."

Frank confirmed that Patheon's biggest initial problem was the bleeding ulcer called Puerto Rico.

In the 1970s, the United States had passed special tax breaks to spur development on the island, an unincorporated territory of the nation. A pharma industry presence emerged in the '70s and '80s. The three facilities Patheon had purchased on the island were part of that miniboom, but they'd never been particularly productive.

"Mova had quality problems," Frank said. "Companies found a very culturally different work ethic in Puerto Rico. They found it to be a great place for tax breaks, but the workforce wasn't strong. It was a hard place to manage people.

"One of Wes's first challenges was to build a management team that didn't previously exist, then figure out how to stop the bleeding in Puerto Rico."

As I shouldered those tasks, the stock market crashed. JLL Partners saw an opportunity, and the private equity firm made a move.

"With Patheon's stock price down and with our conviction in the fundamental strength of the business," Frank reasoned. "We thought, 'Why not buy more?' We wanted to buy anything we could get and knew that it would be worth more when the stock prices rose again."

JLL knew, of course, that the Canadian majority owners would go wild.

"Oh sure, we got a hostile response," Frank confirmed. "They said, 'You can't do that! You can't offer shareowners liquidity!'"

Frank and JLL simply asked, "Where does it say we can't?"

He goes on with his side of the story.

"The primary people involved in bringing Wes on board [JLL] had gone to war with their majority shareholders," Frank said. "At one especially critical point, Wes was no longer on the board of directors, and he was restricted in what he could say to whom, for legal reasons."

Ramsey was right. I was severely hamstrung at the time but I still had a job to do, a company to run.

"We at JLL had brought a lot of money to the table," Frank said. "And keeping Wes engaged really mattered to us."

Frank was blunt about the Canadian majority owners.

"Wheeler was an American," he said. "The Canadians involved in the deal didn't necessarily trust him. They'd look nice, smile, shake your hand, but you could sense an attitude."

Frank vividly saw the effects.

"Wes was not well respected by the Canadian board members," he said. "He couldn't interact with them, and he couldn't interact with us. He was torn in different directions with a lot to fix for the company. And all this time, it was hard to demonstrate true progress, because the economy was so bad."

Frank called that period my "forty days in the wilderness."

At the end of 2009, after a long year heavy with lawyers, JLL prevailed in its ownership bid. The firm closed the tender to go from 35 percent to a 60 percent majority shareowner. On December 1, the litigation settlement was announced. It had very specific terms that would carry the company through 2011 with a new board, among other standstill provisions.

I would remain for ten more months until I was let go by JLL.

Frank himself left JLL Partners in 2012 to set up his own investment company, Amulet Capital Partners, based in Greenwich, Connecticut. In a little more than a decade, he has grown Amulet to be larger than his former firm.

Frank stayed in touch with me through the years. He says he greatly respects the job I did at Patheon and all I've done since.

"It was not a personal thing when Wes was fired," Frank said. "We made it clear we'd provide good references and support for him moving forward.

"What Wes went through was very difficult. It was not what he signed up for. He was on an island by himself with people he didn't know, didn't trust, and who didn't know the business.

"I can only imagine the scars."

A Record to Stand On

Three years had flown by, and worlds had changed—my world, my family's world, the world of pharma.

I had first shuttled from LA to Toronto, then from North Carolina to New York City. Erica had left for college at Michigan. She and Greg would come home on breaks to a new house in Chapel Hill, a place that felt like home to Marianne and me.

Like a good Boy Scout leaving a campsite, I left Patheon in better shape than I found it.

In Chapel Hill, Patheon's new headquarters office had expanded to more than eighty staff, with a new chief information officer, a new head of sales, a new head of tax accounting, and new promise.

The Toronto headquarters closed. I had hired a very able leader to run Puerto Rico operations, and by the time I left nearly every site director in the company had been replaced. I could proudly point to dozens of promotions I approved for worthy people in the organization.

I left with good results for 2010. The company financials in the Patheon Annual Report for that year, shared internally only, reported Patheon revenue of $671 million and EBITDA of $97 million—a 17 percent increase over the prior year. But the company was still experiencing fallout from the economic crisis, the restructuring of the balance sheet, and consulting fees. Even so, volume, revenue, and profit were up. The business was well positioned.

I was hired to lead Patheon out of a difficult financial condition and through an operational turnaround. I shaped a new strategy and a comprehensive change of course, rebuilding the company on a foundation of quality, service, delivery, professionalism, and compliance.

Despite a period of restructuring and the extremely negative market forces—including a global financial meltdown—my team and I improved EBITDA, before extraordinary and onetime charges, by more than 25 percent on marginally flat revenue, as reflected in our financial reports from 2007 to 2010, and which I offer here based on my personal notes from internal sources.

In fact, the company's EBITDA margins, which had grown from 10 percent to 14 percent during my tenure, were among the highest of any finished-dose CMO in the industry, based on my own analysis of internal financials and on data in our annual reports.

PATHEON PHARMACEUTICALS

	$ in Millions				
	Revenue	Gross Margin	%	EBITDA	%
2007	634	130	20.5	64	**10**
2008	717	157	21.8	95	**13.2**
2009	655	144	22.0	83	**12.7**
2010	691	153	22.1	97	**14.0**

Despite all odds, we increased EBITDA margin to 14% during the time I was CEO

I oversaw the replacement of Patheon's entire senior management team. My internal personal notes observe that total staff had been reduced by 850 full-time equivalents (15 percent). Those notes also reflect that I revised and upgraded all corporate governance policies and set up a more professional interface with the board of directors.

Under my leadership, Patheon got a new corporate headquarters in the United States and a new European office in Switzerland. The company benefited from a new tax structure and a simpler corporate legal structure.

Our annual reports and my careful personal notes show that we had recapitalized the company by raising $280 million in new high-yield securities and improving the balance sheet. I centralized Patheon engineering and managed more than $140 million in capital expenditures in my three years, building new management controls for approvals, project management, and the monitoring of all projects.

We divested a small Canadian business with two sites and closed a third. We closed one site in Puerto Rico, prepared a second site for closure, and established a program to restructure the island's remaining plant at Manati.

We rebranded Patheon and rebuilt our entire sales and marketing arm. We retooled all the human resources programs, including short- and long-term incentive programs and US benefits. These complemented a complete new set of financial and operational performance indicators and a new best-in-industry quality management system among contract manufacturing organizations of the day.

And operations?

Our team at Patheon significantly improved on all eighteen of its operational metrics, including the big ones: On-time delivery. Right first-time batches. Inventory turns. Day's sales outstanding. Cycle time. Labor utilization. Batch deviations.

On my first shift as CEO of a public company—and during a restructuring in the midst of the worst world economy since the Great Depression—my personal notes and recollections confirm that Patheon sold more than $160 million in new commercial business and $250 million in new development services business, adding fifty-plus new customers. Much of these data are found in public filings.

In that time, Patheon worked with nineteen of the world's top twenty pharmaceutical companies and two-thirds of all specialty pharmaceutical companies.

I'm proud of those three years of principled leadership. I learned a lot about people. I refined my way of leading a company under extreme circumstances. It prepared me for my next move, perhaps the most important of my career.

LESSONS LEARNED

Sometimes bad things happen. A market crash. A global recession. We have no control over these things, but if we remain true to ourselves and do the right thing for our businesses and people, we can survive and succeed.

During the darkest of days, even while running a company on razor-thin cash reserves, it was important that I kept our employees and customers out of the fray. We had to stay positive, believe in our fundamentals, and continue running the business while keeping the board battles in the background. That positive attitude is what got us through.

CHAPTER 7

MARKEN (2011-2019)

Turning a Complete Financial Write-Off into a Global Industry Leader

The timing of the Patheon exit worked out just fine.

The Next Big Thing arrived—an opportunity that would occupy me for the next eight years and constitute my best work as a corporate leader.

Soon after leaving Patheon, I launched my own consulting practice, WPWheelerLLC (still active today). A company called Apax Partners recruited me as an advisor. After a few months, Apax asked if I would be interested in running Marken, a clinical logistics company it had purchased about a year earlier.

I had no real experience in clinical logistics, but something about Marken intrigued me. It was global, and it had a good reputation for quality.

It took four months to negotiate my contract. I ultimately joined in May 2011, and I was officially appointed to the Marken board of directors in July.

Marken would test all my skills in leading a company.

As it happened, I was equipped with a solid team, and we would lift Marken up from financial ground zero, transforming it into a renowned global player with unrivaled leadership in its sector.

From Manufacturing to Clinical Logistics

Marken's name came, whimsically, from the names of its two founders, Mark Adams and Ken Powell—Mark/Ken.

The company started as a courier that, under strict secrecy, delivered music CDs to sales points before official release. Those shipments required high security, and they were time-sensitive, representing critical income sources for distributors and stores. The company then found similar logistics services valuable for the high-end fashion industry and film studios.

Marken found its true calling, though, when Covance Central Laboratory (now a LabCorp company) hired it to rescue some shipments of blood samples that another delivery company couldn't handle.

Marken delivered the blood on time to Covance's Geneva, Switzerland, laboratory, beginning a long and very profitable relationship. (Marken, in time, would capture 60 percent of the global clinical blood sample logistics market.)

As new revenue flowed in, Marken abandoned the delivery of CDs, sequined gowns, and movie reels to concentrate on this new core business exclusively devoted to the pharma industry.

As pharmaceutical companies, central laboratories, and contract research organizations (CROs) conducted trials of new drugs and treatments, they relied on Marken to shuttle blood samples from clinical trial sites to central labs for analysis.

Marken cultivated a sterling reputation for fast, uncompromised transport of blood samples all over the world.

The end of the first decade of the twenty-first century happened to be a fine time to be in clinical trial logistics. The tightened belts of the Great Recession loosened, and pharma companies started to pump money into R&D again, rushing to refill drug pipelines, which had slowed to trickles by the financial crash. More R&D, of course, meant more clinical trials, with more sample shipments.

Marken stood as one of only three significant players in the niche, roughly a $3 billion global market at the time. Marken and DHL dominated sample movements around the world. World Courier had the lion's share of drug shipments to clinics.

The Apax leaders saw potential in Marken and made a move. Smart money at the time considered Marken a good company, if grossly overpriced by its sellers.

Apax Buys Big

As reported by *Financial Times* (Appendix C7.1), Apax acquired Marken for £975 million in a leveraged buyout on December 8, 2009. The deal closed in early 2010.

According to that *Financial Times* report, Apax would own two-thirds of the equity. The existing mezzanine lender, Intermediate Capital Group, or ICG, earned £170 million from the sale of Marken and would later roll over a portion of its proceeds into the new debt structure.

Apax's portion of the purchase price came in a combination of its own cash, syndicated cash equity, and debt. The syndicated equity came from a clutch of co-investors (AlpInvest Partners, USS Investment Management Ltd., BlackRock Inc., American Financial

Advisors LLC, Scandia Company, and Credit Suisse Group AG). The debt was raised from Alcentra Ltd., ICG plc, The Carlyle Group, and nine smaller firms.

Amazingly, a third of Marken's equity remained in the hands of legacy management, including its former chair, CEO, and five other members of the management team. These equity holders were minority owners but held substantial voting power.

Why such a deal?

The team at Apax, influenced by a senior dealmaker, had grown greatly enamored with the former CEO and with Marken. They convinced the firm that Marken would be a cash generating ATM machine.

There were only two bidders for Marken at the end. Its former CEO, negotiating from a hotel room, negotiated a higher price than the next highest bidder (the cover bidder), named in the press as Hellman & Friedman, another private equity firm. According to rumors at the time, Apax added nearly £100 million to its final bid over a weekend, not knowing that Hellman & Friedman had already backed out.

I would later have access to internal notes showing that the company bought by Apax for more than €1 billion would close its 2009 accounts with about €170 million in revenues, and an EBITDA of about €83 million, a very healthy profit margin. The company only had 382 employees at the time.

Marken came with one big asterisk.

An existential risk lay in its overreliance on a single customer—we'll call it Company 1. In 2009, Company 1 constituted a third of Marken's revenue, which was equal to revenues from all its next four biggest customers combined.

In 2010, the first year of Apax's new ownership, Marken began to slip. Internal records I later saw in my leadership role revealed that revenue stayed essentially flat, just north of €170 million, but EBITDA had declined significantly.

It was a 30 percent profit miss in 2010—the first real sign of a problem.

Apax began to search for a new CEO in early 2011.

I came on board and quickly learned in internal meetings and from notes that not everything presented during my private equity courtship was as it seemed.

I was privy at one point to private internal documents that showed the Marken budget for 2011 was based on projections for a healthy improvement in revenue, with EBITDA growing slightly but still below 2009 levels. Margins were dropping fast, another red flag that warned of performance issues. Those would become all too clear later that year.

Apax was assuming that continued high margins would allow it to reduce debt cover ratio (leverage) significantly. That would have been a very reasonable result. The company was still financially fit and relatively unleveraged, at least on paper.

It would turn out, though, that rosy predictions made by Marken leadership and accepted by the Apax deal team looked like fake news once actual 2011 results came in.

Revenues fell. Margins fell even faster.

Marken's 2011 results would miss again. And EBITDA dropped as the revenue and margins continued to decline.

In its nonpublic March 2011 board report, which I saw before joining, Apax declared, "Marken has had a disappointing first year." But leaders were still optimistic about making the 2011 budget.

Somehow, though, Apax missed the red flags. So did I, even as I agreed to sign on as CEO.

Marken's former chair, CEO, COO, CFO, business development chief, and the head of sales had all made millions on the sale of Marken to Apax. What's more, they still held roughly a third of the equity.

The standing CEO stayed on as Marken's chairman. Two other legacy executives, the COO and head of sales, with millions of proceeds of their own, elected to stay, too, reporting to me.

The chairman wouldn't last long, leaving in 2012.

A Bad Day for Covenants

My first board of directors meeting as CEO took place in July 2011. I sat at the middle of the table. My predecessor, now acting as chairman, stood behind me and didn't take a seat. My inherited team flanked me, and we faced our Apax board members across the table.

I witnessed something completely new in board meetings, at least in my experience.

There were no handouts. There was no agenda. Apax asked for a financial update. The CFO pulled a single sheet of paper from his pocket.

He announced to us that the company would breach its debt covenants in the third quarter—a thunderclap of bad news.

Private equity companies leverage their acquisitions by combining their own cash with borrowed money. Leverage usually ranges from three to five times EBITDA, sometimes higher. To protect this leverage, lenders will set limits, known as "covenants." At the time of the deal and up until this board meeting, the leverage ratio and associated covenants were within the normal range. But now, with

EBITDA and margins falling, the 2011 numbers now pointed to a covenant breach.

No company ever wants to be caught in a covenant breach. So that moment shocked Apax. The chief investment officer resigned from the board of directors immediately after the board meeting. The Apax deal team went into fire drill mode.

I had to go back to the business and do my best to try and avoid a breach.

Cost-saving measures went into place. I scrambled to generate new revenues so Marken could scrape through the year.

Luckily, good things had been happening in the business—the very things that drew me to the job.

In 2010, before I stepped into the C suite, Marken had opened a new office in Tokyo. Marken had also relocated and expanded our Singapore office, cementing itself into a key Asia market.

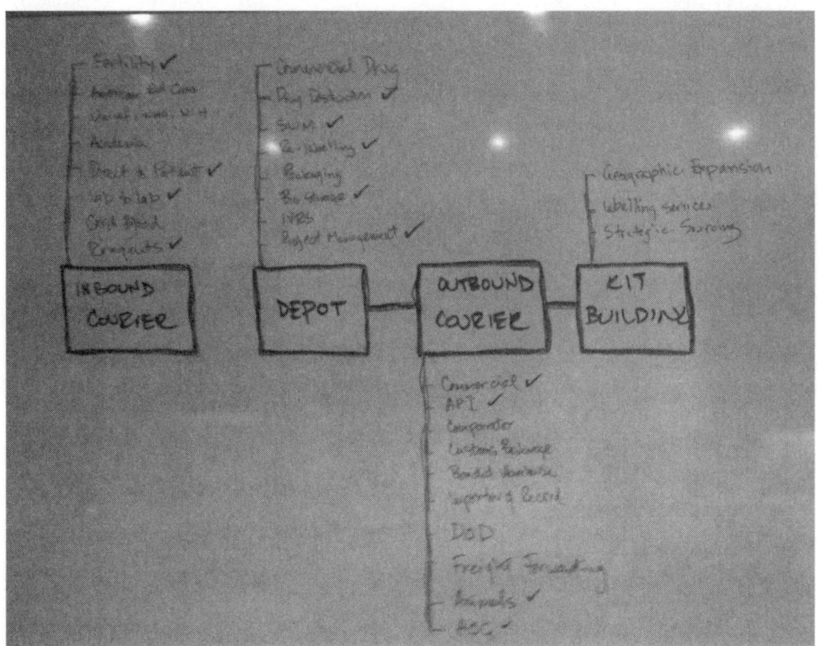

We decided very early on how to expand our portfolio of services

In Singapore, Marken had been completing a GMP "depot"—our term for a drug storage warehouse—marking the first directly owned, purpose-built Marken facility for investigational medical product distribution. The ultraclean, state-of-the-industry, 14,500-square-foot supply site hosted a full range of secured storage options, from ambient to deep frozen. It handled storage/distribution, drug returns and destruction, and biological specimen storage in ultracold conditions.

The standing CEO told me prior to joining that Marken planned to build another ten to fifteen such facilities globally before 2016.

That certainly sounded like growth mode, and those plans ultimately convinced me to join the Marken party. It's what I didn't know before joining that would consume me for the next year.

Death of a Sale Process

I needed help.

In September 2011, Doaa Fathallah came over to Marken from Patheon as general counsel and chief administrative officer. She arrived four months after me, starting work just in time for the fourth quarter Marken board meeting in London.

My C suite now consisted of five executives. Two Marken legacy executives reported to me. The pair was also part of the minority equity holder group, with voting rights that ultimately became a conflict of interest. A new player, who would prove very important in the long run, was Ariette van Strien, newly hired from the pharma industry to lead Marken sales. I had hired a new CFO, from the pharmaceutical industry, and we had Doaa, our new general counsel.

Apax directors, as majority owners, presided over the board.

A dozen investors crowded into the fourth-quarter meeting. Our largest debt holder showed up wearing full hunting gear.

The minority owners, led by their former CEO, called in by phone. Out of nowhere, Apax made an announcement: Marken's headquarters had moved to France, abandoning the London headquarters.

Doaa elegantly described the reaction of lenders. "The banks," she said, "lost their minds."

Doaa, who knew more international law than anyone else in the room, realized what Apax was doing.

"France is the worst place in the world to be if you are a creditor," she said. "But I left the meeting with very clear instructions: 'When the phone rings, Doaa, you say *bonjour*!'"

Our headquarters never moved to France. I chose Chiswick, in West London, as Marken's new headquarters. We already had a small office there, and a number of employees lived nearby. We would eventually move the headquarters to North Carolina.

We worked hard in Chiswick. My team put several delaying actions in place immediately, but we ultimately breached the covenant in the fourth quarter.

That event would throw its long shadow over my Marken turnaround efforts then and for years to come.

Still, not all was lost. By this time, Ariette van Strien and I had gotten a handle on what was happening to Marken's revenue and margin.

Several months before Apax bought Marken, one of our top customers put our entire European business out for bid. It was probably half of our business with that customer at the time. Before the bid process, they had asked Marken for a 5 percent price reduction for the Europe volume, a concession that would have kept the contract from ever going out to bid. But Marken refused, arrogantly, and the business ultimately went to DHL.

Because clinical trials run for 24-30 months, the revenue naturally 'bleeds out' over time and the loss of the European business was not noticeable in the 2010 results. But the decline in revenue and margin in 2011 was significant, and it became clear to me that the loss to DHL was the reason. It was too late. The volumes had been lost in competition, and there was not a thing we could do about it.

Once it was certain that Marken was going to breach, we requested waivers from the lenders to buy time, avoid calling the debt, and come up with a plan.

The lenders collectively granted a waiver with a time limit, and we then asked for a further waiver. In early 2012, as a condition of the second waiver, the lenders requested €100 million be placed on the Marken balance sheet.

I turned my efforts toward raising that cash.

The cash would have to come from existing shareholders. The problem was that Apax held only 65 percent of the company's equity, while the minority shareholders—the former CEO and CFO, et al.—held the rest. The minority holders would need to raise their fair share, which we knew was doubtful. If Apax put in the full €100 million without minority participation, it would dilute Apax's investment even further.

In February 2012, Apax hired Houlihan Lokey, Inc., a Los Angeles-based global investment firm, to support its talks with lenders. The lenders tapped their own global heavyweight banking and investment firm, Rothschild & Co, to seek terms for an agreement.

Doaa was our shuttle diplomacy ambassador, learning to navigate her way around London. She described negotiations with the investors as "World War III."

Apax was being pressured to put in €100 million, but it was leaning toward €50 million, according to a *Reuters* story (AC7.2) from

February, 2012. However, since the minority investors refused to pay their share, Apax simply saw nothing to gain.

"It was a zero/negative proposition," Doaa confirmed. "If Apax invested the entire amount, it would only receive its 65 percent share of that money at exit. But if it didn't pay the €100 million, the lenders could call the loan, which Apax would still have to satisfy."

Doaa was a good emissary. She earned the trust of key figures at Apax and the banks.

"For weeks," she said, "I flew to London over and over, meeting with banks to broker a deal, working for the best outcome. Once I even slept at a hotel in my clothes after negotiating all night with key lenders—a meeting that was supposed to last an hour."

By March 2012, Apax had grudgingly offered to put up half of what the lenders wanted, but that figure was rejected outright. Negotiations came to a stalemate.

And Marken came to the end of its rope.

In April 2012, the board of directors, led by the Apax majority, decided to sell the company. The lenders agreed to provide waiver cover during the sale process.

The board could not have chosen a worse time to sell a troubled enterprise.

The UK had dizzied itself all year celebrating the Diamond Jubilee of Queen Elizabeth II, the monarch's sixtieth year on the throne of Great Britain. The Olympic Games in London in July and August further exhausted and distracted Britons and people of many other nations. Meanwhile, Europeans disappeared for weeks on their coveted summer vacations.

"We worked nonstop, day and night, trying to find a buyer," Doaa said, "with basically just six weeks to do so."

Our board selected Morgan Stanley, a worldwide leader in investment services, to serve as our investment banker in the sales process, which would be conducted as a broad auction.

We hoped the sale would be successful, even though the actual results for 2011 amplified a significant decline in year-over-year profit.

Still, the company had a pulse. Our margins were healthy. We had good cash flow.

The sale process, sometimes referred to as an "auction," stretched into September 2012.

Then, to Marken's distress, someone leaked the auction bids to the media, and this wrecked the careful secrecy we'd cultivated in the entire sale process.

We ended up with just two short-listed buyers.

A midsize US private equity firm was the leading bidder, and there were two others in the mix as cover bids. The deal, if it happened, would allow for existing debts to be paid, and it would bring fresh cash, as it allowed new owners to raise new debt.

Things looked good through the end of October.

Then on November 6, 2012, the day of Barack Obama's second-term reelection as United States president, a financing arrangement that offered five-times leverage with Credit Suisse fell apart. The debt offering was reduced substantially.

The leading bidder declined to proceed. And that was that.

Apax threw in the towel.

The Apax team wrote off its investment, saying goodbye to its €458 million and leaving its co-investors with nothing.

Now a new urgent need obsessed Marken.

"The banks would accelerate the loans and take over the company," Doaa said, "and this had to be disclosed before the end of December for legal reasons and to keep customers from running."

All the previous year, Ariette and I had managed the fallout from rumors of Marken's sale process and then its failed auction. Our competition was telling customers that Marken was already bankrupt. Doaa, our CFO, and I met with lenders. I spent much of my time calming customers and reassuring them that we were still in business.

I issued press releases touting the many improvements and expansions at Marken, doing my best to neutralize the rumor mill. I issued an end-of-year press release to announce that lenders now owned our business. The fact that we were now a lender-led company was bad news, but thankfully that mostly ended up buried during the Christmas holidays.

So, as documented by a private equity newsletter, *AltAssets*, in a December 19, 2012, article (AC7.3), Marken was now owned by its lenders—thirteen of them in all. I now had thirteen bosses, the most complicated ownership situation of my entire career.

Suddenly in charge, the lenders wasted no time in hiring a new chairman of the board at Marken.

His area of expertise?

Turnarounds.

Strange Numbers

Financial struggles and a failed bid process would leave most companies dazed and confused.

Marken proved no exception.

The company burned through three CFOs, three vice presidents of quality assurance, five regional vice presidents, and three chairmen of the board from 2011 to 2016. In this same time, I authorized replacing more than one thousand company positions.

The first hurdle on the comeback trail proved a big one, as my team got back to business with our new owners.

In the final days of 2012, Doaa and I met with our CFO to assess the financials. We noticed something strange happening with the numbers.

It would lead to yet another Marken moment.

I had hired our new CFO in August 2011. He came with experience at a leading supplier of pharmaceutical and medical supplies. He cleared his interviews and had great references. He appeared to be the right fit.

But those strange financial numbers?

"The CFO told me that he was receiving confusing invoices from suppliers, invoices that had originated before Wes's time with the company," Doaa said. "He said that when these big invoices came, nobody seemed to understand what they were."

Many, he told Doaa, were in languages that accountants couldn't read, so instead of accruing the invoices to the P&L, his team would leave them on the balance sheet.

I immediately notified our new chairman while we looked at ways to find the problems and address how to restate the 2012 accounts.

The next board meeting in London was difficult. Our CFO was asked to explain the anomalies. He could not come up with an acceptable argument.

Doaa added, "After the meeting, two whistleblowers came forward to Wes and myself to confirm that costs had, in fact, been moved off the P&L [profit and loss] report and onto the balance sheet."

So it was then confirmed that the balance sheet contained hidden costs that should have been reported on the P&L in 2012.

Doaa's newest dirty job was to get to the bottom of things.

"Were there potential errors in the books? Were we following our accounting practices?" she asked. "I was obligated as general counsel for the company to investigate."

Her investigation involved even more. It had to include me—déjà vu all over again, as at Patheon.

Doaa had worked with me for ten years. She had been by my side through ugly times at Valeant and even uglier ones at Patheon. She knew my morals. She knew my principles.

Still, she had a job to do, and it included investigating me. I was the CFO's boss. Theoretically, I could have instructed him to do whatever he allegedly did.

"You can't ignore the fact that you're under investigation, Wes," Doaa told me. "Just do your job. And I'll do mine. Then it will be over."

Another Day, Another CFO Shake-Up

Doaa finished the investigation. I came out clean.

We had already terminated our CFO. But, somehow, things didn't improve.

From the moment the CFO was outed, the board of directors became suspicious of my management team. Every board meeting was antagonistic.

Our chairman hired a new board member from outside Marken as a nonexecutive director. This new turnaround expert arrived with an attitude of undisguised hostility toward me as CEO.

The chairman also dug up an old friend and installed him as my new chief operating officer. This COO had not worked for some time, and he may have forgotten how the reporting structure works in healthy corporations.

It seemed to me that he thought he was the CEO. He held meetings with my staff and hinted openly that he would eventually replace me as Marken's leader.

Our chairman worked fairly well with me personally during those difficult months, but the company now also needed a new chief financial officer. Marken's board hired a Briton with Rhodesian roots as interim CFO. He came from a uniquely UK collection of financial turnaround "interims," a loose floating cloud of finance people who move from job to job as hired guns.

The new CFO walked in the door, and he, too, was immediately hostile to my management team, especially to Doaa.

He moved into the Marken corporate flat and started hiring his own team to replace our existing finance people.

Put simply, the new CFO and new COO appeared to be trying to run the company I was hired to run.

The new CFO started demanding that changes be made that contravened my instructions. He was hiring dozens of finance people without my authority. He ignored the operations, and it was hard to tell he had an interest in learning anything about Marken.

He was doing some good by reengineering the finance function, but I perceived him building a wall around his team and ignoring all else.

I was living in North Carolina and shuttling back and forth to London during this challenging time. Doaa would cover for me in Chiswick during my absences, which were frequent, as I spent more time with the company, our customers, our lenders, and our board than I spent cloistered in the office. My other steadfast ally, Ariette van Strien, rightly focused on her job, too, selling Marken and looking for new customers.

As the quiet power grab went on, Doaa knew where her loyalties lay and even more where the road to recovery for Marken had to go.

Doaa pushed back—hard—against the overreach. Specifically, she asked to know what authority the new CFO had to hire so many new people without any internal checks and balances.

The legal hand Doaa raised in warning had one effect.

It enraged the CFO.

He had planned a vacation to South Africa. As he set out, he sent an email to Doaa demanding that she approve the hiring of all his new people.

Doaa refused. Instead, she did exactly the opposite. She canceled the requisitions.

That same weekend, I called for a special meeting of the Marken board. I coldly laid out the facts. The CFO's insubordination was clear, even to those directors who didn't care for me.

By vote, the board agreed that he would be terminated as CFO the following Monday.

Another day, another CFO shake-up at Marken. The optics looked bad to many outside the company, including our customers.

Given the smoking clouds now rising over the C suite, I needed to quickly hire a new CFO. The directors agreed.

I tapped into the English secret society called "interims" myself, in search of a new able-bodied candidate.

By Monday morning after the emergency board meeting, I had three CFO hopefuls. I selected Steve Menzies, who had a background in financial turnarounds.

Steve came in only as interim CFO. But it turned out he was exactly the man for the job.

We made him full-time CFO in short order, and he would be a competent member of our team for years.

"It is not the critic who counts; not the man who points out how the strong man stumbles, or where the doer of deeds could have done them better. The credit belongs to the man who is actually in the arena, whose face is marred by dust and sweat and blood; who strives valiantly; who errs, who comes short again and again, because there is no effort without error and shortcoming; but who does actually strive to do the deeds; who knows great enthusiasms, the great devotions; who spends himself in a worthy cause; who at the best knows in the end the triumph of high achievement, and who at the worst, if he fails, at least fails while daring greatly, so that his place shall never be with those cold and timid souls who neither know victory nor defeat."

–THEODORE ROOSEVELT

Surviving a Failed Power Play and Coming Out Stronger

Two leading lenders emerged from the failed auction process as majority equity owners of Marken. Those companies had no real expertise in clinical supply logistics, and they had to completely rely on me, our chair, the new COO, and Steve to run the company.

I was the CEO, of course, but there still were internal rifts and suspicions about my management. So, it remained a very tenuous time.

The greatest tension now came from the lack of clarity between the authority of the newly appointed COO and me as CEO. Our chair still leaned toward the COO. After all, they were old friends.

My staff didn't know what to do about the COO. He was there trying to make decisions for the company. But my team stayed loyal to me.

The antagonistic former CFO was gone, and that took pressure off. Still, the chair remained, the adversarial COO held his post, and unfriendly directors lurked on the board.

Tension flared among board members. Our meetings were very troubled. One ray of positive news is that I brought Tim Tyson onto the board as a new independent. Tim would prove valuable to me in this role.

There was one other little thing.

I did not know anything for sure, but it was my impression that something was going on in the background between our chairman and some of the lenders. It was entirely possible that the chairman was recommending himself as a replacement CEO.

Replacing *me*.

He thought he saw an opening, and he tried to take advantage of it. I had my suspicions because he had abruptly turned from supportive to very antagonistic toward me.

Something had to give. And something did.

For me, it felt like the sun coming up after a long, cold English winter.

The two leading lenders called me to London on a secret trip. I only knew before getting on the plane that the bosses at our two leading lenders wanted to meet me in person.

I remember telling Marianne that I was going to be fired. Things were just that unclear to me.

That day, I looked the two leading owners in their eyes and laid out the facts about Marken, its leaders, and its board as I saw them.

It must have made an impression.

Instead of firing me, they decided to back me. They gave me another six months to prove myself.

This was December 2012. Christmas would not be so merry for some.

By the time I arrived home, the new lender-owners had fired the chairman.

Reading the tea leaves, another of the problematic directors soon resigned from the board. I fired the COO the next day, along with the handful of the "CFO Mafia," as I called them, who had been planted on the finance team.

It was a clean sweep. I would be able to start 2013 as Marken's top executive without the hobbling political impediments of my first two years.

A Like-Minded New Chair

Another ray of light then broke through. The board hired John Pattullo as our new chair of the board on February 1, 2014.

A native of Glasgow, Scotland, Pattullo had previously served five years as CEO at CEVA, a global logistics company (2007–2012), and thirty years before that at Procter & Gamble, the huge US multinational consumer goods corporation.

John was a very mature and capable leader. He first wanted to know what he had to work with. He started at the top. I was brought to London for an eight-hour deep dive into my background, style, and personal history, plus take a battery of cognitive tests.

I passed the audition.

"Wes came across as a fairly typical US corporate professional," John said. "I had spent many years working with US Procter & Gamble executives and had a positive impression of many of them. Wes came across as quite similar—professionally focused, driven—not ruled by his emotions.

"Wes was courting me, in a way. He was looking for somebody he could trust as chair. He wanted an upgrade, and the key elements were trust and an understanding of logistics."

Our new chair had seen enough in his career to instantly smell bad politics.

"It is worth saying that Wes and his senior leadership team had been promised many financial rewards by Apax that were clearly not being delivered," John said. "So they were not happy campers.

"It's also true that the real tension between Wes and the board was that the board just didn't trust *anybody*."

An example?

A new independent director was hired by the board to oversee financial aspects. He would sit directly across the table and stare at me while I was presenting, looking for any body language that might give clues about the real state of the company.

John perceived such problems. He also saw potential solutions.

"It was quite a challenging environment," he said. "But the business was still making a profit. It was not a basket case. We had good people. The question in front of us was: So now what?"

Even with John in place, the zigging and zagging through the wreckage left from the failed auction process and the questionable leadership that followed initially stymied my strategies for development.

We did not meet our 2013 budget, which meant no bonuses for anybody.

I asked the board to consider a compromise and award our leaders something to keep them motivated. John convinced the board to award 50 percent of 2013 target bonuses as an incentive to keep the management team plugging away.

I volunteered to take nothing, myself.

Making Marken Stronger

In May 2014, I negotiated a new incentive plan for the key members of my leadership team.

It took a bit of horse-trading.

We were still in a tough financial situation. I clearly remember that financials, as I personally observed, showed the mark-to-market valuation (the company's true value under current market conditions) was well under 65 percent. The lenders had to write down their investments to that level, which was a huge hit. They decided to leave all the debt on the balance sheet but with better terms and achievable covenants. Still, the debt load restricted our ability to grow as quickly as I planned.

I found an ally in John, a true believer in a motivated management team.

"It was important to get the leadership through the issues about compensation," he said. "Again, they were unhappy campers, and they needed new incentives. Those needed to be attractive, but reasonable, something the lenders could tolerate."

It took John and me close to nine months to nail down a new management compensation package and reach a point where all parties were happy. John represented the owners, and I represented Marken's leadership.

The board wanted us to give up our management contracts. We had very large severance terms, considered problematic to a potential buyer.

John and I negotiated, among other things, an agreement in which management would be paid an incentive when Marken was ultimately sold. A threshold was set as a minimum exit purchase price. Management would divide 15 percent of the proceeds above that level if that threshold were met and exceeded.

That went down well with lenders who needed Marken to show some momentum and hopefully soon position itself for a sale.

At this point, the lenders were desperate to save face with their own company investment committees.

At last, we could park the compensation topic and get on with business.

That year, 2014, also brought a new leading lender from the United States. One of the firm's managing directors joined the Marken board meetings as an observer, making a total of three lenders with observers on the board. The US lender bought the debt at a very low price hoping to make a handsome return on its investment.

I knew that successfully positioning Marken for a sale wholly depended on one factor—top-line company growth.

And somehow, despite all the sideshows of the past three years, John and I had kept our eyes on that prize: growing the company.

John also helped me clarify areas of focus that would allow us to turn the company around.

"First, Wes and I spent quite a bit of time together developing a refined business strategy and finding ways to track our progress. We needed real data that helped us know what we were doing and how we were doing.

"If I brought anything of value to the enterprise, it would be helping the management team develop metrics and monitoring that we could show at every board meeting so people could see what we were trying to achieve."

Second?

"Wes was very strong on what I would label as process management," John said. "This came much more from Wes himself than from our collaboration.

"Wes knew the techniques that make up process engineering, and he drove those into the operations of Marken, setting very high standards of performance for our operating sites. He also brought in Lean practices."

And third?

"The financial systems of our business became a lot stronger under Wes," John said. "Bottom line, the financial center of the business improved greatly.

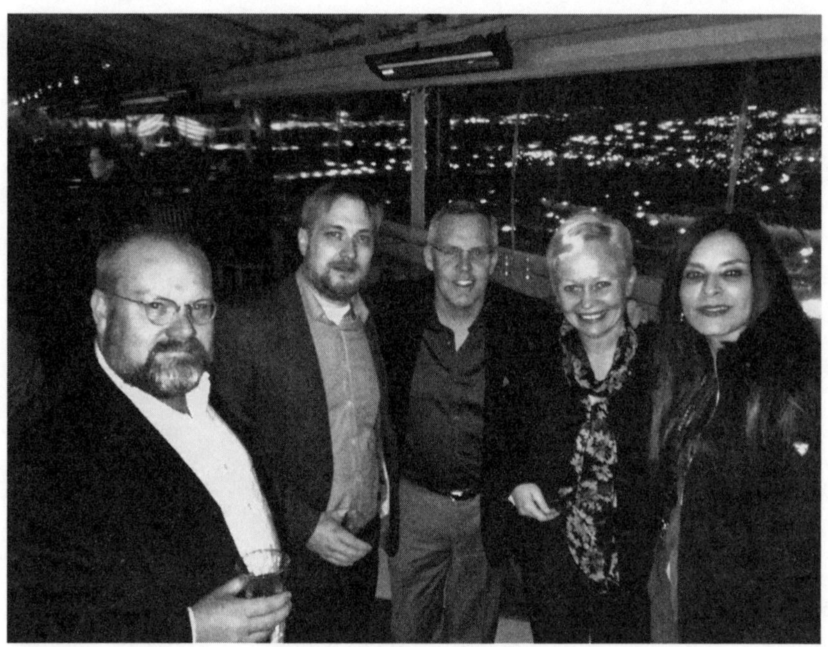

Dan Bell, Gerit Offenhauser, Ariette van Strien, Doaa Fathallah, and I

"As a result of the high-level changes in those three areas, Marken was suddenly a third more profitable than it had been three years before.

"Wes and his team did that. They deserve full credit."

Morale, a rare element at Marken for years, rose perceptibly. Revenue grew. So did profits.

Ariette was building a very credible and highly trained sales team. I was managing the operations and promoting our high-potential young leaders to key roles in the field. We were still considered a very high-quality service provider, moving samples and drugs at better than 95 percent on-time delivery. Months before, we had mapped out a strategy that appeared to be working.

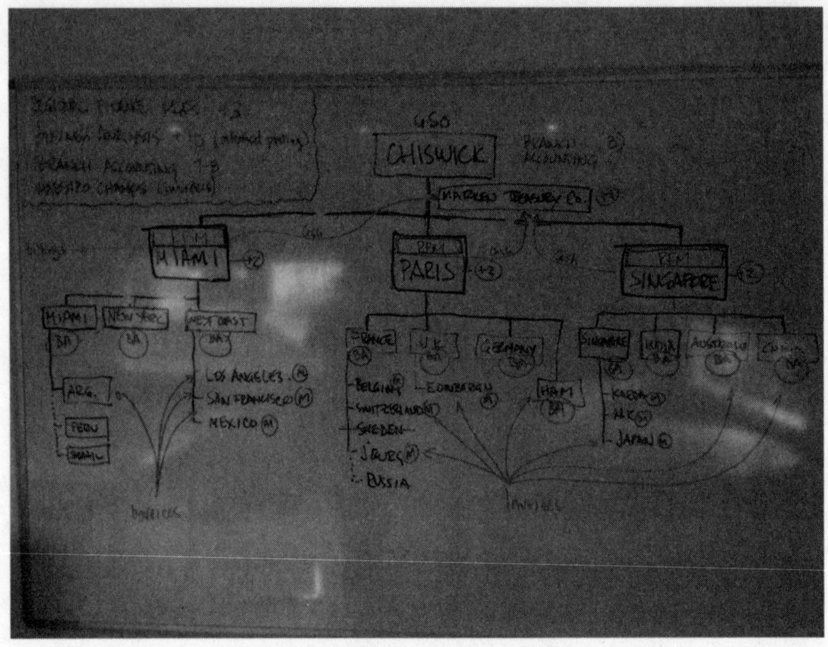

As we refined our strategy, we also developed a complex series of data flows, IT systems, and legal structures

And it was no Potemkin Village enterprise. The management team wasn't simply adding a quick coat of paint to the walls and then hanging out a For Sale sign.

"That was important," John said. "The way Wes ran the business and the way I chaired the business was less focused on the quick sale and more focused on creating a high-performance company."

A Game-Changing Moment with a Key Customer

I continued to rely on Ariette, now our chief commercial officer. She wanted that new title, and I agreed.

Ariette was Dutch. She'd been running global operations for MDS Pharma Services, one of the largest pharma companies in

Europe, when she first heard of Marken in "2003 or 2004," as she remembered it.

Marken made an impression on her.

Some years later, Marken's CEO reached out to Ariette, seeking someone in sales who knew the clinical side of things. Though she had no idea about logistics, transportation, or management, Ariette did have seventeen years of reputation-building performance in the pharmaceutical industry. She knew how drugs were developed, and she knew what companies expected in quality standards and in partnerships.

Ariette got the Marken job in January 2010, just after Apax Partners took over, and nearly a year and a half before I came in as CEO.

She was in for a shock.

"From the outside," Ariette said, "Marken looked like a high-quality, well-organized company. When I joined, I found that there wasn't a database of clients or even an organizational chart."

The balkanization of Marken defied belief.

"Offices were competing with one another for the same clients," she said. "London would put in a bid against New York, offices in the same company undercutting each other."

Examples of fragmentation were scattered across the globe.

"Marken hosted more than 140 conferences in a year. It had fifty different logos, each office with its own branding, pricing, and practices. I was honestly amazed the company could even function."

Hired to lead global sales, marketing, and strategy development, Ariette realized what Marken needed first and foremost.

Adult supervision.

"We needed everything from the ground up. The global CRM system didn't exist. There was no marketing function. Even basic contact information for clients was missing. I was totally surprised."

Once I understood that Ariette had inherited a lazy, maybe overpaid sales organization that constantly missed its numbers, and once I saw the aggressive steps she planned to get that team working on all of our right priorities, we began to work well together.

"We developed a Marken sales strategy together," Ariette said. "My strength was the commercial side and finding ways to grow and win. Wes's strength was restructuring metrics, measurements, and operations. We made a very good complementary pair."

One of our early customer targets was Pfizer. If Marken could win a big account like that on the drug distribution side, it could win any account in the industry. Ariette's team paid a visit to the head of R&D logistics at the pharma giant.

Pfizer's reaction was typical.

Marken? We thought you only moved blood samples?

"We had no brand recognition among many of our target customers," Ariette admitted. "And that was because we depended on one product for a few clients. So, everything Wes and I did was about a race to diversify our services and grow our client base."

By now, I finally had unified a leadership team and a board, and our team had created a new brand, a new brand image, and a new slogan: "Marken Makes it Happen."

The employees loved that slogan and never allowed us to change it.

While I had waged financial battles behind the scenes with the Marken board, Ariette built a competent and professional sales organization. She hired many people from pharma and from laboratories.

"We needed experts to get recognition and to have credibility in the industry," she explained. "And we had to figure out what services to even create."

Marken was finally on a roll (AC7.8)

Ariette and I both felt an urgent need to build out a bigger service portfolio. Marken had historically been so focused on shipping blood samples that it overlooked the growth potential in clinical drug distribution—the "outbound," as we called it—and other potential revenue streams.

We set the bearings of our company toward these and other new destinations.

We worked on a business case to grow the outbound side of our business to match World Courier's dominance in drug delivery. We wanted to take market share from our competitor. So we decided we needed to build ten GMP facilities, including our flagship depot in Singapore.

In fact, we couldn't afford ten. We were in the middle of a financial crisis and a change in ownership. We could only tell our clients that we had such a network in the planning stage.

Since we also couldn't afford consultants to help us, we used the data we had. Then we had to get buy-in from Marken's board to approve capital expenditures and to build. We also needed more offices in more regions, and we had to create a global network under one leadership structure.

Moscow was one of my favorite depot experiences

We needed all that, plus a global pricing strategy and a common purpose.

Ariette's appetite to compete and win matched mine. She brought her strength in sales and marketing to play—creating a message and a unique value proposition for clients, while positioning Marken in the marketplace.

Our annual business strategy meetings were critical to the turnaround—with Frederic Maurice, on the far left

We both knew the moment Marken truly turned the corner.

After Ariette's early first meeting with Pfizer, she artfully cultivated the relationship. Over time, she and her team won the trust of Pfizer decision-makers in a series of meetings and dinners.

In 2014, Pfizer signed Marken as a logistics provider to handle its outbound drug distribution.

It was the customer win Marken had been working for and waiting for.

"We knew that moment that things would be different going forward," Ariette said. "It changed our messaging. It opened up a whole new segment of the industry.

"Winning Pfizer was a game changer."

The Drumbeat of Growth Gets Faster

While Ariette was building a global sales team with a structure, I assumed responsibility for Marken's two largest customers.

I was personally overseeing these accounts and negotiating extensions with each. Ariette had the rest. I had Ernie Batista running Latin America from Miami and Frederic Maurice running Europe from Paris. These two executives on my team would prove critically important to maintaining our two largest customers.

From my perspective, the problems that beset the sales team stemmed in large part from scar tissue caused by all the negative press.

It was tough for us. The market and our competitors all knew we had tried to sell the company and failed. Everyone knew Marken was a "lender-led" company and that we would ultimately be sold. The question was, to whom?

Our team, though, had something to prove, and we had operations that were simply better than anyone else's. I had a team of very competent operational executives reporting to me, particularly Dan Bell in the US and Frederic Maurice in Europe. We had impeccable service levels. Ariette and her growing sales team were out there selling well on the basis of capability, service, and quality.

Marken, in fact, had introduced a solid, freshly enhanced quality system that led our industry. I had hired Navnit Patel from my DSM days to run Quality Assurance. A no-nonsense regulatory compliance operation, run by Dan Bell, also grounded our credibility.

We found the cash, somehow, to continue growing Marken's service footprint—Singapore first, then Frankfurt, Buenos Aires, São Paulo, Shanghai, Moscow. We never hired a consultant, an architect, or an engineering firm to help. We built our depots, which were superior in every way, on a shoestring budget.

We also managed to acquire the assets for assembling customized medical kits from LabCorp (formerly Clearstone) in Hamburg for the princely sum of ONE Euro. That deal came with sixty employees, whom we trimmed to the best-qualified twenty-five.

We were now in the kit-building business. That asset helped distinguish us.

The Hamburg kit building facility

We always focused critical attention on quality, hiring pharmaceutical people with GMP experience at all our depots. This established a reputation for high quality in our warehousing and GMP services and gave us still another competitive advantage.

I worked to restore Marken's frayed reputation by issuing press releases twice a month, conveying new energy and vitality. I wrote most of the press releases myself. They proved effective at squashing negative stories and rumors being spread by our competitors.

All through 2013 and 2014, the drumbeat of growth moved faster.

We opened new offices in Seoul, Tokyo, Melbourne, five cities in India, Lima, Santiago, Zurich, Hamburg, Brisbane, and Stuttgart. I moved existing offices to better locations in nearly all Marken's original nineteen offices, including New York, Miami, Los Angeles, Brussels, London, Edinburgh, Hong Kong, Johannesburg, Sydney, and more.

Singapore got its do-over. We added our own vehicle fleet in New York and Japan, preempting possible glitches in service by third-party delivery partners. Most importantly, we shed many agents who had been taking advantage of the company during the turmoil. We also dismissed a number of old-guard employees who had been actively working against new strategies. In fact, I carried a list of these people for many months, waiting for the most opportunistic time to terminate them.

We made all this happen with our own cash flow. Marken never borrowed a cent from anyone, even with all the debt left on the balance sheet.

Our fierce focus paid off.

Marken hit its budget numbers in 2014—that year was a success—and then hit 2015 revenue targets, though we fell just short of our profit goal. Regardless, my vision had brought a spirit of promise to Marken for the first time in years.

We were growing, and growth was accelerating.

My longtime personal coach and organizational expert, Dr. Terry Tipple, could add that I was growing as a leader too.

"One of the things that separated Wes from others was that he'd gained international experience at far-flung places around the world," Terry said. "He had worked in the UK, in Europe, in the United States, in Japan. By the time he reached Marken, he was much more the multinational citizen and much less a hard-charging engineer."

Terry could see that I surrounded myself with the best people possible, wherever I found them.

My leadership team in the UK: Frederic Maurice (second from left), Ernie Batista (fifth from right), Navnit Patel (fourth from right), Dan Bell and Doaa (both far right)

"Wes had an odd lot of direct reports," Terry said. "To him, it didn't matter where people lived or worked, as long as he saw something in them. He didn't care if they showed up in the office at eight in the morning or at midnight. Wes was all about production and performance.

"To me, that demonstrated his new blend of skills—the combination of now being a global executive and still being a get-it-done technical person."

Terry did perceive one hiring bias.

"What Wes learned on his paper route as a kid never left him," Terry said. "He understood the discipline and the determination it took to do that early morning work.

"If somebody in an interview told him that his first job came at X or Y Corporation after spending years in classes then earning an MBA, Wes didn't want the guy.

"'What was the first job you ever had?' Wes would ask.

"Wes just loved it when somebody told him, 'My first job was a paperboy.'"

The Global Leader in Clinical Logistics

By 2015 and 2016, Marken was generating enough cash to accelerate the growth of our infrastructure.

We added to our capabilities with direct-to-patient services and a new IT operating system, Maestro, to support them. Maestro had replaced an older green-screen system, and it was now being upgraded. A new depot operating system called Solo had been introduced years earlier and was also undergoing expansion.

Marken developed our own brand of packaging, yet another differentiator, and we negotiated an exclusive arrangement with a GPS tracking provider that let customers know where their shipments were at any time.

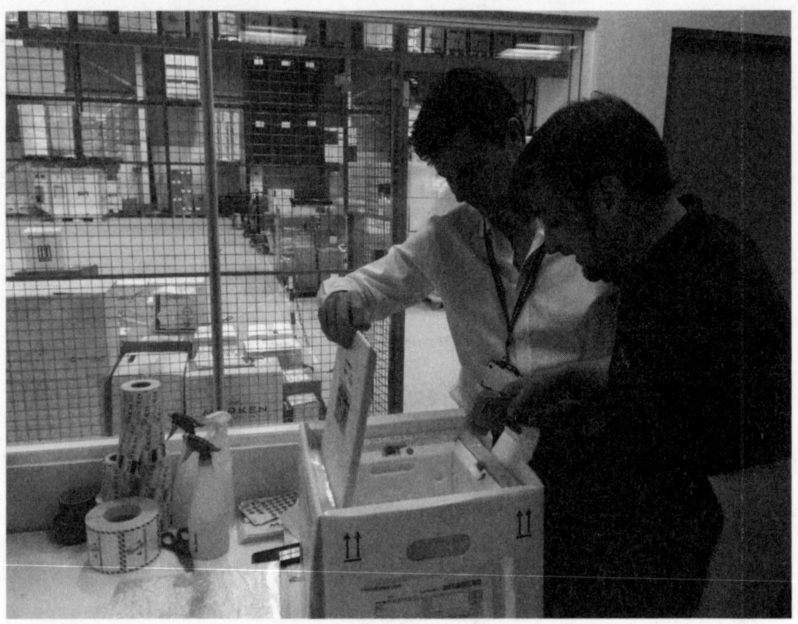

We were one of the first courier companies to adopt special thermal boxes for moving samples—Michael Culme-Seymour ran Asia from Singapore, and Gerit Offenhauser ran depot operations from Hamburg

At this point, we were competing head-to-head with World Courier on the outbound drug delivery side of the market. Marken already dominated the inbound side of the market—we controlled an estimated 60 percent of the inbound and easily 15 percent of the outbound drug shipments.

We had the first-ever direct-to-patient service, and we were gaining market share in kit building. We would also build a global at-home nursing service.

All this came as Marken emerged as the best service provider and rapidly moved toward a market-leading depot service position in the industry.

By 2023, Marken would declare victory as the global leader in clinical logistics.

We put together a global supply chain for clinical trials that was simply better than anything offered by anyone else in the world.

And, finally, to the relief of its long-suffering lenders, Marken would be a sure bet in a sale.

MARKEN FINANCIAL TRANFORMATION

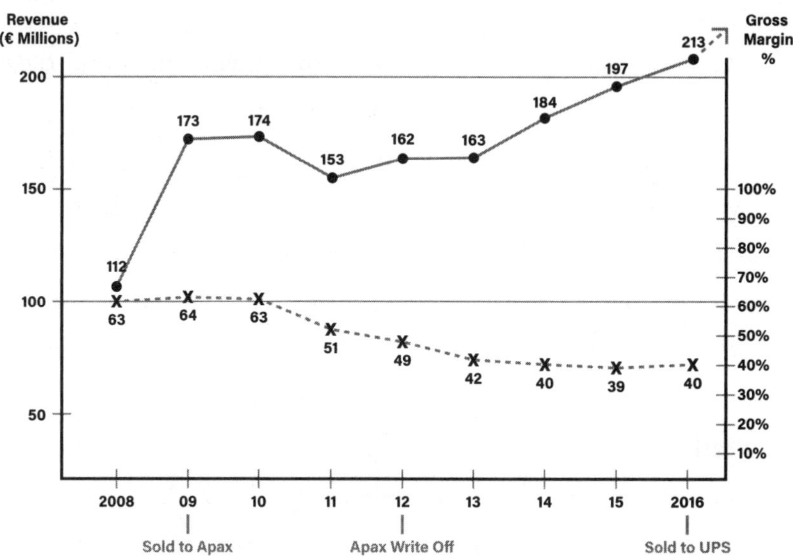

Paradoxically, we decided early on to reduce margins to enable growth

Sold to One of the World's Most Trusted Brands

Marken's board of directors approved a new sale process in 2016. Hopes were high, but, as the old adage goes, *mistakes were made.*

We set out to hold another broad auction process. Somehow, though, we decided to send teasers out to strategic *and* financial sponsors (AC7.6).

We received solid interest in the auction process—at first. But when financial sponsors got wind that strategics were involved, we lost them. Financial sponsors knew they could not be competitive with strategics that would be able to benefit from cost synergies.

By the final stage of the process, Marken had three leading bidders.

Champagne corks would soon pop.

We were clearly going to exceed the threshold required to trigger payout to management. That meant a great deal to people who had worked so hard to turn things around.

Marken was sold to UPS on the winter solstice, December 21, of 2016 (AC7.4). The sale price remains confidential, but from my direct involvement I can say that we ultimately sold the company at an EBITDA multiple that almost certainly went above our minimum threshold and well beyond what anyone would have predicted two years earlier.

Marken's senior debt? Completely paid off. All the original lenders who stayed in the game after the failed auction bid in 2012 made money on their investments.

Companies that entered the investment at 65 percent mark-to-market made substantial returns in just two years.

UPS To Acquire Marken, A Leader In Global Clinical Supply Chain Solutions

Acquisition to complement UPS healthcare logistics solutions

November 07, 2016 09:25 ET| Source: UPS 

The word was out on the UPS-Marken acquisition (AC7.7)

At the sale, my management team and I received rewards well above the threshold levels.

Everyone was happy with the all-cash deal. All debts were satisfied, and UPS was now our new owner.

The bottom line?

Once upon a time, I had walked into a corporate version of a booby trap. I faced rebuilding a company at the same time I encountered rebellion and hostility from most of its leadership.

As power shifted and shifted again, executives mismanaged the books. Whistleblowers came from nowhere to tell dirty secrets. Power grabs, suspicion, and court intrigues turned Marken, for a time, into a corporate *Game of Thrones*.

But in just five years, against all odds and nearly all expectations, a key cadre of loyal employees and I had transformed Marken into an unchallenged world player in its specialty, clinical trial logistics, and a global leader in healthcare logistics generally.

Marken added brawn to UPS. At the time of the sale, we had fifty-three locations in twenty-five countries and hundreds of pharma clients and service providers engaged in clinical trials. The workforce tripled in size, from 382 to more than 1,000, and our new people brought UPS professional skills and a dedication to excellence the clinical logistics world had never known before.

Marken's turnaround was my best work as a professional. With the help of a few remarkably capable and steadfast leaders, we took the company from a complete financial write-off to a respected and reputable success.

Next would come three years as CEO under a new brand—Marken, a UPS Company.

In that time, Ariette, Doaa, myself, and the rest of our team worked as a loosely connected ("tethered," as my new boss, UPS Chief

Operating Officer Jim Barber, described it) part of the $100 billion-plus UPS, the worldwide leader in transportation logistics.

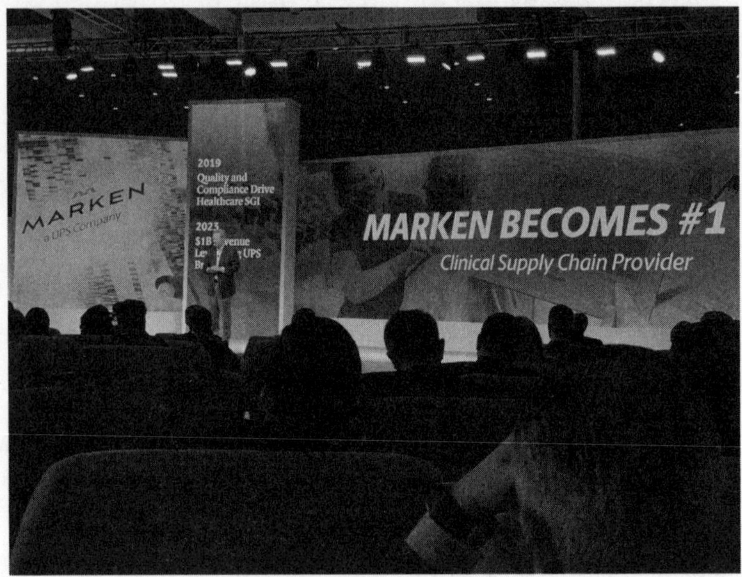

UPS management conference with Jim Barber

The Big Brown machine gave us the freedom to operate, allowing Marken to continue growing.

Nothing changed in how Marken was allowed to operate, except that we now had the financial backing of a Fortune 500 organization with global brand recognition second only to Disney.

I would report to four bosses during my three years as a UPS executive, but it was Jim Barber who saw early on what Marken could do for UPS.

Jim and I grew close during these three years.

He allowed me to run Marken as a relatively independent company. We began leveraging resources we never had before to drive rapid growth.

We made use of the UPS air fleet, the eighth-largest in the world, shipping on UPS "brown tails," as the jets were called, instead of expensive air cargo carriers like British Airways, Lufthansa, and American Airlines. Marken could also use the excellent UPS customs brokerage resources instead of expensive third parties.

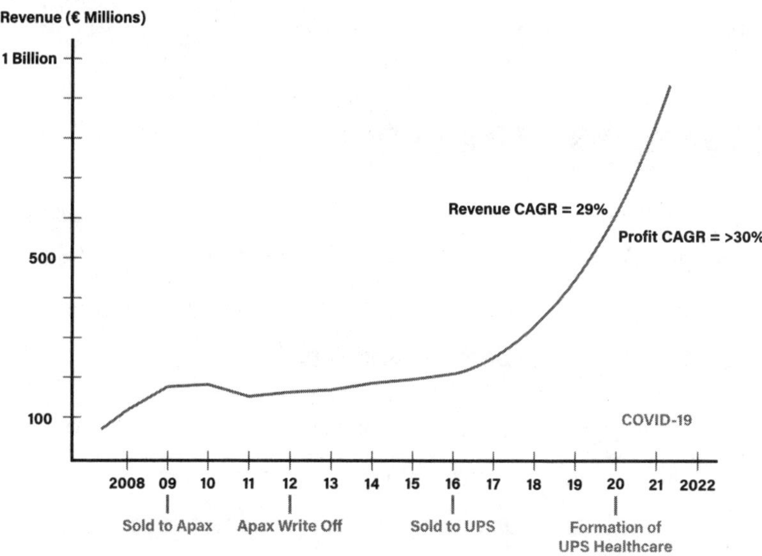

We used anything and everything we could from the UPS network without compromising quality. And very soon this new hybrid service model would be the key to taking market share leadership from World Courier.

Naturally, our transition to UPS didn't come without a hiccup or two.

Marken missed its budget numbers in 2017, but given the disruption of becoming a part of UPS, we were allowed to continue the mission.

That was wise because we grew substantially from 2018 through 2021. We became one of the best-performing parts of all the vast UPS global businesses, and with margins which were accretive to its parent company.

Not bad for a company that had been a financial write-off, flirting dangerously with bankruptcy and ruin, only a few years earlier.

About the time I left UPS in May 2023, Marken had exceeded all financial expectations with more than twenty-eight hundred employees in sixty-five locations. It remains the undisputed leader in global clinical trial logistics (AC7.5).

LESSONS LEARNED

In business, quality and service win. One can take a failing company and turn it into a business that truly cares for customers. When we learn to speak the language of our customers, they speak to us in return.

We must purge the blockers from our organizations as quickly as we can and then build a loyal team around us that believes in our vision and our passion for service.

Above all, never minimize the value of strong leadership when faced with adversity, ill-willed people, and misaligned board members. When all the leaders are aligned around a common objective, any business can survive.

MARKEN'S PATH TO GLOBAL LEADERSHIP

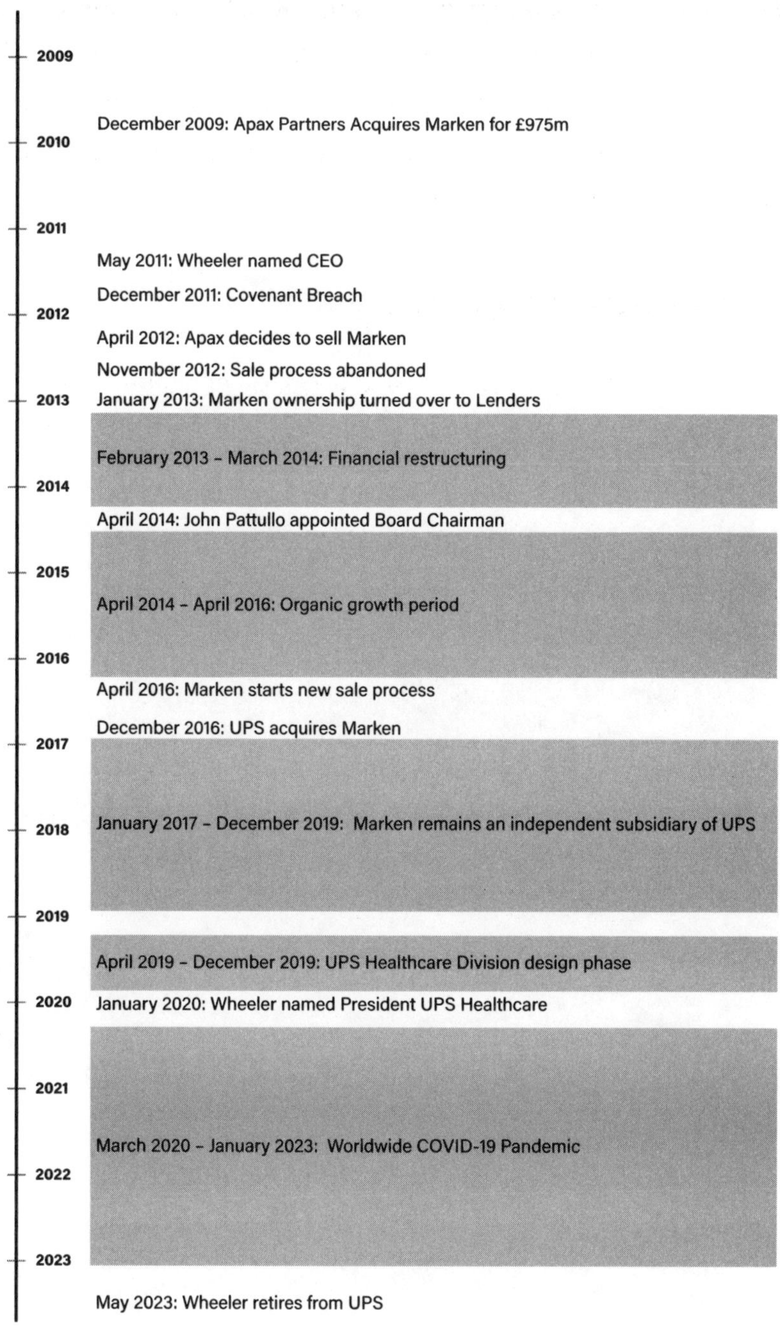
2009
December 2009: Apax Partners Acquires Marken for £975m
2010
2011
May 2011: Wheeler named CEO
December 2011: Covenant Breach
2012
April 2012: Apax decides to sell Marken
November 2012: Sale process abandoned
2013
January 2013: Marken ownership turned over to Lenders
February 2013 - March 2014: Financial restructuring
2014
April 2014: John Pattullo appointed Board Chairman
2015
April 2014 - April 2016: Organic growth period
2016
April 2016: Marken starts new sale process
December 2016: UPS acquires Marken
2017
2018
January 2017 - December 2019: Marken remains an independent subsidiary of UPS
2019
April 2019 - December 2019: UPS Healthcare Division design phase
2020
January 2020: Wheeler named President UPS Healthcare
2021
March 2020 - January 2023: Worldwide COVID-19 Pandemic
2022
2023
May 2023: Wheeler retires from UPS

N

CHAPTER 8

BUSHU PHARMACEUTICALS LTD. (2017-2021)

What Not to Do When Hiring a Consultant

In the years I led Marken, I also helped out a Japanese company called Bushu. The story demonstrates the power of experience, partnership, and leadership in solving problems that appear intractable.

Bushu started out in 1981 as a packaging operation, Sandoz Yakuhin KK, in Saitama, a city just north of Tokyo. In 1985, Sandoz moved into the promising field of drug manufacturing. International distribution began in Canada (2007), and in the United States and Europe (2010).

In 1999, Shionogi, a leading Japanese pharmaceuticals company, acquired a plant from Sandoz and rebranded it Bushu Pharmaceuticals Ltd. Then Bushu sold to a local private equity firm in 2010 and was expanded further with the purchase of a second plant from Eisai Pharmaceuticals.

The two manufacturing facilities specialized in oral solid dosage drug products and sterile drug product packaging. They lacked, however, sterile fill-and-finish capacity, which would have been the best investment they could have made.

Late in 2014, another private equity company, today consolidated with the Swedish global investment firm EQT, bought Bushu. At the time, Bushu was the number two contract manufacturing company (CMO) in Japan. The new owners in Hong Kong and the deal team in Tokyo looked forward to the typical healthy returns expected by private equity investors over a normal hold period of three to five years.

Bushu looked like a prize. Internal financial records (that for a private company can't be shared or used for citations and sources) showed that operations in 2014 employed about one thousand people. It generated about 26 billion yen ($230 million USD) in overall revenue, a healthy 26 percent EBITDA margin.

The company's good health began to fail almost immediately after the private equity firm's purchase.

Bushu's CEO (we'll call him Executive One), was a top-tier former consultant with a solid resume, excellent English, polish, and poise. But he had an Achilles' heel—two, in fact. First, he lacked experience in pharmaceuticals. Second, he also lacked experience in contract manufacturing.

Executive One was a nice man and a professional manager with a respectable track record. He was short, though, on industry credentials. This proved to be more important than anticipated. In the pharma industry, connections to decision-makers and knowledge of the language of the business are critical.

With his consulting background, Executive One was more comfortable focusing on costs than investments. As a ship captain, he'd have watched more closely for leaks than for islands of opportunity.

Internal financial records that I have seen and noted but that remain private with a privately held company showed that in 2016 Bushu's revenue had declined slightly but held its EBITDA stable, thanks to cost-cutting..

Bushu was going nowhere. A sudden push by the Japanese government to produce generic drugs was also an unexpected headwind for the Japanese Contract Development and Manufacturing Organization (CDMO) industry.

The private equity firm's purchase of Bushu suddenly looked more like a turnaround deal.

In April 2017, two years after the Bushu purchase, the private equity owner brought me into the company as a nonexecutive director of Bushu Holdings Ltd, the holdings board. The private equity team recruited me through a personal contact I made while serving previously as a board member at Sunsho Pharmaceuticals, another Japanese manufacturing company.

I brought Bushu an asset that would prove invaluable.

My long-ago Exxon assignment in Japan gave me a good working knowledge of how Japanese business leaders thought and reached decisions. It happened at social gatherings, not in the office. All the raucous late-night meetings over whiskey and water to bond and build commitments during Exxon's Sakai project gave me insights rare for a gaijin (a non-Japanese person).

That Japan experience, along with previous turnaround work at DSM, Valeant, and Patheon—work that included international engagements in Japan and other Asian nations—rewarded me with a clear vision of how to get Bushu back on course.

With my first appointment in April 2017, I worked alongside the local private equity executives on the holding company board. Very little got done at that level. It would take two frustrating years before I was in a position to make changes.

Still, with energy and optimism, I watched for a chance to put my turnaround ideas into play.

Prior to my arrival on the board, Executive One hired one of the world's best-known management consultancies as an advisor. The CEO must have believed an old industry adage that nobody ever got fired for hiring that fabled consultancy.

For me, it was not happy news. I'd already been burned twice before with this consultancy's projects, at Valeant and Patheon. I had two trash bins full of good reasons to doubt the consultancy so many other executives considered the gold standard for management advice.

The third time was not a charm.

The renowned consultancy had identified four actions for Bushu:

- Improve yields in formulation at the two Bushu plants from 96.2 percent to 97.7 percent.
- Reduce the number of full-time employees in packaging operations by 34 percent.
- Reduce the number of quality control and quality assurance employees at the two plants by 70 percent.
- Reduce utility costs by 30 percent.

The consultancy projected these measures would save one billion yen in expenses. Without delay, Executive One launched an improvement initiative called Teppen (which means "the summit").

I sensed trouble.

Later, in July 2017, shortly after joining the holdings board, the private equity owner made its first bolt-on acquisition, buying Takeda's drug development unit in Osaka. With its new building came scientists and pilot scale equipment and Takeda's projects-in-progress. The private equity team called the new company Spera Pharma Inc.

It was another strategic mistake.

At this same time, the board decided to sweep its cash and pay down debt. This came at the expense of investing in capacity. In the contract pharma business, the only way to survive is to invest in new equipment and create new capacity. Without new capacity, there's no new business and no new growth. Bushu's capabilities and capacities were, in effect, capped. Rather than grow, Bushu reduced staff in critical areas.

As part of that staff reduction, and, on the basis of the renowned consultancy's recommendations, Bushu had slashed the number of sterile inspectors by 50 percent to save money. This further hampered the company's ability to grow into new business. Without inspectors, no sterile vials move through a plant.

Meanwhile, the Spera acquisition wasn't creating any opportunities for the two plants, and there were no cost synergies. Nothing was in sync. Spera was in Osaka, while Bushu was northwest of Tokyo, so even board meetings were difficult. Spera did not bring a single new piece of business to Bushu as a result of the acquisition.

I, along with the two other holding company directors, offered ideas to bend the curve. We passed those to our private equity firm's senior leadership in August 2017, eight months after I joined.

Our suggestions:

- Strengthen the sales team.
- Open a Tokyo sales office.

- Expand high-potency capabilities.
- Leverage Spera's relationship with Takeda.
- Refocus cost-reduction work.
- Appoint a restructuring officer.
- Look for new acquisitions for capacity and growth.

I got no reaction from the CEO, and the holding company board was deferring to him on all decisions.

By 2018, after another year without financial improvement, the handwriting—the hiragana—was on the wall for Bushu.

Its private equity owners had seen enough. In February, they positioned Bushu for sale.

It may not have been a fire sale, but you could smell smoke.

The private equity team would grow even more determined to shed the firm after learning Bushu misled it on 2018 growth. While the private equity owner expected revenues of about 28 billion yen, roughly 10 percent growth, Bushu brought in only some 25 billion yen, a further decline from 2017.

Bushu did hear me out on one point.

Jefferies Group LLC was hired as the investment banker, based on my suggestion. Jefferies is a respected US-based global full-service investment banking and capital services firm.

Even then, frustratingly, Bushu continued to keep me at arm's length. From the holding company board, I had no access to real business strategizing. The sales process was a broad auction, but management presentations proceeded without me. I never had a chance to review and comment on the critical confidential information memorandum, the CIM, as it's known in business.

Jeffries built a nice book and went ahead on the sales process.

Then came a new shock.

The sales process failed. No buyer came forward.

If a warning light was flashing before the abortive sale, now the entire Bushu control panel blazed red.

Something had to change.

And something did.

Bushu brought me out of the shadows.

The Man for the Job

The path to progress opened in January 2019, when our private equity owner appointed one of its top Tokyo executives, Tadashi Maruoka, to lead the Bushu Pharmaceuticals Ltd. board of directors. Soon after, the equity owners brought three other savvy investment professionals, Takanobu Hara, Nino Gorla, and Teruyuki Asaoka, to launch a new Bushu team.

Tadashi Maruoka's mandate was crystal clear—he was a fixer. He must stop the Bushu bleeding and help the private equity owner recover as much of its initial investment as possible.

Maruoka-san, as I fondly grew to call him, proved to be the man for the job. (The respectful "san" ending to a Japanese name is the equivalent of "Mr." or "Mrs." in English.) A Japanese gentleman with a long banking and securities resume, Maruoka-san first heard of me during my recruitment to Bushu's holding company board, though we didn't really get acquainted then.

That moment came at the 2018 JPMorgan Chase & Company Annual Healthcare Conference in San Francisco. Maruoka-san approached me in the lobby of the conference center. I was expecting someone else, not a Japanese stranger.

"Nice to meet you," said Maruoka-san.

"Who are you?" I answered, with trademark directness.

"It didn't make me feel uncomfortable at all," Maruoka-san later told me, laughing. "It made me feel open to speaking with you."

Business in Japan runs on trust, on personal relationships. I had learned this truth in Japan in my Exxon years. When Maruoka-san answered candidly in return, I knew he was inviting my trust.

Things moved quickly after that.

The private equity owner pressed me into active duty—from the holding company board directly onto the Bushu Pharmaceuticals board. Now I had a relevant, hands-on role in turning the company around.

Guided by our private equity leadership, the Bushu Holdings Board also relieved CEO Executive One of decision-making, though he kept his title. The board elevated Tadao Takano to chief operating officer, making him the company's top executive. (Takano-san was an Executive One lieutenant, hired by the sidelined CEO.)

Takano-san seized the moment. He had pharma industry expertise, running operations in the United States and Japan. As COO, he took charge of details and made well-advised decisions that would soon stop the company's slide.

The reversal came too late to save Executive One, who always meant well. But the business needed a new leader and a fresh start. Executive One decided to leave and make way for Takano-san in November 2019.

The Turnaround Team

In Takano-san, I at last found a leader who spoke the language of pharma. This was the situation I'd wanted—me offering seasoned, smart, real-world recommendations and Takano-san, the acting leader of Bushu, listening and acting.

The private equity owners and I set up an executive committee that met twice monthly for the next two years. It became Bushu's primary governance team.

With the private equity team and Takano-san, I undertook detailed reviews of the company's inner workings. I hired a reliable colleague from my past, Ken Somers, to look into the internal workings of the supply chain. (To no one's surprise, Bushu quickly cut off the agreement with the renowned consultancy.)

We reviewed customer contracts, pricing, internal workflows, inventory, financial policies, weak and strong players in the company, and just about everything else. Not only were Takano-san and his team cooperative, but they also actually relished this opportunity to engage.

We increased capital expenditure spending and advocated for expanded capabilities. We built a new cold-chain warehouse, expanded the marketing team, modernized the brand, relaunched the website, hired a US sales director, and created a new pricing policy. We also started attending industry conferences with a conspicuous presence.

We sold Spera for a handsome profit, and the cash was put to work.

Bushu felt rejuvenated, vital. Suddenly, no improvement was too small.

On my advice, Takano-san translated the Bushu quality system into English. He built up the technical transfer team so that Bushu could move new business into its plants. Takano-san was mortified to find out Bushu had fired half its sterile inspectors. He immediately began to hire them back.

On July 1, 2020, the private equity owner asked me to take an even more important position as chair of the Bushu board of directors—the INEC, as they called it, for independent nonexecutive chair.

I accepted with a grateful bow.

This new role came as the COVID-19 pandemic rolled across the globe. No matter. For the next two years, I helped Bushu make constant enhancements. A new head of marketing came on board. Management attacked supply backlogs and investigated workflows. The conclusions from Ken Somers more or less went into practice.

The biggest challenge? Bushu needed a permanent CEO. After one false start with a leader who didn't work out, Bushu returned to its roots and found the right leader hiding in plain sight.

Bushu tapped Takano-san.

Ready to Sell

Bushu by now had momentum despite the dampening effects of COVID-19 and all its economic complications.

Sales picked up. A big US pharmaceutical company contracted with Bushu to introduce a major new drug into the Asia region, using Bushu as its regional launch platform. Revenue was already streaming in. Other new opportunities arose as we made clear we were willing to buy equipment and invest in capacity.

Bushu ran out of packaging space, so Takano-san went outside the company to lease a facility. He approved capital spending to build new packaging sites off-site, then hired people to run them. To reduce expenses, Bushu chose to use leases to reduce capital expenditures. Some fifty new projects gobbled up cash, but the company remained under good control. The monthly reporting was greatly enhanced by the company's capable CFO, Tetsuya Morikawa.

We were hitting a brick wall with our lenders, who had already held debt for too long and were starting to take a more cautious view on the whole Japanese CDMO industry. New capital would not be forthcoming. We had to use our own cash for expansion.

The private equity owner, with Takano-san and I, kept our focus on positioning the company for a sale. We aggressively pursued acquisitions. In March 2022, Bushu bought a Fukushima plant owned by Sanwa Kagaku Kenkyusho Co., Ltd., greatly expanding our ability to meet demands for oral solid dosage formulations.

Still, even with all the new vitality, Bushu's balance sheet hadn't quite recovered from its swoon years.

In 2021, Bushu's internal—and nonpublic—records showed gross revenue at slightly over 23 billion yen, below the level of the private equity firm's initial investment. But Bushu's EBITDA held firm, and margins were quickly improving. Even more promising, the product pipeline was full. Many new projects and contracts already produced added revenue.

The private equity owners decided to salvage what it could of its investment. For them, the Bushu project had reached its shelf life and had to close out.

We ran out of time, just as we were picking up real speed with the financial health of the company.

In fall of 2021, Bushu went up for sale a second time.

The board agreed to hire New York–based JPMorgan, among the largest, oldest, and most reputable financial companies in the world. The firm has a strong Tokyo team, and we thought we could attract international buyers.

As it turned out, Bushu hadn't had quite enough time to internationalize its brand. The company just wasn't widely enough known outside Japan. As well, Japan can be insular and protective—a tough market for international businesses to penetrate.

We appreciated—and pragmatically leveraged—how much Bushu had learned from its previous failed sale.

This time we spent a lot of time developing the confidential information memo and the data room to support value statements. Our financials had greatly improved, and the expanded capacity allowed new bidders to appreciate our growth potential.

A detailed management presentation was drafted in Japanese and translated into English.

Takano-san practiced his presentation dozens of times, getting it pitch-perfect. Central to future growth was a plan to expand the sterile manufacturing suites, in which we had already started to invest when we ran out of time.

Bushu also timed its sale more wisely. In 2022, business wasn't just picking up, it was hitting a whole new gear. That year, our internal records and my own notes and conversation showed that Bushu would report revenue of about 29 billion yen and nearly 9 billion yen in EBITDA.

In two short years since the arrival of Maruoka-san as the board director, with Takano-san's strong leadership, my role as the company's INEC, and through dozens of executive committee meetings—we sold Bushu for a very respectable multiple of EBITDA on a constant currency basis.

The buyer was a power player, the US-based global investment company KKR & Company (Kohlberg Kravis Roberts & Co) (Appendix C8.1).

The deal pleased the private equity owners, but I wish we could have waited longer, given the momentum we had. Also, the yen had started to rapidly depreciate around this time, diminishing dollar-based returns for the private equity firm's fund. Still, Bushu would be well positioned to grow for its new owner. And employees breathed a sigh of relief, trusting a well-known, well-managed owner's oversight.

I felt pride in our Bushu work. Even so, I couldn't help but ponder a few "what-ifs."

Honestly, I wanted to wait and witness the true effects of our turnaround.

Had the Japanese yen not fallen so much versus the US dollar, and had the Japanese banking environment at that moment been more robust, I'm strongly convinced we would have well exceeded all expectations. That would have made Bushu one of the best-performing companies in the private equity owner's portfolio.

Still, I finished the job at Bushu with a deep sense of satisfaction. Another troubled company, another turnaround.

I didn't have long to savor a job well done.

I suddenly needed to give undivided attention to another challenge, the biggest and most important of my career—and my lifetime.

Saving the world.

LESSONS LEARNED

Consultants can be helpful but also can be dangerous. Decisions based solely on a consultant's report to a board of directors should be challenged before impractical actions damage a company for years to come.

We hire CEOs for the ability to set a vision and a strategy. Consultant input is valuable, but a good CEO will know how to use that information, or disregard it, before charting a course for the future.

CHAPTER 9

UPS HEALTHCARE

(2019-2020)

The Design and Launch of a New Vertical Business Unit

UPS, the world's largest and most important logistics company, started in 1907 as a bicycle courier service headquartered over a saloon in rainy Seattle, Washington.

The logistics giant had taken several important positioning steps into healthcare logistics before the December 2016 Marken purchase.

In 2000, UPS bought Canadian companies Livingston Inc. and Livingston Healthcare Services Inc. With a solid Canadian supply chain business already in place, the Livingston acquisition brought new good manufacturing practices (GMP) and Good Distribution Practices (GDP) compliant warehouses to the UPS network, a first move into healthcare logistics.

After the Livingston purchase, UPS put up its first pharma facilities. In 2005, the company launched a healthcare campus in Louisville, Kentucky, that would prove important as UPS developed its

Worldport facility there. In the next few years, UPS built or bought healthcare warehouses in the Netherlands, Singapore, and China, and it acquired four companies to fill service gaps in Europe: Poltraf (Poland), Cemelog (Hungary), Pieffe (Italy), and Polar Speed (UK).

These nascent UPS Healthcare logistics efforts, though, fell short of their potential.

From my Marken vantage point, I saw UPS's healthcare logistics efforts simply as a collection of client accounts with a "healthcare" tag in the global sales book. It was an internal committee-supported function with no real authority, no separate P&L, and no refined or unified strategy. Jim Barber, UPS's chief operating officer, saw the problems too. Early in 2018, wanting change and a new strategy, he decided to replace a retiring thirty-year "UPSer" with his own new man, a non-UPS executive with a solid career of nearly two decades at one of the big pharmaceutical companies.

This was a rare outside hire for UPS. Almost always, Big Brown kept leadership promotions all in the family. And, as it turned out, Jim's handpicked healthcare guy wasn't the right fit for this job at this time.

It was then that Jim took a closer look at Marken. He decided to build a quality management system (QMS) using Marken's industry-best quality standards as a model and as a foundation for UPS's healthcare operations.

When Jim invited me in, I recommended a consultancy with which I had worked in the past. Setting up our QMS strategy, design, and standards was a collaborative effort with implementation left to UPS under the consultant's oversight and audit.

UPS launched an industry-leading quality management system in fall 2019. Tom Page, another veteran UPSer, led the function and reported directly to Jim.

A Big New Idea

With Marken going great guns in 2018 and 2019, I found myself in more and more meetings in UPS's C suite.

I became central, in fact, to a Big New Idea taking shape.

Jim began to lean toward setting up a whole new business vertical within Big Brown that would be dedicated to healthcare logistics. Carved out of an existing UPS P&L, it would become the first independent industry-focused business unit *ever* within the century-old integrated UPS network.

It was a bold idea, but that's who Jim Barber was, a unique leader at UPS.

It took two full months of negotiation and persuasion, plus some real horse-trading, to convince UPS CEO David Abney and the majority of the UPS Management Committee that a new freestanding division dedicated to healthcare logistics would be in the best interests of the company.

One part of the horse-trading greatly appealed to UPS leaders.

"We committed to grow the division at double the rate of the market," said Paul Vassallo, whom I would eventually appoint as our vice president of healthcare strategy.

"We also committed to a very high profit margin, where we previously had margins

David Abney, former UPS CEO, and I

similar to the rest of UPS. At that time, healthcare at UPS had been growing slowly year after year, and we were actually losing market share.

"That convinced the organization to make a bet on us."

In late November, Jim asked me to be president of the new division—history in the making at Big Brown.

I accepted the UPS job. In December 2019, I started work.

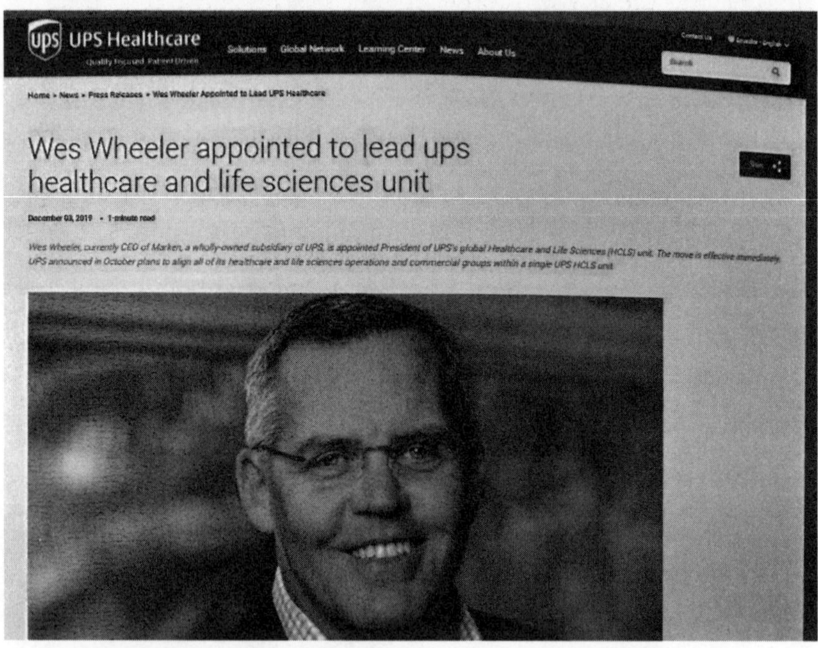

The decision to lead UPS Healthcare would prove fateful (AC9.1)

Why Marken Mattered

Jim Barber would soon announce his retirement from UPS despite the healthcare division setup.

Jim later reflected on his efforts to convince UPS to expand healthcare logistics.

"For a century, UPS operated under a completely different model from Marken's," he said. "We moved things from point A to point B, and all we did was based on delivering things in that kind of network with as few complications as possible.

"So UPS based business decisions on the nature of the network. What was the best product to move? Was it easier to ship a horse or a brick? A sofa or a one-foot cubic package? Easy decisions, right? The elegance was the lack of complexity, the fact that an average package might only be touched three or four times. The less touch, the more efficiency and speed.

"Before we bought Marken, some people at UPS considered healthcare as a shipment of simple medical devices and over-the-counter products. Those move very nicely through the network. They don't talk back to you. They don't get old. They don't need to be a certain temperature," Jim said.

"Then we went after Marken, and we were suddenly in the clinical trials business. In fact, we were on the front end, where Pfizer and Moderna play, where new drugs are created and connected to networks. The really fun stuff.

"And I'll be honest. We stumbled through the door. It was the right door, but we stumbled in—all of us but Wes Wheeler.

"Wes saw the future. He told me and many others that there was a time coming when healthcare would be delivered to people's homes—the majority of it. We have an aging population, a huge percentage of people living into the eighties, women at home by themselves who want somebody they trust to come to the door.

"And who better than UPS to trust? Why create another brand and spend tons of money trying to create the trust we already had? So that's why we set up a separate UPS Healthcare division—one of the most trusted brands in the world would allow us to penetrate new markets.

"Marken was the front end of a spear. The UPS Healthcare division would follow," Jim emphasized.

"When we bought Marken," he added, "we didn't really understand what it was really going to take to blossom inside UPS. But Wes did. Like all sellers, he hoped the buyer would have the fortitude, discipline, and strategic vision to see the jewel they bought, to say yes over and above the money. Ultimately, Wes thought UPS would pay attention to the healthcare sector and lean into it.

"So here we are, weighing the mediocracy of yesterday versus the glory of tomorrow. Wes and I are proposing that we move away from the simple stuff, fighting Amazon for book shipments and the like, swimming against the tide of decades that wanted the elegance of the easy package. Some had concerns. And why not? What's in that UPS package? Somebody's *blood*?

"That shift would be radical. We're talking about the tail wagging the dog here. It sometimes felt like we faced the unwillingness of 99 percent of the company to recognize the potential of healthcare logistics.

"Wes saw its potential long before I did. It was powerful, and we'll look back fifty years from now and know going into healthcare was the right thing to do."

Jim shrewdly found a path through the thorny UPS politics.

"At last, they got it," Jim said. "And then I was gone.

"I left in the first inning of a nine-inning game. So the credit for what the UPS Healthcare division would do goes entirely to Wes Wheeler. He created that organization by sheer dint of personal force.

"It was a really cool ride with Wes. He's a hell of a leader."

The Coming of COVID-19

Jim departed in November 2019, a month before I started as president of the newly created healthcare logistics organization.

I was suddenly left with no boss. I asked David Abney if I could work with Kate Gutmann, the company's executive vice president of sales and solutions.

Kate had strongly supported the healthcare stand-up. She was also the only C suite executive with a truly global role that could support me, a carved-out solutions team, and a new sales team.

David Abney agreed. And Kate gave me a call. She was, she said, "all-in."

Then came the COVID-19 pandemic. It became a building crescendo in my mind.

We watched what was happening in China, as everyone did. UPS played its part helping the Chinese with face masks and Tyvek suits. At this same time, I was busy building a team and a strategy. But when it became clear that the virus was spreading beyond China, I knew we had to play a bigger role. This was, after all, a healthcare crisis, maybe without parallel, and we were a freshly branded healthcare division of UPS.

I wanted us to jump in with all the power and resources we could muster as a new team. We would do exactly that.

Jim Barber looks back on that shock to the world.

"The pandemic proved the case for a dedicated UPS Healthcare logistics organization, didn't it?" he said. "The world moved instantly to 'I'm not going out; I'm staying in. Whoever wins my threshold—that's my trusted provider.'

"It's an amazing testimonial to Wes Wheeler, what his organization did in the pandemic. And it won't end there. If UPS can stand tall, healthcare could be the greatest market the company ever discovered."

For me as the new division's president, it would also be the greatest challenge of its kind in my career.

Jim understood, "It always amazed me, and still does, how Wes got this done," he said. "He wasn't born in the logistics world, and he was no spring chicken when he took over at Marken and turned that business around. Wes had a great pedigree, but this was UPS, with the biggest hill he'd ever had to climb.

"At least ten times as COO, I'd go home at night and ask myself, 'Why does Wes stay? Why does he put up with it? When is enough, enough?'

"But," Jim added, "Wes is the kind of leader who's going to fight for something he believes in. As tough as it was along the way, Wes was even tougher. He persevered. He grew Marken, and now who knows in the years and decades to come what will happen at UPS? More than anything I envisioned, I'm sure.

"Wes is the guy who brought this across the finish line to make UPS the trusted healthcare logistics champion of the world."

Standing Up UPS Healthcare

My new organization would have its own finance function, its own marketing function, its own engineering function. It would have independent departments for information technology, human resources, communication, legal, and sales.

I would lead it all, and still oversee operations at Marken as an independent clinical logistics arm of my new organization.

Our business model basically came down to making our division its own network-within-a-network. Speed and flexibility were the backbone of our high-speed operation.

Kate Gutmann was providing needed support as our unit's champion among the UPS top leadership.

"UPS had experience in healthcare for years, but it was heavy in medical devices," Kate said. "We needed more specialization, and that came with Wes. He built the division to create a healthcare ecosystem that would bring out the best of our global intelligence network and the best of our people."

By this time in my career, I could spot true talent a mile away. I created a small core team to carry out our strategy: Paul Vassallo, Tom Page, Dan Gagnon, Will Jacques (my new chief financial officer), Ariette van Strien (from Marken), and consultant Jonathan Hanak.

The new UPS division would be founded on two capabilities that would set it apart from industry competitors.

First, the new quality management system (QMS) would be deployed worldwide, using customized software. (Marken had its own QMS, and it would complement the expanded system.) The QMS would be crucial in managing without compromise a flood of new time-sensitive and temperature-sensitive biologic drugs and treatments from pharma companies.

Second, we licensed a new shipment tracking technology, based on Bluetooth and RFID technologies, from a start-up company in California. That would give UPS and our customers full visibility to shipments at any facility in the world, in real time.

UPS Premier, as our visibility and monitoring product would be known, was superior to any similar offering by Federal Express or DHL, our two major global competitors.

UPS Premier became a differentiator.

We quickly made other key moves. In January 2020 we started with a new brand and a new name for our new division.

We were UPS Healthcare.

We focused on complex healthcare customers: pharmaceutical and medical device companies, laboratories, hospitals and clinics, diagnostic testing companies, and other companies that supported these.

Audaciously, our team even made a logo change.

For the first time in UPS's proud 115-year history, the UPS shield was allowed to use a color other than brown. We made it blue, to distinguish the new division for our customers and within UPS itself.

I put Dan Gagnon in charge of marketing. I asked him to break the rules. Nothing was off the table.

"In our first working session as a staff," Dan recalled, "we participated in a workshop where we wrote notes on 3M sticky pads—ideas that could make us successful as a new division. We posted to the wall more than a hundred new ideas and thoughts.

"At the end, as Paul Vassallo and I were pulling them off the wall, we found one sticky note clearly written by Wes.

"It read: 'Push back on norms. Let Wes take the heat.'

"I took that note and kept it in my desk for a rainy day," Dan said. "I never had a chance to use it because Wes was constantly by our sides, helping us to push back on internal bureaucracy and resetting our internal focus back to the customer.

"He was out front in the fight, which did not make him a very popular person at UPS corporate, but he was certainly very popular within UPS Healthcare and with our customer base."

After leading the effort to give UPS Healthcare that new brand, Dan then set up new UPS Healthcare websites in more than thirty countries. He launched a new Instagram site, a LinkedIn handle, and a Facebook page.

Everything we did was meant to remind the world, including our own internal one, that we were different. We needed to be bold, distinct, best-in-industry. We needed new collateral materials, new training materials, and new internal presentation formats. As soon as we finished those things, we went to work on events, training sessions, proposal formats, and even business cards.

Operationally, we split UPS Healthcare warehouses off from the existing warehouse network in the UPS's Supply Chain Solutions (SCS) segment. We carved out only the warehouses operating under GMP (FDA) regulations and therefore dedicated to healthcare. Then we hoisted brand-new blue UPS Healthcare–branded signage on every building around the world.

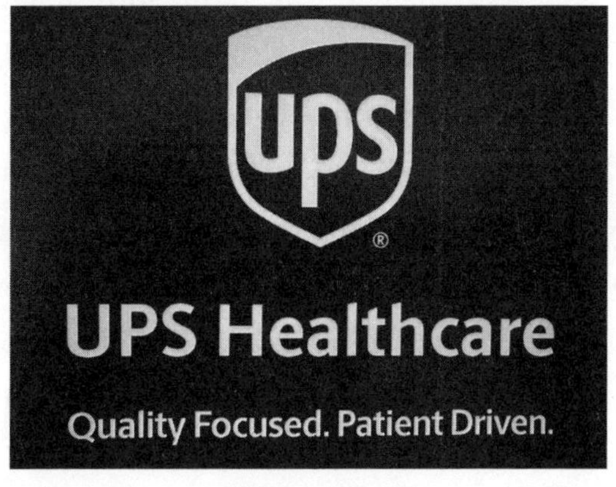

Our new brand

We found able-bodied help by sifting out a solutions team from the existing UPS sales organization. These experts focused on designing unique shipping lanes and warehouse configuration solutions for healthcare customers.

Organizationally, we also set up separate operating units for Marken and five other acquired businesses. Jim Barber had asked me to take responsibility for Polar Speed, a United Kingdom acquisition. I appointed Doaa Fathallah, my trusted legal colleague at two prior companies, to fix it.

The change to a stand-alone healthcare unit involved intense teaching and training.

I insisted that everybody in the division, especially the sales team, learn to speak "the language of pharma." It was clear to me that if we were to be successful in the market, we had to speak the language of our customers.

"To sit down and confidently do business with pharma customers," Dan confirmed, "you need the right vernacular. It shows you understand their risks and that you know what you are doing. It simply gives you credibility."

Our sales team and solutions engineers also had to learn the QMS and how to talk about it, because I was convinced that UPS Healthcare had built a best-in-class quality system, and our customers would see it as a differentiator and a logical reason to switch to us.

As we designed this entirely new business unit within UPS, Will Jacques, our new CFO, and his team set up a P&L for healthcare. It was another first at UPS.

We tagged every customer in the UPS accounting system that was dedicated to healthcare. We included pharmaceuticals, medical devices, laboratories, animal health, over-the-counter medicines, hospital systems, and clinical trials.

UPS Healthcare had 114 facilities in twenty-five countries and seven thousand employees. That's where we started life, in March 2020.

And that's where we started saving lives as a great pandemic swept the world.

LESSONS LEARNED

Established companies build cultures that are deeply rooted in the souls of their leaders. Sometimes, such strong company cultures stifle entrepreneurial thinking internally and kill unique ideas. A strong leader is willing to step out of a cultural quagmire and create something unique and different for the greater good.

N

CHAPTER 10

UPS HEALTHCARE

(2020–2023)

Battling a Global Pandemic

Shortly after the new year, the World Health Organization (WHO) announced a disease outbreak in Wuhan, China. A fast-spreading coronavirus affected victims with flulike symptoms, only more lethal, especially for elderly populations and people with compromised immune systems.

In February 2020, the virus had a name: COVID-19.

By March, more than one hundred thousand cases were reported. Intensive care units in hospitals overflowed, and the death toll soared.

China seemed far away until, suddenly, Europe was the epicenter of outbreaks. The epidemic had morphed into a pandemic, a worldwide illness.

By spring, the United States had declared a national state of emergency.

Researchers feverishly began looking for an effective vaccine. A dozen companies pushed the development of potential drugs, using approaches largely unique to their labs and trials.

Among the first to launch clinical trials with a novel mRNA vaccine were Moderna from the United States and BioNTech out of Germany. Pfizer had entered a collaboration with BioNTech years before, a decision that would shortly elevate Pfizer's brand into a global household name.

Marken, our company, was a preferred courier for all of Pfizer's clinical work. We actively supported US clinical trials for the Pfizer-BioNTech COVID-19 vaccine.

I had ambitiously assembled UPS Healthcare during this time, but when COVID-19 hit, we were still young, gathering all the pieces, getting to know each other, and still building the knowledge base.

We'd had exactly one sales meeting—one—though strategy implementation had begun. The UPS Premier product, a new system to track packages in real time, was in its infancy, still being installed and largely untested—like the entire UPS Healthcare division.

One thing was clear. Whatever UPS Healthcare would do, we had to do without delay—and without rehearsal.

I woke up motivated every morning.

By April, the United States reported one million COVID-19 cases. Stores and institutions shuttered. The economy stalled, except for online businesses.

The world was in lockdown.

PPE, Test Kits, and Vaccines

UPS Healthcare would become essential to three major COVID-19-era logistics efforts, each of unprecedented scale and paramount urgency:

1. **Personal protective equipment (PPE)**: We created a logistics pathway to deliver and store all the PPE that we could.

2. **Test kits**: We created a logistics program that could deliver COVID-19 test kits anywhere.
3. **Vaccines**: We built a global supply chain to store and deliver COVID-19 vaccines.

These initiatives undoubtedly saved many millions of lives.

The PPE work came first, as the speed of COVID-19's spread caught global suppliers shorthanded.

In the United States, PPE for healthcare workers, as well as ordinary citizens, ran desperately low. A fair portion of the US national stockpile had been shipped to China at the beginning of the outbreak, hoping to contain the virus there.

UPS Healthcare made calls to the US government to offer assistance. We had a warehouse called New Cut Road under construction in Louisville, near our Worldport facilities. I offered this entire five-hundred-thousand-square-foot facility for storage and distribution of any PPE imported into the United States.

The impressive UPS Worldport hub in Louisville played a critical role during COVID-19 operations

On cue, the UPS Freight Forwarding team brought chartered aircraft from Shanghai mostly through Chicago, then to Louisville. UPS Freight Forwarding and UPS Healthcare worked as close partners.

Paul Vassallo watched our new healthcare organization act with astonishing speed and foresight.

"We resolved to find PPE around the globe, wherever it was, and fly it where it needed to go," Paul said. "Where was that? We did something no other company did—we sent our salespeople everywhere to find out."

In the end, UPS Healthcare would move nearly forty-one million items through New Cut for the Federal Emergency Management Administration (FEMA), the government agency charged with locating and distributing PPE to protect US citizens. We scheduled 250 charter flights and moved more than twenty-four million pounds of materials.

Considered an essential services provider, UPS Healthcare became a key part of the US Strategic National Stockpile. That designation enabled a communication pathway between UPS Healthcare and the US government. The connections established through that channel would soon prove extremely important to the nation and bolster our reputation.

Working with the Government

I worked closely with Laura Lane, then head of UPS corporate's global government affairs, to set up a COVID-19 communication network with the right contacts in government, science, and the private sector to effectively operate in this code-red situation.

Laura took a first call on January 28, 2020, hearing a plea to make a humanitarian delivery of PPE to Wuhan.

That was the beginning.

Another urgent call came during early March, as COVID-19 spread to United States shores.

"My family and I were literally at Disney World, the happiest place on earth, when President Trump made the decision to close off US borders," Laura remembered. "I knew my sole task now was to keep UPS's network going despite the closure."

Laura would spend intense months coordinating efforts to get PPE to the right people and right places.

"We needed to make sure that critical PPE could be available around the world," Laura said. "We had to keep our package cars and trucks and planes moving. We were an essential service.

"That's when we got the first call made by the government to join what would become known as Operation Air Bridge, a mobilization of resources to help the nation, first responders, and vulnerable communities get the hand sanitizers, masks, and other PPE that could keep them safe and limit COVID-19's spread."

Laura took calls, she said, "every single day" from senior White House officials and key military figures mobilized to stop the pandemic. Members of Congress called about their constituents needing supplies, and foreign leaders asked UPS for help in standing up new supply chains for PPE and ventilators.

"Calls came from just everywhere," Laura said, "asking how to get PPE using UPS's infrastructure and expertise.

"The Canadian government had trouble getting supplies, and we helped them, moving shipments just in time to places in need. We worked country by country to remove cross-border barriers impeding the flow of needed goods."

UPS Healthcare kept up with the demands. Medical ventilators were high on the list of critical items needed. Laura spearheaded

UPS's partnership with GM, the US automaker, which retooled its entire production line to manufacture ventilators. Other companies followed suit. We were there to deliver the PPE to hospitals with critical shortages.

I made a lot of very important connections during these early days. I had to quickly find people I could call on, rely on and trust. I wanted people around me who would do whatever had to be done. I found them. My team, these people whom I barely knew, would run through walls for me. We were doing something very special, and we all knew it. I built a fortress with these people, and in the exhilaration of our mission, we honestly felt capable of doing anything. The pandemic moment was life-changing for us. We felt this every day.

Backing our twenty-four-seven work, Laura and the UPS team delivered hope and help.

"Because of our performance in Operation Air Bridge," Laura said, "We developed the trust and respect that led us into Operation Warp Speed, the sweeping and groundbreaking initiative to develop and create the vaccines against COVID-19.

"Marken's work with Pfizer on their clinical trials gave Wes the knowledge we would need to add to our capabilities to deliver with zero loss of product. That, in turn, would lead us to accelerate the widespread availability of UPS Premier, the solution that differentiates UPS Healthcare from our competitors today."

Laura felt that "all that was the result of Wes and his team thinking through the critical logistics and standing up the supply chain it took to develop and then deliver vaccines with almost flawless service levels.

"Wes brought expertise and partnership instincts that made sure everybody was integrated in the effort. It was never about a single person—it was about teams executing together.

"In crises," Laura said, "great leaders foster that kind of collaboration and problem-solving."

Always Ready, Whatever It Takes

One UPSer enjoyed a unique front-row seat in efforts to deliver vital PPE to the world.

Jim Coughlan, a veteran UPS professional, came out of retirement to serve the company's humanitarian projects, largely in Africa. When the pandemic struck, Laura, with Kate Gutmann's approval, moved Jim to Washington, DC, to a Federal Emergency Management Agency (FEMA) Command Center.

"My role with FEMA was to coordinate all international shipments and all charter flights of PPE equipment," Jim said. "That work involved multiple cities out of China and South Korea where equipment was sourced for US companies."

Jim could be considered the first responder's *first responder*.

"I took information coming into the agency and fed it back to the UPS Healthcare team who were on all-day Zoom calls, working with freight forwarding, and making anything happen," he said. "We coordinated PPE supply chain and logistics solutions for aircraft, boats, for transports across the nation, customers, and brokerage."

Our UPS Healthcare team managed everything. The FEMA people would turn to Jim and say, "What do we do here?" He'd have the luxury of telling them, "I'll have three subject matter experts here on a call within the hour." Then our people would get on the line and explain exactly what was needed to do to get a shipment of PPE out of Asia.

"There was not one call I ever made to UPS and Wes," Jim said, "that I wasn't given access to anybody I needed and told yes to whatever needed to be done."

With efforts like these, UPS stepped into clear view as a partner of the US government.

"We were like consultants," Jim said. "FEMA was a government agency, but previously only responsible for *domestic* emergency responses for the United States. The agency didn't know how to move product out of Asia, so we worked with UPS transportation solutions and leveraged our capabilities to support FEMA.

"There were no other partners in this effort—just UPS."

A Billion COVID-19 Test Kits Delivered

The second great UPS Healthcare initiative was the COVID-19 test kit. Every household and every individual would potentially need them at some point. Healthcare leaders came to understand that testing for the virus could slow its spread.

Kits rolled out of factories in China and in the United States, with Abbott taking an early lead in developing a rapid PCR (polymerase chain reaction) test device and, ultimately, the more popular antigen tests later in the pandemic.

Aside from Abbott, dozens or even hundreds of companies made test kits, though not all were approved for emergency use authorization (EUA) by the FDA. Part of our job would be navigating the FDA website to determine which kits were real. We partnered with several of the winners.

Now the question: How to get the kits close to users?

UPS Healthcare offered our airline and our forwarding operations from any manufacturer anywhere in the world with delivery to any point of use, anywhere in the United States.

Paul Vassallo points out that the outreach during the PPE delivery taught UPS Healthcare a great deal about swift action.

"We called Laura Lane in Washington," Paul remembered. "We told her, 'We want to do something different. We want to call all the state departments of health and city health departments and their labs. We'll let them know we have test kits, and the logistics to deliver them, next day air.'

"In a matter of weeks, we became the number-one logistics provider in twenty states. Cities like Los Angeles needed help testing their homeless populations. Others were setting up local or mobile test sites. And we got the kits to them.

"When states started testing," Paul said, "we were entrenched. Every state we called got our message: even if we're not your official logistics provider, we are happy to consult with you. Overnight, I became friends with people from two dozen states."

UPS Healthcare engaged the UPS air fleet. Pilots made regular runs from Shanghai to Anchorage, Alaska, then on to Louisville and UPS's massive Worldport central air hub at the end of the Muhammad Ali International Airport runway. Pilots under charter were running from Shanghai to Chicago.

Ultimately, UPS Healthcare would transport, store, and deliver more than one billion Abbott Binax and ID Now COVID-19 test kits and devices in the United States. We supported testing in thirty-eight states. Partnering with the testing companies, we proactively reached out to universities and food supply chain companies, like meat packers, to support testing their employees.

The Choreography of Healthcare Logistics

Todd Snyder, vice president of solutions and healthcare operations, was my right-hand operations expert during the pandemic.

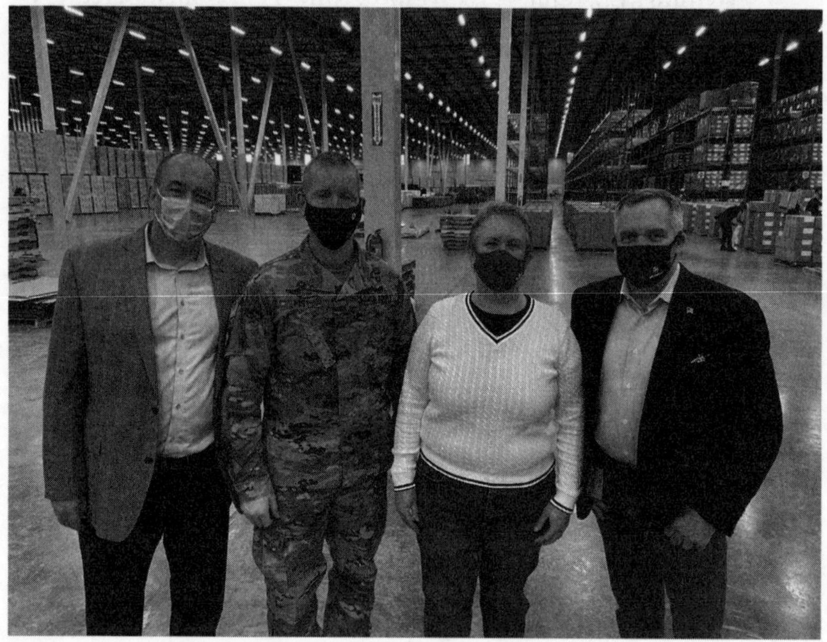

Todd Snyder and I with US Army chiefs at McKesson

Todd and I were on calls with government officials and their teams nearly every week. As the executive on my senior team, he rallied our lieutenants to come up with solutions for every single delivery required to satisfy the US government. He chased packages all over the country and beyond, reported the daily details, and built a command center that, in my mind, is the best-managed twenty-four-seven operation I have ever seen.

He was a masterful leader and a loyal part of my team, and I still miss those heady days when we believed we were helping save the world.

Todd quickly realized that UPS's first government engagement, with Operation Air Bridge, really centered on two capabilities.

"Flexibility," he said, "and being fast."

Todd and his team choreographed the multiple charters in and out of Asia each day. They synchronized scheduling with freight forwarders, creating a master of charters that leveraged all the UPS brown-tail fleet with existing capacity. Millions of tons of PPE moved out of Asia, setting down at New Cut, a site that was still "just four walls and a roof," as Todd described it.

"Think of Operation Air Bridge as bringing all bulk materials into the United States—masks, test kits, etcetera," Todd said. "UPS then broke down the bulk and shipped it as per government directions across the nation."

A Command Center like No Other

First, we managed the PPE. Next came test kits. Last would come vaccines.

All were received, processed, and tracked by UPS people and technology, overseen by the brand-new and separate command center. It gave "state of the art" a new meaning.

"We knew that the command center would be the key to our success," Todd said. "We set up a single entity to monitor every shipment and to track it. We set it up in just two months, between August and October."

The UPS Healthcare Command Center was set up like a movie theater, with big screens on walls. Some screens showed the weather.

Some showed breaking news. Some showed the actual tracking of shipments, every one of the screens crucial. We ultimately streamed data from Pfizer and connected to Washington.

Our UPS people watched every screen, every setup. We could see airport operation configurations, planes coming in, planes departing. Todd and the team knew, of course, what was on every plane, down to the number of masks and vials. They knew when planes were on time or delayed.

Also, UPS had multiple tracking systems, including those for UPS Premier shipments that had ping sensors in facilities, for redundancy and for richer information. Operations could prioritize decisions based on all this information.

"The command center was a huge differentiator for UPS," Todd reported.

To engage with the government through the command center and at other levels, Todd said UPS focused on three crucial things.

"First, we spelled out our capabilities. We outlined UPS's warehousing and cold-chain capabilities, which were not well understood by government officials.

"Second, we planned and mapped the operational strategies we would use, regardless of whose product we would move. We published a written manual—Wes called it a 'user encyclopedia'—that detailed mapping and operations. That degree of foresight and design greatly impressed officials.

"Third, we designed and sold the government on our delivery system. That system was national and international, creating new lanes for deliveries and setting their timetables."

No amount of work was too much for the upstart UPS Healthcare team.

Saving the world was serious business.

The UPS Command Center that monitored vaccine deliveries impressed even Operation Warp Speed leadership

Operation Warp Speed

UPS Healthcare had the good luck and good planning to be well positioned for work with the lifesaving COVID-19 vaccines.

Marken was already engaged with nearly every one of a dozen vaccine clinical trials. (The outlier, Moderna, worked with our competitor, Kuehne & Nagel, and its last-mile delivery company, QuickStat.)

In April 2020, just more than a month after the WHO declared COVID-19 a global pandemic, my trusted longtime associate Ariette van Strien, now president of Marken, and I got a copy of the clinical trial protocol for the Pfizer-BioNTech COVID-19 vaccine. Making clinical trial protocols publicly available was new, a precedent in the pharmaceutical industry.

We read the Pfizer-BioNTech protocol closely, and at that time learned the vaccines would be shipped at -70° Celsius. The mRNA technology used by the two companies required that extremely demanding storage and shipment temperature.

The shelf life of the Pfizer-BioNTech vaccine was unknown at the time, and the vaccine molecules were fragile. All the other vaccines—Johnson & Johnson's, AstraZeneca's, and the rest—came from differing technologies, but we knew those would likely be stored and shipped at about -20° Celsius, about the temperature of a household freezer.

Ariette and I spotted something else important in the Pfizer-BioNTech protocol.

In pharma, a phase 1 test is the first time a drug is tested in humans. A phase 2 test first introduces a drug to humans who have the actual disease being combated. These two phases can take years in traditional clinical trial settings. Phase 3 trials, also called pivotal trials, collect the extensive data that companies present to the FDA for potential approval for production and marketing.

With appropriate urgency, the COVID-19 pivotal clinical trials would move straight to phase 3 by fixing the dose early and after the safety trials. Much of the typically required phase 2 data would be drawn from the pivotal trial. To do that, the FDA required that thirty thousand patients of various demographics be included in each clinical trial.

By now, the US government had formed a COVID-19 task force.

Moncef Slaoui, MD, PhD, a Moroccan-born executive who had been chair of GlaxoSmithKline's global vaccine research and development arm was named by the Trump administration to lead the initiative. It would be called, famously, Operation Warp Speed.

Dr. Slaoui hit on an inventive way of speeding up the vaccine development process. He selected only six from the large number of ongoing clinical trials. He chose two trials from each of three separate technologies and let them race to come out on top in terms of efficacy and safety. Dr. Slaoui pressed the US government to invest in those six trials.

Pfizer's and BioNTech's vaccine development efforts with the mRNA technology were well underway, and Dr. Slaoui selected the Pfizer-BioNTech and Moderna trials to represent mRNA technology.

The official Operation Warp Speed logo

In effect, Dr. Slaoui put bets on six horses, hoping one would be a winner. He forced all the clinical trials to adopt a very similar protocol, but each with their own nuances. All were required, however, to select the dosage early, and all the trials had to recruit thirty thousand patients from a similarly diverse patient population.

Nothing like this had ever been tried as part of a government-led project before, but there had also not been a global pandemic in five generations.

Shortly after Dr. Slaoui's appointment, the administration of President Trump named a second leader of Operation Warp Speed, Four-Star General Gustave Perna.

The thinking was that the US military would be best to run logistics and even be responsible for delivering the vaccine. General Perna was named chief operating officer of Operation Warp Speed.

General Perna had put in a full career as a military leader. Most recently, he'd headed the US Army's Materiel Command. He'd been preparing to retire to his home and private life in Alabama when the call to duty came again.

General Perna quickly went to work building his team.

Retired Army Lieutenant General Paul Ostrowsky was put in charge of supply, production, and distribution. General Perna appointed Major General Chris Sharpsten as General Ostrowsky's deputy director. Both men had previously served under General Perna's command.

Laura Lane and I had been making calls to the White House COVID-19 Response Team and to Health and Human Services contacts several times a day. We were trying to figure out how UPS could help with logistics. We had made some progress, but it wasn't until I met General Ostrowsky on Zoom, thanks to an introduction from my long-trusted friend, colleague, and West Point man Tim Tyson, that things started to gather steam.

I offered Operation Warp Speed the full cooperation of UPS Healthcare, all our assets, and a dedicated team.

That pitch stood out, for the same reasons UPS Healthcare stood out in the healthcare logistics industry.

We had a quality management system like no other, and we had UPS Premier. We had space in our warehouses. We had the UPS airline. And we had the best healthcare logistics team in the world.

In no time, I was having conversations with General Sharpsten and General Perna. Questions persisted about nearly every part of OWS, but one thing was crystal clear.

The operation now had a willing partner in UPS Healthcare that could deliver anything, anywhere, and we were well prepared to do so as soon as a vaccine was approved. We were partners with OWS by late April.

General Perna valued a commitment like that.

"I had three tenets to make sure the vaccine was ready, and distribution occurred," General Perna said of his role as Operation Warp Speed COO.

"First, my vision was that the administration of the vaccine would be in comfortable places. There should be a sense of normalcy. Think drugstores. Walgreens. CVS. Familiar places for people.

"Second, we shouldn't create a whole new playbook for distribution. Why would we want to? We had great companies that already knew how to deliver packages, get to houses, get to small places. We could rely on their expertise and capabilities.

"Third, and essential: Whoever we chose to work with on distribution had to have the capability and capacity to get the vaccine out to all of America simultaneously—not just one state, not just one group of people. Everywhere in the country, from Maine to Puerto Rico to the Pacific territories.

"I gave those tenets, set that vision—then I put the monkey on the backs of the team. Leaders like Wes Wheeler were successful because they took the mantle, took responsibility—and figured it out."

Building a Battle-Ready Cold-Chain Network

In May 2020, General Perna decided that the US military would not need to handle vaccine deliveries. He recognized that UPS had the full capability to deliver vaccines any place in the United States and its territories with complete visibility to each shipment, and with guaranteed delivery within twenty-four to forty-eight hours after doses left the factory.

Of historic significance, General Perna and Dr. Slaoui announced that OWS would be declared a "public-private" partnership. Under public organizational direction, private industry would develop and distribute the vaccines.

Big questions remained.

Which vaccine would win approval? When? Where would it be manufactured? What temperature? How long would approval take? How was patient enrollment for the clinical trials going? What kind of packaging would be needed to ensure vaccine stability?

Under Todd, UPS Healthcare's solution team went to work on those questions far in advance. We researched every possible manufacturing location where the vaccines could be made and crossed these origin locations with every major city where vaccines would be needed. We created an encyclopedia of supply lanes that comprehensively compiled first-mile pickup, air routing, storage location, and final-mile delivery. Our team simulated more than seven hundred different combinations of lanes and solutions that might be needed, and we mapped all the major supply chains in advance. It was an incredible effort by Todd and his team.

By this time, I had been named as the first private member of the OWS team. Meetings took place with General Sharpsten and the US Army team he led. I also set up a private UPS-only meeting with the OWS team every Friday to provide additional behind-the-scenes intelligence. Todd, Paul, and I led those meetings for more than a year.

The proactive thinking made a huge impression. When we showed General Sharpsten and his team our advance supply chain mapping, he was amazed we had already undertaken such an initiative.

Other foresight made a difference too.

Anticipating the cold temperature requirements of all the vaccine candidates, our team began to build out a cold-chain storage system made up of large coolers and freezers designed to handle drugs at 28° Celsius and at -20° Celsius.

UPS Healthcare then partnered with Sterling Inc. to manufacture and deliver ultracold storage units capable of storing at -70° Celsius. We installed these in the New Cut Road warehouse where we had earlier managed storage and distribution of PPE and test kits. This new use of the New Cut warehouse would become generically known as a *freezer farm*, a term the industry and media embraced.

We were prepared to store anything at any temperature in Louisville, then ship it overnight from Worldport to any zip code in the United States. The UPS Premier label would go on every shipment.

The UPS Healthcare planners also had the foresight to recruit key people in each region of the nation who connected to the command center to ensure final-mile deliveries and to intervene if shipments got delayed. From Worldport, the command center directly interacted with OWS systems, UPS Flight Operations, and UPS Premier tracking systems.

Keeping shipments ultrafrozen at -70° Celsius would be crucial for the Pfizer mRNA vaccines. Moderna's would be handled at -20° Celsius.

There were concerns about the amount of dry ice (CO2) that would be required to move these mRNA vaccines to maintain constant ultracold temperatures during transit. We were hearing estimates of dry ice requirements in the media that far exceeded the total amount of dry ice available in the world marketplace. Also, due to CO2 sublimation, we had to deal with very real constraints on how much of it we could safely carry on each UPS aircraft.

Our preemptive solution? Use ground delivery for the nearby East Coast deliveries and use air for the rest of the country.

But how could we solve for the dry ice volumes needed?

We did the most practical thing possible. We built our own dry ice factory in the Louisville warehouse.

My head of engineering, Felix Chang, had been building warehouses for me as fast as he could write checks. Now, Felix was in the freezer farm and dry ice business. He just kept on delivering whatever we needed and at speeds rarely before seen at UPS.

The dry ice saga serves as a sort of UPS Healthcare parable, an illustration of derring-do at a moment when others sat paralyzed and doubtful.

In one of the OWS meetings, General Sharpsten raised a critical question to a room filled with a chosen few assembled to rescue a nation from COVID-19.

"If we launch with an mRNA vaccine, how will we handle the dry ice needed to maintain -70° Celsius during transit?" General Sharpsten asked.

Paul Vassallo sat in that meeting.

"At first, no one breathed," Paul said. "You heard nothing but crickets.

"The first voice was Wes Wheeler's. 'We can handle it,' Wes said. 'We'll manufacture dry ice ourselves, and we can move it to facilities that need it within three days.'"

Paul stared. "Wes just looked at us and said, 'We can figure this out. We can do this.' He committed us to manufacture and distribute dry ice, when we had never done it.

"UPS became the sole supplier of dry ice for the follow-on shipments of all the mRNA vaccines."

We weren't done being audacious.

I asked Felix Chang to procure every ultracold freezer *in the world* capable of holding temperatures at -70° Celsius.

"We figured out the mechanics of managing it all," Paul said. "We worked out which aircraft to use, the supply lanes from the front-end production to the downstream destinations, all the vehicles, and the freezers—all handled by UPS."

That meant when any of the six temperature-sensitive vaccines still in clinical trials were approved, UPS Healthcare would have our cold chain ready. The shipping containers would be capable of handling any of the vaccines at any of the three temperature ranges.

If the Pfizer-BioNTech or Moderna vaccines were first to launch, UPS would have dry ice ready. Every distribution would even have a chaser shipment, just to make sure vaccines stayed at -70° Celsius. Those shipments would include instructions on how to handle dry ice, how to keep safe using gloves, shovels, masks, etc.

"I had worked at UPS for thirty-four years," Paul said, "and I had never seen a thing like that. Wes had the foresight and the vision to know … it's not going to get done if UPS doesn't do it."

We created a team in Louisville dedicated to manufacturing, procuring, and storing thousands of pounds of dry ice every night in the Kentucky facility. Men and women in UPS gear shoveled dry ice into bags and loaded planes and vehicles through the hours. In all, 2.4 million pounds of dry ice shipped through UPS, protecting fragile vaccines.

Stephen Hydrick was the hero of the Louisville operations during this time. He and his team did everything we asked.

By the end of the pandemic, we had deployed 169 freezer units in eighteen countries.

Decisions with the cold chain transcended the pandemic. We asked a whole different kind of question even in the middle of the plague: Where is the medicine of tomorrow going to be built? How do we go ahead and create our network so we're there already?

"Because Marken was already in the clinical trial pharma space," Paul said, "Wes knew the drugs being developed there, and where they would ultimately be manufactured. We took that knowledge to the UPS leadership and convinced them that the time to build out the healthcare logistics network of the future was *now*. That's the real win.

"If you're sitting in an MBA class somewhere," Paul said, "and you're talking about leadership profiles, this is about as good an example as I have ever seen."

General Perna Praises Vaccine Delivery Preps

The top brass at Operation Warp Speed paid an on-site visit to New Cut in July 2020.

"It was immediately clear to me that Wes was in charge," said General Perna. "I saw a quiet professionalism. You could tell instantly. And as soon as I walked into the room, that team he led was ready to brief me—excited to brief me.

"They had done a lot of fricking work, but they were ready to get my update and get my guidance. They weren't closed-minded. You could tell it was a team effort, that the UPS folks were really vested and proud of what they'd done, but with humility.

"I heard them say, 'We've got this all set, but we need to work faster here, do more here.' They self-reported. That's the sign of a great organization, that awareness.

"Wes wasn't the one talking the whole time. His leaders spoke, the collective team, all of them ready, walking around with purpose, eyes up, shoulders back, not dragging around, nobody watching the clock.

"I could see the *organization* was ready, not just one person. UPS was excited about contributing to the nation. It was really, really impressive."

UPS Healthcare's strategic plan proved equally impressive.

As we presented it to General Perna and Dr. Slaoui, Todd, Paul, and Dan were by my side. The leaders of Operation Warp Speed returned to Washington convinced that we were ready when a vaccine was ready.

A few days later, General Perna called me with a question.

"Will you be set to launch by October 1?"

"Yes, sir," I answered.

Pfizer: First Out of the Gate

Though no one yet knew which vaccine would be the first one ready to launch, we had a gut feeling.

Pfizer, with BioNTech, appeared to be ahead. That was reinforced when Tanya Alcorn, vice president of BioPharma global supply chain for Pfizer Pharmaceuticals, joined the OWS team.

Tanya and her team conveyed confidence.

"We just had a feeling," she said. "As we focused on getting everything in order, we understood we were the largest company developing a vaccine, we had the largest scale, we had the most experience. I kept telling our team, 'If anyone in the world can do this, we can.'" Tanya understood that partnership would be the key to vaccine distribution.

"We knew this would be very different from a supply chain perspective. We had to start designing something on a massive scale that did not yet even exist.

"How were we going to ship a vaccine? How would we store it at a distribution site? How could we keep it at the ultralow temperature it required? Every dose was precious, and we had one clear goal: No dose wasted due to distribution or storage. We knew we couldn't solve these problems alone."

Pfizer wouldn't be alone.

Tanya met with me and our UPS team. A confident partnership emerged.

"Wes was usually one question ahead of us," she admitted. "He and UPS already had plans and tools in place to do real-time monitoring and to have a control tower to guide shipments. Our minds were always in sync. And UPS made a lot of knowledgeable people available to partner in the design of the vaccine supply chain."

Given the scale of the project and the speeds and special conditions required, "Things went a lot more smoothly than I ever expected," Tanya said.

"UPS from the beginning was running scenarios and planning mitigations. I knew they were all over it.

"UPS took a lot of risks to build the infrastructure we would need. They were one of the few that were constantly thinking ahead.

"For example, we didn't at first know absolutely for sure we'd need a solution that required dry ice, but UPS went ahead. And I saw the UPS team thinking just as much about vaccine delivery to sub-Saharan Africa as it did to the United States, globally creating new lanes that didn't exist to create faster pathways that also didn't yet exist."

Tanya also praised the teamwork we showed with marketplace rivals.

"I never once got the impression that UPS was trying to beat out Federal Express or DHL," she said. "It was all-in with those other companies on the common goal of saving lives."

Showtime at the White House

As Pfizer plans shaped up, I sensed that the Moderna vaccine was a close second in development. Other contenders lagged at that time.

By now, the White House had given OWS full authority to manage vaccine logistics.

In the run-up, UPS Healthcare worked closely with Pfizer, Johnson & Johnson, and Novavax on their clinical trials. All those companies had agreements in place with UPS Healthcare for vaccine storage and distribution.

UPS Healthcare would be ready the moment OWS gave the green light.

On December 7, 2020, I attended President Trump's Vaccine Summit in Washington, DC. On December 10, I also appeared before the Senate Transportation Subcommittee. At both meetings, I assured elected officials and other leaders that UPS Healthcare was prepared.

On the day I represented UPS Healthcare at the White House Vaccine Summit, Pfizer and BioNTech received emergency use authorization for its COVID-19 mRNA vaccine.

All systems go.

Ahead of my White House appearance, I called Tanya Alcorn to ask a favor; I wanted to borrow one of Pfizer's shipping containers.

As the Pfizer-BioNTech vaccine would get first approval, it made sense to present the Pfizer shipping container at the summit meeting.

Pfizer agreed. Over the weekend, that company's training department coached me on the container's proper use. I had it shipped overnight to Washington, DC.

It was a product made by Softbox, Inc., custom-designed to hold 195 vials with 1,170 total doses of the Pfizer-BioNTech vaccine and to maintain their integrity at -70° Celsius for as long as ten days. It held thirty pounds of dry ice to keep the vials at temperature and without risk of compromise in transport.

Every box carried a tracking device made by Controllant, a company based in Iceland. Those devices connected to the OWS Command Center and to the UPS Healthcare Command Center.

We would have two sets of eyes on every container. And every container would proudly carry the UPS Premier label.

With the Softbox by my side, I waited at the White House for my summit appearance.

President Trump gave opening remarks. He then departed, leaving OWS to carry out our business.

General Perna and Dr. Slaoui gave incredible presentations on all the preparations made for the vaccine. Shawn Seamans from McKesson spoke. Marc Casper, the CEO of ThermoFisher, brought out his company's freezer.

Then it was time for UPS Healthcare and FedEx to present.

It was a watershed day for our UPS team. We took the audience through details of the shipping container, and how we would move, protect, and monitor vaccine deliveries. We got the lion's share of time and the lion's share of media attention.

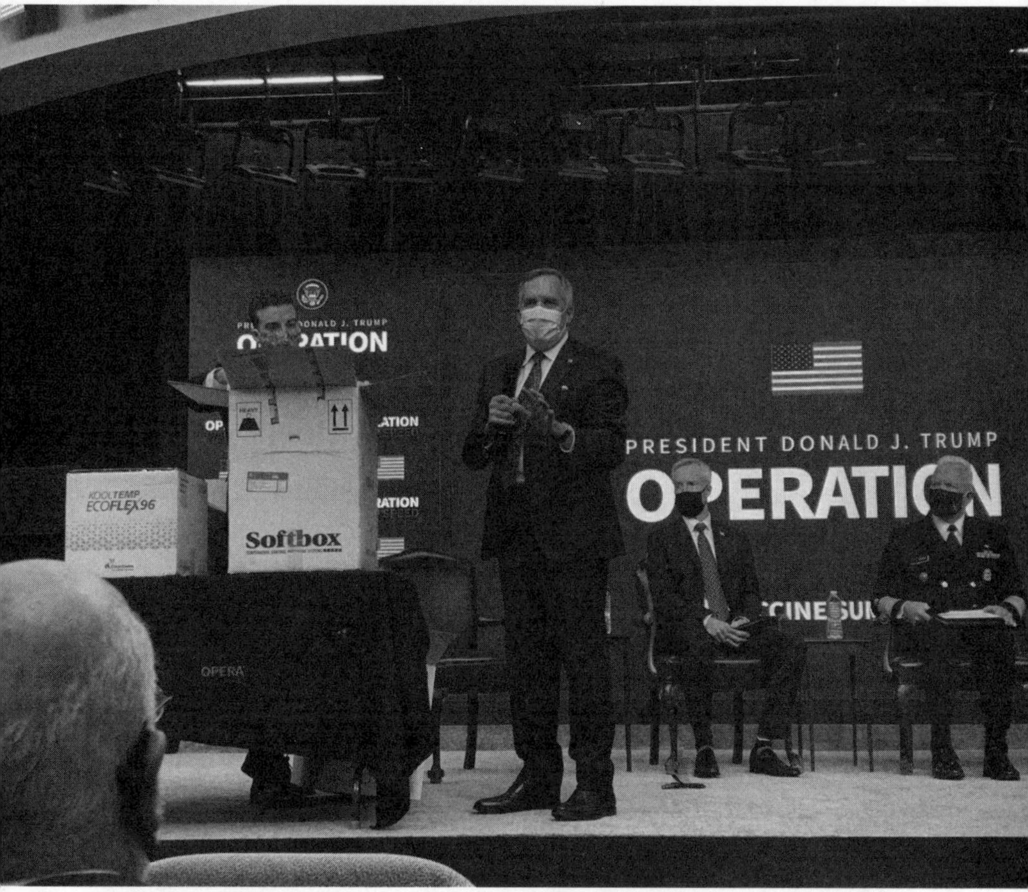

Presenting at the White House Summit

Shortly after the summit, I presented in front of the US Senate Committee on Commerce, Science and Transportation, assuring the senators that we could do this. I think they were caught off guard by our confidence. They left the hearing satisfied.

DEB FISCHER
NEBRASKA

UNITED STATES SENATE
WASHINGTON, D.C. 20510

December 10, 2020

Mr. Wheeler:

Thank you for testifying before the Senate Transportation and Safety Subcommittee on December 10, 2020.

I appreciated your thorough responses to the Subcommittee's questions about UPS's work on vaccine distribution. As you know, there are numerous challenges and logistics hurdles to transporting the COVID-19 vaccines. The insights you provided about the preparation that has taken place to ensure the safe and quick transportation of millions of vaccines were encouraging to hear.

I look forward to continuing to work with you and UPS on other transportation priorities going forward. More importantly, I hope you and your employees at UPS stay safe throughout this process.

Sincerely,

Deb Fischer
United States Senator

The Senate testimony was unique for me

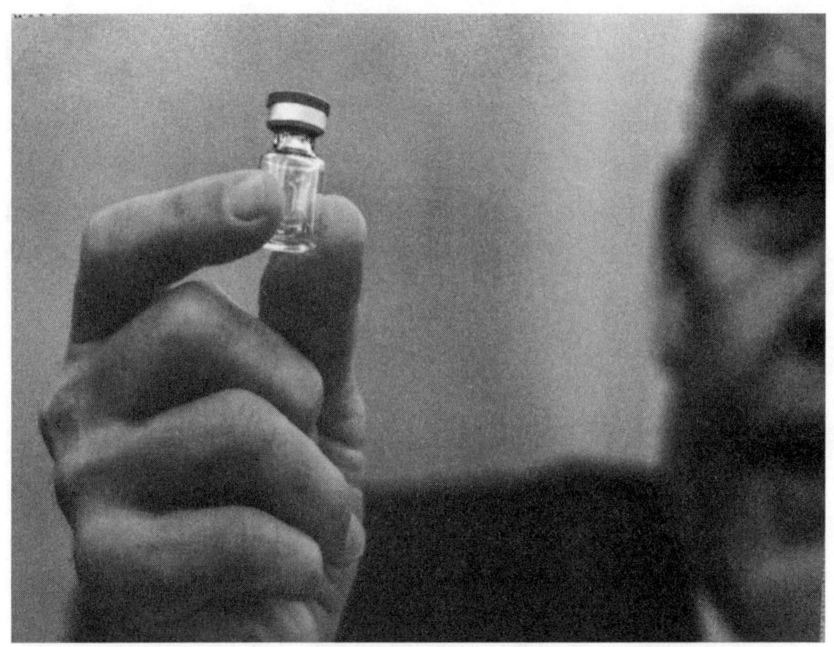

At the Senate hearing, introduction of this tiny vial holding eight doses of vaccine created a sensation. This photo went viral, spurring global hope in the fight against COVID-19.

First flight with Pfizer vaccines arrives at Worldport

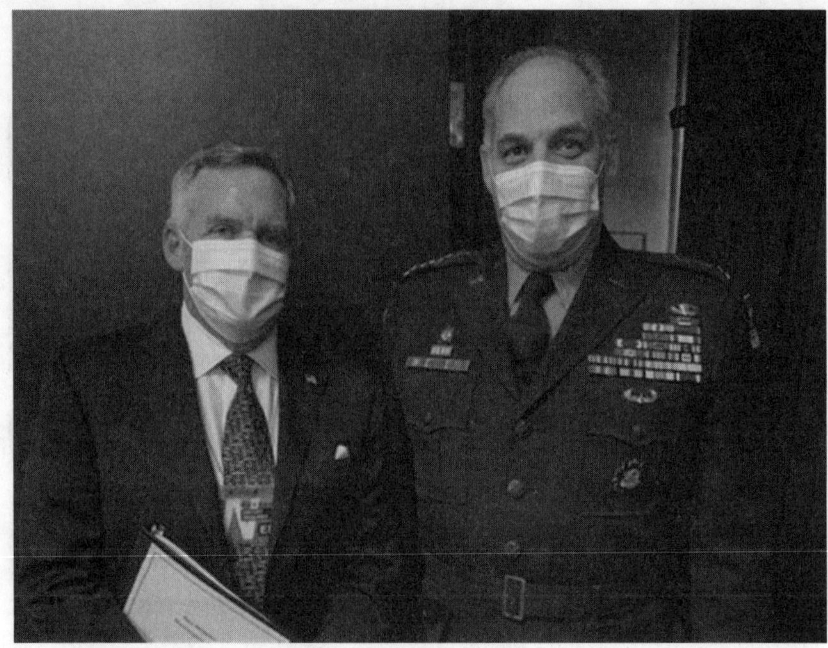

Four-Star General Gustave Perna and I at the White House Vaccine Summit. The general and I spent a lot of time together coordinating our roles in Operation Warp Speed.

Within hours of the emergency authorization, a UPS trailer carrying the first doses of the COVID-19 vaccine in the United States left Pfizer's manufacturing site at Kalamazoo, Michigan. The trailer flew on a special charter from Lansing to Worldport. It arrived the next morning in Queens, New York.

A critical care nurse named Sandra Lindsay at Long Island Jewish Medical Center received the first dose of the Pfizer-BioNTech COVID-19 vaccine. This frontline responder became the first US resident immunized against the COVID-19 virus. She humbly—but proudly—represented frontline responders everywhere.

The hour of celebration would be tempered by reality—billions of doses remained to be delivered to a waiting world.

Competitors Team Up for the Greater Good

General Perna recognized the achievement of UPS and a small team of uniquely capable leaders with Operation Warp Speed.

"Wes was a key leader and part of a larger team that assured our success," General Perna said. "I credit his direct leadership, his persona, his holding himself and his team accountable, his coming through for us.

"If you had to put up a wall and showcase the ten or fifteen leaders who held the baton and ran the laps, Wes Wheeler would be on that wall. Knowing him, he'd give credit to everyone else around him.

"When Wes told me something, I knew I could trust it. When there was a problem, he always came to me with a solution ready.

"Would Wes Wheeler be a good general?

"He can visualize. Then he can figure out how to operationalize the vision. He can lead through adversity. Those are all qualities needed to be a good general. Because he was that kind of leader, his team was able to accomplish all that it did."

General Sharpsten's praise for our work at UPS was equally generous.

"In my time in the army, I grew up in elite units," General Sharpsten said. "I got better every day, not only learning from the best but wanting to contribute and be relevant, not look like a fool. Every day, I went to work trying to get better and better.

"When I met Wes and his UPS team, I thought, 'Hey, I'm back home. I've got to be at my peak now—I don't want to walk into a meeting and not rise to their level.'

"Wes is one of those people who made me want to work harder each day. And, in my opinion, Wes Wheeler is a patriot who stepped up when the nation called."

For the sake of the greater good, General Perna decided to split vaccine logistics for the country in two. UPS Healthcare was given first choice, and we opted to handle vaccine shipments east of the Mississippi River. FedEx would handle the US West. UPS also handled all the military outposts in the Pacific.

Federal Express Senior Vice President Richard Smith and I met over Zoom weekly once FedEx came onto the OWS team. We really bonded, though, at the White House and later at the Senate hearing. I never considered him a competitor at this time. We were doing important work together.

General Perna deeply respected the working relationship our rival companies created.

"I remain impressed at how Wes and Richard figured out how to work together without involving me," General Perna said.

"I'm a big fan of people solving issues at their own levels. Don't bring me into tactical problems you should be able to fix yourselves. These two leaders spent countless hours working things out together for the greater good.

"This couldn't have been done by just one company. And if Wes and Richard hadn't found a respectful way of working together, it could have been such a crap storm."

The accommodations involved more than just personalities. Pfizer chose to split the country its own way, and we ended up with a hybrid set of states for the Pfizer-BioNTech distribution out of Pfizer's Kalamazoo manufacturing site.

In the end, UPS handled about 60 percent of all Pfizer-BioNTech COVID-19 vaccines in the United States, and about 50 percent of all Moderna shipments. We also handled 100 percent of the dry ice chaser shipments, almost two million pounds of that solid form of carbon dioxide.

By November 2020, OWS had designated forty thousand distribution locations, known as "point of use sites," where vaccines would be dropped. These sites included hospitals, clinics, pharmacies, and medical centers.

Sections of the country—more than sixty of them—were labeled "jurisdictions," and each had its own share of vaccines for distribution. Native American reservations made up a jurisdiction all its own, and so did military posts. Distribution allocations were determined by the Centers for Disease Control and Prevention and communicated in real time to the OWS team in Washington.

Our plan also included vaccine shipments to far-flung US territories. In multiple complex moves, including re-icing and site coordination, we would deliver vaccines to American Samoa, Guam, and the Northern Mariana Islands, building huge credibility for the US government.

Thirty Thousand Zip Codes in All Kinds of Weather

The UPS Healthcare participation in OWS continued through the end of the Trump administration. By the time President Biden took charge in January 2021, all the shipping lanes had been mapped, all the nodes in the supply chain worked seamlessly, and more than one million vaccine doses had already been delivered, with more on the way.

Around the clock, UPS trucks left Pfizer's Kalamazoo plant and Moderna's (Catalent's) Bloomington plant. McKesson managed inventory and packing for Moderna and sent out those vaccine shipments via UPS and FedEx.

Pfizer took a different approach. It managed its own inventory and packed its own vaccines, which were shipped by UPS and FedEx, depending on jurisdiction.

UPS Healthcare, Moderna, Johnson & Johnson, Pfizer, McKesson, FedEx, and the OWS team in Washington had become a well-orchestrated team, meeting at least twice a week. This team moved vaccines to thirty thousand of the forty thousand zip codes in the United States, starting with efforts to reach the elderly and the immunocompromised, next focusing on deliveries to those age sixty-five and over, and finally delivering lifesaving doses to all the US population.

We had the process down pat. It became almost routine … most of the time.

Exceptions called out the best in us. Delivery efforts ran into one of the worst nor'easters of the season just before Christmas 2020.

"Our operations team and command center worked feverishly through the day to ensure all vaccine packages were delivered," said Todd Snyder. "We were determined to deliver each and every one.

"We found one last remaining shipment on a parked aircraft at shut-down Boston Logan International Airport. Our operations team used our UPS Premier locator to determine that the package was on that aircraft. Two employees unloaded it and shuttled that single remaining package to Cambridge for delivery. That's a testament to how personally our operations took these lifesaving shipments."

Another weather event, a brutal freeze, shut down much of Texas, but not the UPS vaccine deliveries. Next, storms in the South knocked out power and took lives, but UPS vaccine deliveries never stopped.

Whether the skies were crystal clear or there were severe storms, UPS delivered vaccines at a near-perfect 99.9 percent on time before 10:30 a.m. Every shipment was tracked by a human being. We left nothing to chance. If a shipment appeared to be stuck, we moved heaven and earth to rescue it.

Our UPS people became heroes in their own small towns and cities. They all felt a sense of duty to our country.

"That was true for every UPS Healthcare worker around the world," said Kate Gutmann. "It comes from the premise that we hold here: it's a patient, not a package. That spirit of service is in the fiber of UPSers. We take it to heart."

UPS efforts went far beyond US borders too.

Marken had already worked with more than one hundred countries, distributing vaccines for clinical trials to clinics and patients' homes.

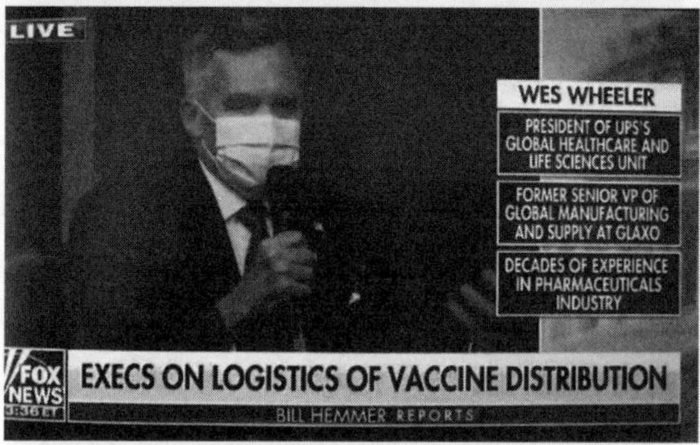

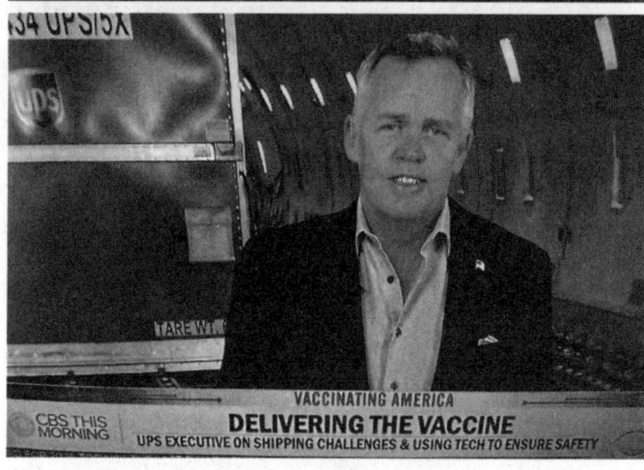

Top: Media coverage came nearly every day
Middle: Fox News
Bottom: CBS News

With that powerful network in place, UPS worked with the Global Alliance for Vaccines and Immunization (GAVI), the COVID-19 Vaccines Global Access organization (Covax), and the United Nations Children's Fund (UNICEF) to deliver vaccines internationally. Some success would come, though not enough.

We met with the African Union trying to forge a distribution deal. It was rejected by UNICEF. The African nations then suffered for months and even years due to incompetence and politics.

I personally had dinner with ambassadors from six African nations in UPS's Government Affairs townhouse in Washington DC, listening to their complaints about not having vaccines. UNICEF never delivered for them. And, as of spring 2023, only 37 percent of the African population has been vaccinated.

Elsewhere, things went better.

As this book was written, UPS Healthcare has delivered more than 1.48 billion doses of vaccines to more than 108 countries. The network remains in place for new vaccines that will counter COVID-19 variants.

We worked our process until the COVID-19 public health emergency was declared over. We used the same supply chain design and the same command center while maintaining a 99.8 percent on-time by-day performance.

It was a project like no other. UPS Healthcare is very proud of its role. It was an honor to serve as part of the overall effort to vaccinate the world during this once-in-a-century health crisis.

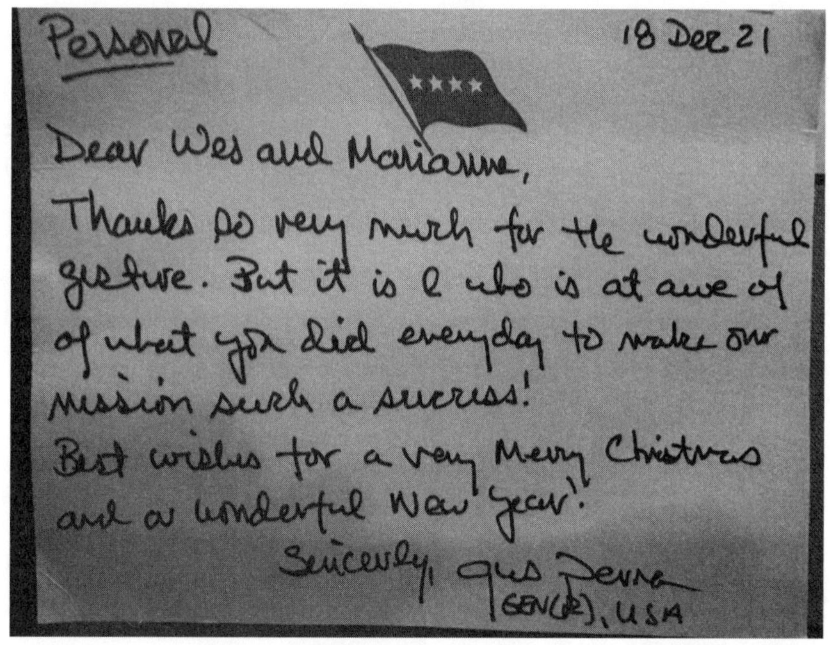

Personal 18 Dec 21

Dear Wes and Marianne,

Thanks so very much for the wonderful gesture. But it is I who is at awe of of what you did everyday to make our mission such a success!

Best wishes for a very Merry Christmas and a wonderful New Year!

Sincerely, Gus Perna
GEN(R), USA

General Perna's note to me

Post-COVID-19 Progress

Meanwhile, life went on for UPS Healthcare, the business.

Anticipating the age of biologics, and proven so spectacularly right by our COVID-19 preparation, UPS Healthcare industriously built out our cold chain around the world.

"Our balance sheet afforded us this opportunity," explained Kate Gutmann. "We had righted the business and freed up capital for investment and growth. We moved with speed, and that's the part that our competitors couldn't match—the amount of our spend and the speed with which we moved.

"UPS Healthcare's leadership role in preparing the nation's defenses against the COVID-19 virus gave us our right to win in the cold-chain market. It vaulted UPS into prominence against DHL, its biggest international competitor, as a leader across the globe."

We added ten million square feet of GMP-compliant warehouse space in the United States, UK, Italy, Australia, Germany, Ireland, Netherlands, Poland, Czech Republic, Hungary, Singapore, and South Korea.

We also established a Proposal Factory. We brought all proposals in-house to a team of specialists trained in the development of professional, consistently excellent proposals for clients. This innovation saved thousands of hours of salespeople's time and helped us build a massive pipeline of new business.

Our network-within-a-network boomed. UPS Premier operated in more than forty-five countries. The command center expanded to the Netherlands and Singapore.

UPS Healthcare pioneered a new concept called UPS LabPort, a three-hundred-thousand-square-foot facility near the Louisville Worldport air hub. UPS LabPort houses as many as eight diagnostic laboratory clients with their own wet lab—a facility where clients test and analyze drugs, chemicals, and other types of biological matter using different liquid agents. UPS Healthcare became the landlord and the logistics service provider to these clients.

In 2022, UPS Healthcare also acquired Bomi Group, headquartered in Milan, to supplement our cold-chain network in southern Europe and Latin America.

The BOMI acquisition was the third largest in UPS history, adding three thousand skilled professionals to our ranks.

On April 17, 2023, I retired from UPS at the zenith of my forty-five-year corporate career.

My team just before I retired from UPS

We had ten thousand employees worldwide and had exceeded all expectations when we first promised UPS CEO David Abney that we would double the rate of growth of the industry.

In fact, in the three years I was president, our growth was *triple* the rate of industry growth. We had also built the industry's best global cold-chain network, with 114 facilities in thirty-five countries and expanded UPS Premier to forty nations.

"All this happened," Kate said, "because Wes forged a team that knew its mission and saw a little farther into the future than our competitors. Its specialized training and Wes's day-to-day leadership cemented UPS Healthcare's place in our industry."

Today, UPS Healthcare's classic blue logo is now a globally accepted brand representing excellence in cold-chain logistics.

And Marken, the company my team and I built from the ashes up, is now the undisputed global leader in clinical trial logistics. It stands as one of the most successful acquisitions UPS ever made.

Now it's up to UPS to maintain the healthcare division and preserve the reputation we have built.

I will be watching.

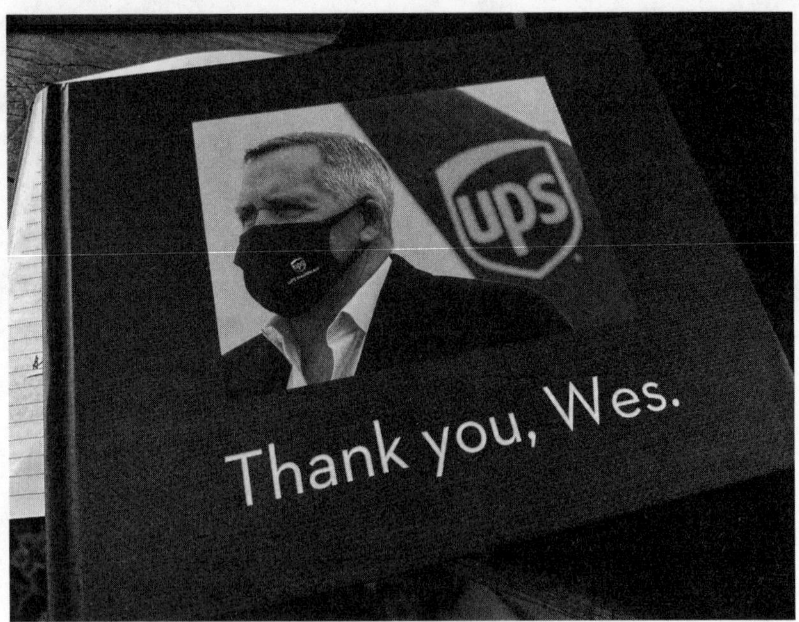

I retired from UPS with a deep sense of accomplishment

LESSONS LEARNED

A global crisis, for all the harm it does, can hold a silver lining. It can drive needed changes by making it easier to break restrictive rules. My advice? Run *to* the fire, not away from it. Use the power of a leadership position to forge bold new practices. Take charge; people will follow. It's impossible to be prepared for everything, but it's essential to adapt as the unexpected happens.

CHAPTER 11

WHAT'S NEXT

(2023 AND AFTER ...)

Building Boats and Beyond

I'm certain the next phase of my life will be filled with more business ventures. My top priority, though, will involve reviving a solid family brand and building boats.

The rebirth of *Pilar*, Ernest Hemingway's fishing boat, never crossed my mind when I was age seven, twelve, or even thirty. Somewhere along the line, though, it occurred to me that the family had never spoken of Hemingway when I was growing up.

"We built lots of boats," I would hear them say dismissively when I mentioned *Pilar* or its famous owner.

Curiosity grew inside me as I began to wonder about the writer and the fishing boat he captained with the Wheeler name on its bow.

My dad seemed particularly proud of the family's involvement in World War II, with the thousands of boats we produced, and the five Navy-E Awards granted to the business for our outstanding contributions. Dad wrote several papers on the subject, and I still have copies. But he never talked about Hemingway or *Pilar*.

Wheeler built hundreds of ships for the World War II effort

Why?

I still don't know. It's a question I still ask myself every day.

An idea came to me, though, after I got a call from Hilary Hemingway, the writer's niece, in 2009.

Hilary and actor Andy Garcia had cowritten the script for a movie, *Hemingway and Fuentes*. It would never get made, but Hilary and I had a meeting on the deck of *Elhanor*, another 1934 Wheeler Playmate like *Pilar*.

She and I had a long talk, recorded on video, about her famous uncle. Hilary told the whole story of *Pilar*, and fishing, and Bimini, and the Finca. We remain friends to this day.

So that led to my big idea: the Wheeler Yacht Company.

I decided that if anyone was ever going to recreate *Pilar*, it would have to be me. If anyone was ever going to bring Wheeler boatbuilding back from the ashes and preserve my family's boatbuilding reputation, it would be me. I would do it for wooden boat aficionados everywhere, and for Greg and Erica, and for the Wheeler legacy.

The idea started there, and it has never gone away.

A Legacy Lives On

My great-grandfather, Howard E. Wheeler, started the Wheeler Yacht Company in 1910. After World War II, three of his five children ran the business.

My grandfather, Wesley L. Wheeler, was one of the three. He graduated from Pratt Institute as a naval architect and immediately took a role as the company's design chief. He drew up all the Playmate series boats, all of them made of wood, including *Pilar*. The other two brothers managed business and sales.

From the end of the war until 1963, the three brothers did their best to grow the business, turning out hundreds of high-quality wooden yachts, many for the rich and famous. Trouble arrived, though, with fiberglass. Boats made with fiberglass could be mass produced, were less expensive, and were less trouble to maintain.

The Wheelers tried unsuccessfully to build boats with fiberglass to answer the market demand, but it proved both difficult and expensive to pull off. We had to convert the yard to satisfy New York Fire Department requirements, which were still evolving. My dad told me a few times that the problem might have gone away with a certain "donation" to the fire department.

The family business suffered. Then the brush fire in the Bronx, its source never discovered, destroyed the shipyard and a half century of Wheeler boatbuilding.

As described in chapter 1, my dad never got over the loss of the Wheeler Yacht Company.

Dad had gone to the University of Michigan to get a naval architecture and marine engineering degree. He intended to come back to run the family business. Instead, unmoored, he drifted from job to job and marriage to marriage. He ran his own business, but never the business of his dreams. He died a few years ago, bereft of the purpose he'd once had for his life.

Dad shortly before his passing

So it has come down to me to resurrect the Wheeler boatbuilding craft and name.

I reincorporated Wheeler Yacht Company in 2011. Our first vessel might have been a 1960 sport fisherman model. I had seen an article in *Sea* magazine written by Tom Fexas, a well-known boat designer, about the Wheeler he grew up on (Appendix C11.1). It told the story of a Wheeler sportfisherman his dad owned that his family had loved for most of his childhood.

I read the article and called Tom and introduced myself. I ended up working with him to design a new Wheeler fifty-five-footer from the 1960s era, and I got excited about building one. But Marianne and I would have needed a second mortgage on our California home to do so. Thankfully, we canceled the project when the economy sank the real estate industry and dragged down most everything with it. I had also just changed jobs, from Patheon to Marken. It just wasn't the right time to build that boat.

Elhanor, *now* Pilar, *with brother Jon and Cousin Eugene "Tut" Wheeler*

One day, the phone rang. It's the story of my life.

The call came from from Hilary Hemingway, followed within minutes by one from Andy Garcia. They explained that their screenplay focused on Ernest Hemingway's last twenty-five years in Cuba, when *Pilar* was the center of the writer's life. In fact, the boat had been written into their script as a central character.

Garcia wanted an authentic duplicate of *Pilar*. I enthusiastically said yes. I found *Elhanor*, a 1934 vintage thirty-four-foot Playmate designed by my grandfather and built by the Wheelers (AC11.2). I then helped Andy restore it at Moore's Marine boatyard in Beaufort, North Carolina.

When we sea-trialed the boat with its new engines and hull planking, it sent chills through me. I took videos and shipped them to my dad.

Andy Garcia renamed the craft *Pilar*. He told me it would be his movie model.

The experience inspired me to design an exact copy of the original *Pilar*. For research, Marianne and I traveled with Hilary and her family to Cuba. I was allowed on board the *Pilar*, and we took hundreds of measurements. I then spent five years researching and designing the new boat.

It took another two years to find a builder, and then, in September 2020, we launched what my family would call *Legend*. Marianne designed the interior beautifully. She wanted it to look true to the period but be comfortable enough to live in. And it is.

Marianne at Legend's *launch*

We have come to consider *Legend* a member of our family. It has taken us up and down the East Coast more than seven thousand miles, from the Gulf of Maine to the Florida Keys and back. Twice.

The Wheeler boatbuilding business is back, albeit at a much smaller scale.

Legend's *first trip from Maine*

The Wheeler Yacht Company today has two new Wheelers under construction, each fifty-five-feet long and both inspired by a 1931 Wheeler Playmate of the same size. One of the new yachts has already been sold. They're both made of African mahogany, and each carries the vibe of the 1930s. We're looking for boat owners who love the look of classic boats but who want no compromises on performance, comfort, and modern amenities.

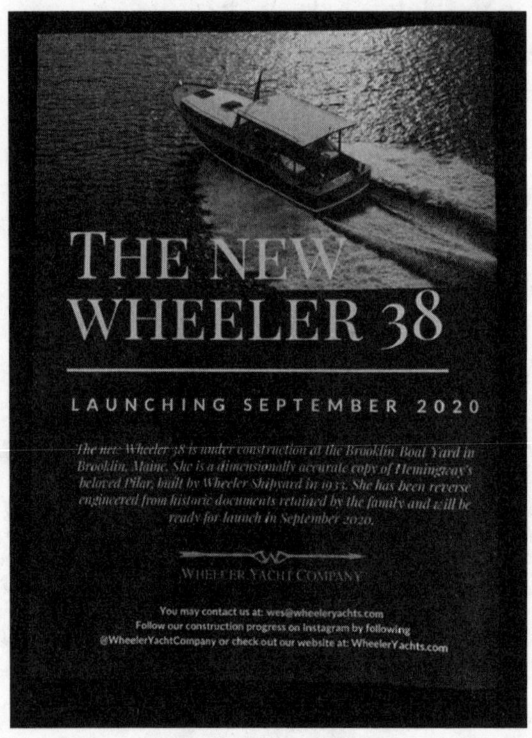

THE NEW
WHEELER 38
LAUNCHING SEPTEMBER 2020
The new Wheeler 38 is under construction at the Brooklin Boat Yard in Brooklin, Maine. She is a dimensionally accurate copy of Hemingway's beloved Pilar, built by Wheeler Shipyard in 1933. She has been reverse engineered from historic documents retained by the family and will be ready for launch in September 2020.
WHEELER YACHT COMPANY
You may contact us at: wes@wheeleryachts.com
Follow our construction progress on Instagram by following
@WheelerYachtCompany or check out our website at: WheelerYachts.com

Legend *launch ad*

You'll understand by now what drives me.

I see that my purpose—my love—is fixing things. Families, after my dad left. Businesses, struggling to survive. Boats, deserving of glory instead of ashes.

It now seems so clear. I started my life remembering the burning embers of my family's legacy. I spent most of my life after college building something new or repairing something broken and in need of revival.

The boatbuilding business—restoring the family legacy—has become another chapter in my life. It could be my greatest challenge of all.

Greg and Erica

Above all, I will devote the rest of my life to my family: my wife, Marianne; my son, Greg; and my daughter, Erica, and their spouses—and, one day, our grandchildren.

My children know me better than anyone on earth besides Marianne. They mean the world to me.

Greg lives with his wife, Natalie, in Newport Beach, California, in Orange County, not far from where he was born in 1989, while I worked at Exxon.

My son studied history and political science at Miami University of Ohio, then took a law degree at Elon University in North Carolina. Greg handles business contracts for a clinical research company, IQVIA. Natalie manages a portfolio of assisted living facilities for Berkshire Hathaway.

They're very honest about life in the Wheeler family, and about me.

"Dad is a natural leader," Greg said. "He's self-reliant. He has a hardworking constitution. He believes you need to find confidence in yourself. In my career, I've taken that to heart.

"He leans on my mom a lot and maybe depends on a few other colleagues he trusts. He's traditional in the ways he does things—he may have a little romanticized view of the past, in fact, Dad believes in hard work and honesty, and in telling the truth directly, New York-style. Telling the truth even if it upsets someone. But he's a caring dad, and he wasn't ever afraid to show us that."

Some of Greg's favorite memories are also favorites of mine.

"One great time together," Greg said, "was our scouting trip to Philmont Scout Ranch, the Boy Scouts of America's premier camping site.

"Dad came with me, and we spent twelve days backpacking. One day, I led the troop. We had to crisscross a river several times and, on one crossing, the log over the river broke. I fell in the water, and Dad jumped in after me.

"Another time, we went camping for ten days. We were sitting on a mountaintop looking over an open valley, and we were so hungry. All we had were crackers and Cheez Whiz. I had never tasted Cheese Whiz so good. That day was amazing."

Greg also understands something else important about me.

"The Wheeler heritage is a big thing," Greg said. "The family is super important to Dad, the Wheeler shipbuilders, and Mom's Italian family too.

"Dad is the patriarch now. He drives to reunions, goes to graduations, gets people together for Thanksgiving, pulls together all the cousins. We all see how hard he tries to hold things together that were broken once when the shipyard burned, and his own dad left the family when he was twelve.

"And I believe all that work is important to Dad's sense of identity. It's why I don't think he will ever fully retire. He's a man that needs to stay busy."

My daughter Erica works in England, a place she learned to love as a kid when we lived there three years for my overseas work with Glaxo. Erica was baptized in one of the oldest churches in England. Chuck Bramlage is her godfather.

She works in London as a management consultant with Ernst & Young. Her husband, Josh Kule, works as chief commercial officer for a start-up in Copenhagen.

"Honestly, the England years of my childhood were some of my most memorable," Erica said.

"We went to places all over Europe, kissed the Blarney Stone, looked for the Loch Ness Monster, and I just had all these fantastic first experiences in life. It was all so memorable that I'm back here again now, living and working."

Erica studied psychology and minored in global media studies at Michigan, graduating in 2013. She was on the university water polo team. She calls herself a "water baby," since she has swam since age four.

We have much in common.

"I'm just as sensitive as my dad," Erica said.

"He gives this gruff exterior to the world, but he's a very sensitive person. And in good and bad ways, we're a lot alike. We can get hotheaded. We can be reactive in certain situations. The reason he and I butted heads at times was because we're so similar. It's taken me years to admit it."

When you ask Erica what people should understand about Wes Wheeler, she answers instantly.

"What you should know about Dad," she said, "is that things didn't come easy for him. Nothing was ever handed to him on a silver platter. Dad had to work really hard for everything he's earned.

"He's been successful. Every decision he's made led to better results and happier lives. But it's never been easy.

"And I'm not discounting the support of colleagues and friends, his family, us. We're still tight-knit and present for one another."

My family: Mom, brother Jon, sister Debbie, and their families

My Marianne

When I hear my children say words like those, I know my life has been a success, no matter what else has happened or will happen.

I know my life will go on through Greg and Erica; the Wheeler life will endure. I am happy knowing that the values and tools they have will give them a good chance to define what happiness is for them—and to then successfully find it.

Of all the things I've built, I value above all the marriage I've built with Marianne. Nothing else, no other accomplishment, even comes close.

Marianne means the world to me.

"Wes has grown so much, changed so much … but Wes has stayed true to himself too," Marianne said. "He's seen the world and made his biggest dreams come true, but he still opens the door for me, he still goes on adventures with me, he still puts his arms around the family and his friends and the kids and me. In a world filled with ordinary people, Wes is truly one of a kind."

The Stuff I've Learned

The stuff I have learned throughout my career is chronicled in this book.

Hopefully, the next generations of leaders can find it helpful.

Reflections

By the time you read this book, I may be retired. Perhaps not. My approach to life has always been inspired by challenges whether they happen by chance or by design. Life's challenges make you alert and sharp—and keep you busy. They occupy your mind. They occupy your spirit. I gladly move on to that next challenge, whatever it may be.

Erica, Greg, me, and Marianne

APPENDIX

Chapter 1: Beginnings

AC1.1 Wheeler Yacht Company, "News & Events," https://wheeleryachts.com/news/.

AC1.2 Steve Dougherty, "The Rebirth of a Legend," *Florida Sportsman*, March 2023, https://wheeleryachts.com/app/uploads/2023/02/Wheeler_FloridaSportsman_3-23.pdf.

AC1.3 Staff, "Naval Submarine Base New London," CurrentTops.com, https://currentops.com/installations/us/ct/nsb-new-london.

FOR FURTHER REFERENCE

Captain Bob Cerullo, "Wheeler Yachts Reborn," Boating World, January 2022, https://liboatingworld.com/wheeler-yachts-reborn/.

Art Paine, "Wheeler 38: The Spirit of Hemingway's Boat Comes Alive in a New Build," MaineBoats.com, 2022, https://maineboats.com/print/issue-164/wheeler-38.

Chapter 2: Exxon (1978-1989)

AC2.1 Nicholas Lemann, "So You Want to Be Chairman of Exxon?," *Texas Monthly*, December 1978, https://www.texasmonthly.com/news-politics/so-you-want-to-be-chairman-of-exxon/.

FOR FURTHER REFERENCE

Exxon Company USA Staff, "Development and Production Plan (Cumulative Updates) Santa Ynez Unit Development," Exxon Company USA, Unit Operator, September 1987, https://www.boem.gov/sites/default/files/about-boem/BOEM-Regions/Pacific-Region/DPPs/9A3---1987-09-Platforms-Harmony-Heritage-Hondo---Santa-Ynez-Unit-Cumulative-Updates.pdf.

ExxonMobile staff, "ExxonMobile Santa Ynez Unit Facilities," ExxonMobile, 2024, https://www.syu.exxonmobil.com/history.

Exxon Mobile Corporate Website, https://corporate.exxonmobil.com/.

Chapter 3: Glaxo (1989-2002)

AC3.1 "Heroes of Medicine." Special issue, Time 150, no. 19 (October 1, 1997).

FOR FURTHER REFERENCE

Claudia Winograd, "GlaxoSmithKline: A British-Based Company," *Encyclopaedia Britannica,* Updated 2024, https://www.britannica.com/topic/GlaxoSmithKline.

GSK Corporate Website, https://www.gsk.com/en-gb/company/history-and-heritage/.

Andrew Ross Sorkin with Melody Petersen, "Glaxo and SmithKline Agree to Form Largest Drugmaker," *New York Times*, January 17, 2000, https://www.nytimes.com/2000/01/17/business/glaxo-and-smithkline-agree-to-form-largest-drugmaker.html.

Kirsten Birkett, "Inside the Glaxo Wellcome and SmithKline merger," Thompson Reuters Practical Law, May 1, 2001, https://uk.practicallaw.thomsonreuters.com/2-101-4509?transitionType=Default&contextData=(sc.Default)&firstPage=true.

Staff, "Glaxo Wellcome and SmithKline Beecham Merge at Last," Pharmaceutical Online, January 18, 2000, https://www.pharmaceuticalonline.com/doc/glaxo-wellcome-and-smithkline-beecham-merge-a-0001.

Associated Press, "Clinton Leads Gala Honoring Time," *Los Angeles Times*, March 4, 1998. https://www.latimes.com/archives/la-xpm-1998-mar-04-mn-25446-story.html.

Kasper Zeuthen, "FDA Loosens Restrictions on Drug Ads on TV, Radio," *Los Angeles Times*, August 9, 1997, https://www.latimes.com/archives/la-xpm-1997-aug-09-mn-20766-story.html.

Chapter 4: DSM Pharmaceuticals, Inc. (2002-2003)

AC4.1 Bloomberg News, "Company News; DSM to Acquire Catalytica for $800 Million," *New York Times*, August 4, 2000, https://www.nytimes.com/2000/08/04/business/company-news-dsm-to-acquire-catalytica-for-800-million.html.

AC4.2 Staff, "Food and Drug Administration CFR Title 21 Part 11," Microsoft, January 26, 2023, https://learn.microsoft.com/en-us/compliance/regulatory/offering-FDA-CFR-Title-21-Part-11.

AC4.3 Internal sources and interviews.

AC4.4 Internal sources and interviews.

AC4.5 Internal sources and interviews.

AC4.6 Internal sources and interviews.

AC4.7 Kyle Blankenship, "The Top 20 Drugs by Global Sales in 2019," Fierce Pharma, July 27, 2020, https://www.fiercepharma.com/special-report/top-20-drugs-by-global-sales-2019.

AC4.8 Erica Pandey, "America's Adderall shortage," Axios, November 15, 2022, https://www.axios.com/2022/11/15/adderall-shortage-adhd-diagnosis-prescriptions.

AC4.9 Internal sources and interviews.

AC4.10 Oscar Wilde, "Lady Windermere's Fan," Britannica.com, Act 1. Four-act play first performed February 20, 1892, https://www.britannica.com/topic/Lady-Windermeres-Fan.

FOR FURTHER REFERENCE

Official Website of Pitt County, North Carolina, https://www.pittcountync.gov/.

"About DSM Fine Chemicals," ChemEurope.com, https://www.chemeurope.com/en/companies/15237/dsm-fine-chemicals.html.

DSM 2002 Annual Report to Shareholders.

DSM 2002 Annual Report to Shareholders.

DSM Pharmaceuticals Website, https://www.dsm.com/human-nutrition/es_LA/pharma.html.

Chapter 5: Valeant Pharmaceuticals International, Inc. (2003-2007)

AC5.1 Form 10-K for ICN Pharmaceuticals, Inc., "Annual Report Pursuant to Section 13 or 15(d) of the Securities Exchange Act of 1934." Securities and Exchange Commission. Fiscal year ended December 31, 2002. Commission File Number 1-11397.

AC5.2 Staff, 2002. "Panic Attack," Forbes, September 30, 2002, https://www.forbes.com/forbes/2002/0930/400052.html?sh=6feb78f46385.

AC5.3 Form 10-K for ICN Pharmaceuticals, Inc., "Annual Report Pursuant to Section 13 or 15(d) of the Securities Exchange Act of 1934."

AC5.4 ICN Pharmaceuticals, Inc. Annual Report to Shareholders, 2002.

AC5.5 Form 10-K for ICN Pharmaceuticals, Inc., "Annual Report Pursuant to Section 13 or 15(d) of the Securities Exchange Act of 1934."

AC5.6 Ronald D. White, "ICN's Sale of Russia Operations Is Finished," *Los Angeles Times*. July 1, 2003, https://www.latimes.com/archives/la-xpm-2003-jul-01-fi-icn1-story.html.

AC5.7 Ronald D. White, "ICN Sells Unit to Global Dosimetry," *Los Angeles Times*, October 2, 2003, https://www.latimes.com/archives/la-xpm-2003-oct-02-fi-rup2.6-story.html.

AC5.8 Form 10-K for ICN Pharmaceuticals, Inc., "Annual Report Pursuant to Section 13 or 15(d) of the Securities Exchange Act of 1934," Securities and Exchange Commission, Fiscal year ended December 31, 2003, Commission File Number 1-11397.

AC5.9 Ibid.

AC5.10 Ibid., p. 81.

AC5.11 Staff, "Valeant Buys Amarin Unit in $38M Deal," Pharma Letter, February 23, 2004, https://www.thepharmaletter.com/article/valeant-buys-amarin-unit-in-38m-deal.

AC5.12 Admin, "FDA OK's Valeant's Zelapar for Parkinson's," Fierce Biotech, June 14, 2006, https://www.fiercebiotech.com/biotech/fda-ok-s-valeant-s-zelapar-for-parkinson-s.

AC5.13 Ana de Barros, "Tasmar (Tolcapone) for Parkinson's Disease," Parkinson's News Today, August 24, 2023, https://parkinsonsnews-today.com/tasmar/#:~:text=Roche%20originally%20developed%20the%20therapy,have%20been%20available%20since%202015.

AC5.14 American Spa Staff, "Courteney Cox to Represent Kinerase Skin Care," American Spa, May 18, 2005, https://www.americanspa.com/courteney-cox-represent-kinerase-skin-care.

AC5.15 Form 10-K for ICN Pharmaceuticals, Inc., "Annual Report Pursuant to Section 13 or 15(d) of the Securities Exchange Act of 1934," Securities and Exchange Commission. Fiscal year ended December 31, 2004, Commission File Number 1-11397.

AC5.16 Archives of the New York Stock Exchange.

AC5.17 Bloomberg News, "Company news; Valeant to Buy Xcel Pharmaceuticals for $280 million," *New York Times*, February 3, 2005 https://www.nytimes.com/2005/02/03/business/company-news-valeant-to-buy-xcel-pharmaceuticals-for-280-million.html.

AC5.18 Form 10-K for ICN Pharmaceuticals, Inc., "Annual Report Pursuant to Section 13 or 15(d) of the Securities Exchange Act of 1934," Securities and Exchange Commission, Fiscal year ended December 31, 2005, Commission File Number 1-11397.

AC5.19 Staff, "Valeant Pharmaceuticals is Soldiering On," Pharmaceutical Executive, November 1, 2005, https://www.pharmexec.com/view/valeant-pharmaceuticals-soldiering.

AC5.20 Form 10-K for ICN Pharmaceuticals, Inc., "Annual Report Pursuant to Section 13 or 15(d) of the Securities Exchange Act of 1934," Securities and Exchange Commission, Fiscal year ended December 31, 2006, Commission File Number 1-11397.

AC5.21 Ibid.

AC5.22 Form 10-K for ICN Pharmaceuticals, Inc., "Annual Report Pursuant to Section 13 or 15(d) of the Securities Exchange Act of 1934." Securities and Exchange Commission. Fiscal year ended December 31, 2007. Commission File Number 1-11397.

AC5.23 Ibid.

AC5.24 Calisha Myers, "GlaxoSmithKline and Valeant Pharmaceuticals Announce Worldwide Collaboration Agreement for Retigabine," Fierce Biotech, August 28, 2008, https://www.fiercebiotech.com/

biotech/glaxosmithkline-and-valeant-pharmaceuticals-announce-worldwide-collaboration-agreement-for.

AC5.25 Nathan Vardi and Antoine Gara, "Valeant Pharmaceutical's Prescription for Disaster," Forbes, May 9, 2016, https://www.forbes.com/sites/nathanvardi/2016/04/13/valeant-pharmaceuticals-prescription-for-disaster/?sh=45057627206c.

AC5.26 Ibid.

AC5.27 Ransdell Pierson and Amrutha Penumudi, "More Trouble for Valeant as Possible Debt Default Looms," Reuters, March 15, 2016, https://jp.reuters.com/article/idUSL2N16N1DO/.

AC5.28 Nathan Vardi and Antoine Gara, "Valeant Pharmaceutical's Prescription for Disaster," Forbes, April 13, 2016, https://www.forbes.com/sites/nathanvardi/2016/04/13/valeant-pharmaceuticals-prescription-for-disaster/?sh=45057627206c.

AC5.29 Biotech and Pharma News Staff, "Ex-Valeant, Philidor Executives Get Prison for Fraud," CNBC, October 30, 2018, https://www.cnbc.com/2018/10/30/ex-valeant-philidor-executives-get-prison-for-fraud.html.

AC5.30 Nathan Vardi and Antoine Gara, "Valeant Pharmaceutical's Prescription for Disaster," Forbes, May 9, 2016, https://www.forbes.com/sites/nathanvardi/2016/04/13/valeant-pharmaceuticals-prescription-for-disaster/?sh=45057627206c.

FOR FURTHER REFERENCE

Valeant 2003 Annual Report to Shareholders.

Valeant 2004 Annual Report to Shareholders.

Valeant 2005 Annual Report to Shareholders.

Valeant 2006 Annual Report to Shareholders.

Valeant 2007 Annual Report to Shareholders.

Valeant Website, https://www.valeant.com.

Valeant Promotional Materials.

Chapter 6: Patheon, Inc. (2007-2010)

AC6.1 Staff, "Patheon Adds Capacity," *Globe and Mail*, November 23, 2004, https://www.theglobeandmail.com/report-on-business/patheon-adds-capacity/article1144489/.

AC6.2 Staff, "Patheon Announces $150m Investment by JLL Partners," Fierce Biotech, March 2, 2007, https://www.fiercebiotech.com/biotech/press-release-patheon-announces-150-million-investment-by-jll-partners.

AC6.3 Michael Flaherty, "Patheon gets $150 Mln Injection from JLL Partners," Reuters, August 9, 2007, https://www.reuters.com/article/idUSN02226649/.

AC6.4 Toronto Stock Exchange, https://www.tsx.com/.

AC6.5 The Board of Directors of Patheon, Inc., "Patheon Names Wheeler CEO, to Replace Trecroce," BioSpace, November 21, 2007, https://www.biospace.com/article/releases/patheon-names-b-wheeler-b-ceo-to-replace-b-trecroce-b-/?keywords=GlaxoSmithKline.

AC6.6 Health & Pharmaceuticals Staff, "Patheon to Divest Some Canadian Operations," Reuters, April 17, 2007, https://www.reuters.com/article/idUSN17331202/.

AC6.7 Staff, "Patheon Completes Sale of Niagara-Burlington Commercial Manufacturing Business," BioSpace, February 1, 2008, https://www.biospace.com/article/releases/patheon-completes-sale-of-niagara-burlington-commercial-manufacturing-business-/.

AC6.8 Staff, "Patheon Unveils New Brand Image," BioSpace, June 17, 2008, https://www.biospace.com/article/releases/patheon-unveils-new-brand-image-/.

AC6.9 Staff, "Patheon Announces Japanese Subsidiary Patheon, K.K.," BioSpace, June 3, 2008, https://www.biospace.com/article/releases/patheon-announces-japanese-subsidiary-b-patheon-k-k-b-/.

AC6.10 Staff, "Patheon Reaches Agreement with BSP Pharmaceuticals for Development and Manufacture of Cytotoxics," BioSpace, July 3, 2008, https://www.biospace.com/article/releases/patheon-reaches-agreement-with-bsp-pharmaceuticals-for-development-and-manufacture-of-cytotoxics-/.

AC6.11 Staff, "Patheon Establishes European Headquarters in Switzerland," BioSpace, November 6, 2008, https://www.biospace.com/article/releases/patheon-establishes-european-headquarters-in-switzerland-/.

AC6.12 Staff, "Patheon Announces Closing of Carolina Facility," BioSpace, February 2, 2009, https://www.biospace.com/article/releases/patheon-announces-closing-of-carolina-facility-/.

AC6.13 Andrew Ross Sorkin, "JP Morgan Pays $2 a Share for Bear Stearns," *New York Times*, March 17, 2008, https://www.nytimes.com/2008/03/17/business/17bear.html.

AC6.14 Laura Rodini, "What Happened to Lehman Brothers? Why Did It Fail?," TheStreet, July 14, 2023, https://www.thestreet.com/banking/what-happened-to-lehman-brothers#:~:text=On%20September%2015%2C%202008%2C%20Lehman,11%2C%202001%2C%20terrorist%20attacks.

AC6.15 Caroline Valetkevitch, "Key Dates and Milestones in the S&P 500's History," Reuters, May 6, 2013, https://www.reuters.com/article/idUSBRE9450WL/.

AC6.16 Business Staff, "TSX Down 35% in 2008," *Canadian Press*, January 1, 2009, https://www.cbc.ca/news/business/tsx-down-35-in-2008-1.814643.

AC6.17 Toronto Stock Exchange, https://www.tsx.com/.

AC6.18 PE Hub staff, "JLL Partners Wants Rest of Patheon Inc.," PE Hub, December 9, 2008, https://www.pehub.com/jll-partners-wants-rest-of-patheon-inc/.

AC6.19 Staff, "Patheon Board Recommends Rejecting JLL Offer," Contract Pharma, March 26, 2009, https://www.contractpharma.com/contents/view_breaking-news/2009-03-26/patheon-board-recommends-rejecting-jll-offer/.

AC6.20 Agence France-Presse, "Swiss Pharma Supplier Lonza Bids for Canada's Patheon," IndustryWeek, August 23, 2009, https://www.industryweek.com/leadership/companies-executives/article/21935891/swiss-pharma-supplier-lonza-bids-for-canadas-patheon.

AC6.21 Business Staff, "JLL Bid for Patheon Expires," CBC News, August 27, 2009, https://www.cbc.ca/news/business/jll-bid-for-patheon-expires-1.859323.

AC6.22 Staff, "Lonza Group Ltd., Patheon Extend Takeover Talks Deadline," BioSpace, September 28, 2009, https://www.biospace.com/article/releases/lonza-group-ltd-patheon-extend-takeover-talks-deadline-/.

AC6.23 Gareth Macdonald, "Lonza Withdraws Patheon Bid, but Still Keen on CMOs," OutsourcingPharma, October 20, 2009, https://www.outsourcing-pharma.com/Article/2009/10/20/Lonza-withdraws-Patheon-bid-but-still-keen-on-CMOs.

AC6.24 Patheon Annual Report to Shareholders 2009.

AC6.25 Staff, "Patheon Announces Offering of $280 Million of Senior Secured Notes," BioSpace, April 5, 2010, https://www.biospace.com/article/releases/patheon-announces-offering-of-280-million-of-senior-secured-notes-/.

AC6.26 Ontario Securities Commission. In the Matter of Patheon Inc. And In the Matter of an Offer to Purchase for Cash Any and All of the Restricted Voting Shares of Patheon Inc. by JLL Patheon Holdings, LLC: Reasons for Decision. August 6, 2009, https://www.osc.ca/sites/default/files/pdfs/proceedings/rad_20090806_patheon.pdf.

FOR FURTHER REFERENCE

Patheon 2007 Annual Report to Shareholders.

Patheon 2008 Annual Report to Shareholders.

Patheon 2009 Annual Report to Shareholders.

Patheon 2010 Annual Report to Shareholders.

Patheon Website: https://www.patheon.com.

Patheon Promotional Materials.

Chapter 7: Marken (2011-2019)

AC7.1 Martin Arnold, "Apax Pays £975m in Marken Buy-Out," *Financial Times*, December 8, 2009, https://www.ft.com/content/aad49dda-e367-11de-8d36-00144feab49a

AC7.2 Isabell Witt and Tessa Walsh, "RLPC-Apax to Stump Op 50 Mln Stg for Marken," Reuters, February 16, 2012, https://www.reuters.com/article/marken-restructuring-idUSL5E8DG41F20120216/.

AC7.3 Staff, "Apax to Hand Embattled Drug Courier Marken to Lenders," AltAssets, December 19, 2012, https://www.altassets.net/private-equity-news/by-news-type/deal-news/apax-to-hand-embattled-drug-courier-marken-to-lenders.html.

AC7.4 Jeff Berman, "UPS's Acquisition of Marken Is Made Official," Logistics Management, January 3, 2017, https://www.logisticsmgmt.com/article/upss_acquisition_of_marken_is_made_official.

AC7.5 Internal Sources and Interviews.

AC7.6 O'Donnell, Carl and Hirsch, Lauren . "Medical courier Marken up for sale: sources." Reuters, July 1, 2016. https://www.reuters.com/article/idUSKCN0ZH5P5/.

AC7.7 Globe Newswire. "UPS To Acquire Marken, A Leader In Global Clinical Supply Chain Solutions." GlobeNewswire, November 7, 2016. https://www.globenewswire.com/news-release/2016/11/07/887350/0/en/UPS-To-Acquire-Marken-A-Leader-In-Global-Clinical-Supply-Chain-Solutions.html.

AC7.8 Manufacturing Chemist 87, no. 11 (November 2016).

FOR FURTHER REFERENCE

Marken Website and Marken Social Media Posts.

Marken Promotional Materials.

GOV.UK, Companies House: MAZE 1 Limited, Company Number 08325021 for the years 2012–2016.

GOV.UK, Companies House: Marken Limited, Company Number 01485138 for the years 2009–2013.

GOV.UK, Companies House: Iridium Topco Limited, Company Number 07089805 for the years 2009–2011.

Confidential Interviews and Investment Documents.

Chapter 8: Bushu Pharmaceuticals Ltd. (2017-2021)

AC8.1 Deals Staff, "Private Equity Giant KKR to Buy Japan's Bushu Pharmaceuticals," Reuters, December 20, 2022, https://www.reuters.com/markets/deals/private-equity-giant-kkr-buy-japans-bushu-pharmaceuticals-2022-12-20/.

Chapter 9: UPS Healthcare (2019-2020)

Content in Chapter 9 has been reviewed for accuracy and approved for use by all sources, contributors, and subject matter experts.

AC9.1 Marken. "Wes Wheeler Appointed to Lead UPS Healthcare and Life Sciences Unit." Press release, December 3, 2019. https://www.marken.com/wes-wheeler-appointed-to-lead-ups-healthcare-and-life-sciences-unit/.

FOR FURTHER REFERENCE

UPS Healthcare Website: https://www.ups.com/us/en/healthcare/aboutus.page#:~:text=UPS%20Healthcare%20is%20launched%20as,99.9%25%20on%2Dtime%20delivery.

Chapter 10: UPS Healthcare 2020-2023

Content in Chapter 10 has been reviewed for accuracy and approved for use by all sources, contributors, and subject matter experts.

FOR FURTHER REFERENCE

United States Senate, "The Logistics of Transporting a COVID-19 Vaccine: Hearing before the Subcommittee on Transportation and Safety of the Committee on Commerce, Science, and Transportation," December 10, 2020, https://www.govinfo.gov/content/pkg/CHRG-116shrg52857/html/CHRG-116shrg52857.htm.

Bryce Shreve and Eileen Street, "First Shipments of Pfizer's COVID-19 Vaccine Arrive in Louisville," Spectrum News 1. December 14, 2020. https://spectrumnews1.com/ky/louisville/news/2020/12/13/pfizer-coronavirus-vaccines-ups-worldport.

Terri Moon Cronk, "Operation Warp Speed official: First COVID-19 Vaccines to Arrive Monday," Air Force Medical Service, December

14, 2020. https://www.airforcemedicine.af.mil/News/Display/Article/2445371/operation-warp-speed-official-first-covid-19-vaccines-to-arrive-monday/.

Dr. Carlo de Notaristefani, "Special Report: Operation Warp Speed: A View From The Inside," *Pharmaceutical Engineering*, May/June 2022, https://ispe.org/pharmaceutical-engineering/may-june-2022/special-report-operation-warp-speed-view-inside.

Staff, "UPS Crosses One Billion COVID-19 Vaccine Delivery Milestone," TLME News Service, December 18, 2021, https://www.transportandlogisticsme.com/smart-logistics/ups-crosses-one-billion-covid-19-vaccine-delivery-milestone.

Press Release, "UPS Healthcare Announces UPS® Premier," UPS. May 28, 2020. https://about.ups.com/ca/en/newsroom/press-releases/customer-first/ups-healthcare-announces-ups-premier.html.

Matt Leonard, "UPS Offers Tracking Tech, Logistics and Warehousing in Pharma Cold Chain service," Supply Chain Dive, May 27, 2021, https://www.supplychaindive.com/news/ups-cold-chain-pharmaceutical-supply-chain-biologics-covid-vaccine/600905/.

Max Garland, "UPS Plans to Open 7 Healthcare Logistics Facilities in 2023," Supply Chain Dive, May 3, 2023, https://www.supplychaindive.com/news/ups-health-care-logistics-facilities-2023/649236/.

UPS Press Release, "UPS Completes Acquisition of Bomi Group Multi-National Healthcare Logistics Provider," Globe Newswire, November 16, 2022. https://www.globenewswire.com/en/news-release/2022/11/16/2556810/30428/en/UPS-Completes-Acquisition-of-Bomi-Group-Multi-National-Healthcare-Logistics-Provider.html.

David Adler, "Inside Operation Warp Speed: A New Model for Industrial Policy," *American Affairs*, Summer 2021, https://americanaffairsjournal.org/2021/05/inside-operation-warp-speed-a-new-model-for-industrial-policy/.

Chapter 11: What's Next (2023 and After ...)

AC11.1 Christian Gullickson, "Boating: Recasting a Classic," Robb Report, July 1, 2005, https://robbreport.com/motors/marine/boating-recasting-a-classic-239357/.

AC11.2 Staff, "Ernest Hemingway's Boat Pilar Reborn as Legend—Wheeler 38," Wheeleryachts.com, October 31, 2022, https://wheeleryachts.com/in-the-news/ernest-hemingways-boat-pilar-reborn-as-legend-wheeler-38/.

FOR FURTHER REFERENCE

Danna Voth, "Resurrecting the Family Business Pt.1: Wheeler Yacht Company: A Fourth-Generation Member of an Inspired Boat-Building Family Seeks to Revive its Legacy," *Robb Report Worth Magazine*, March 2006, https://wheeleryachts.com/app/uploads/2020/07/WorthMagazine_March2006.pdf.